SAVE THE LAST BULLET FOR YOURSELF

SAVE THE LAST BULLET FOR YOURSELF

A Soldier of Fortune in the Balkans and Somalia

By
ROB KROTT

CASEMATE
Philadelphia & Newbury

Published in the United States of America in 2008 by
CASEMATE
1016 Warrior Road, Drexel Hill, PA 19026

and in the United Kingdom by
CASEMATE
17 Cheap Street, Newbury RG20 5DD

ISBN 978-1-932033-95-3

Cataloging-in-publication data is available from the Library of Congress
and the British Library.

Some information in this book has appeared in *Soldier of Fortune* magazine as
"Looking for War in All the Wrong Places," "Achtung, Baby," and
"Little Nancy and the Big Bad Mercenaries."

Printed and bound in the United States of America.

For a complete list of Casemate titles please contact:

CASEMATE PUBLISHERS
Telephone (610) 853-9131, Fax (610) 853-9146
E-mail: casemate@casematepublishing.com
or
CASEMATE UK
Telephone (01635) 231091, Fax (01635) 41619
E-mail: casemate-uk@casematepublishing.co.uk

CONTENTS

For the family story teller, my grandfather,
Ed Krott, 1914–2001

IN MEMORIAM

Captain Lance Eugene Motley, aka "Gene Scroft," USMA 1979
Foreign Correspondent, *Soldier of Fortune* magazine
Advisor, Karen National Liberation Army
KIA, Komura, Burma, 31 May 1989

Lance Corporal Domingo Arroyo
3/11 Field Artillery, USMC
KIA, Mogadishu, Somalia, 12 January 1993

Andreas Kolb
International Volunteer, King Tomislav Brigade
KIA, Gornji Vakuf, Bosnia, 15 November 1993

Colonel Robert Callen MacKenzie aka "Bob McKenna" and
"Bob Jordan"
CDR, Sierra Leone Commando Unit
KIA, Malal Hills, Sierra Leone, 24 February 1995

First Lieutenant David "Rocky" Eales, USMC
Oklahoma Highway Patrol Tactical Team
Killed in the Line of Duty, 24 September 1999

Jimmy A. Riddle
Security Contractor, SOC SMG
KIA, Ashraf, Iraq, 03 March 2005

Master Sergeant Thomas D. Maholic
2d Bn, 7th SFG (A), US Army Special Forces
KIA, Kandahar Province, Afghanistan, 24 June 2006

"Only the dead know the end of war."
—Plato

FOREWORD

By

JIM MORRIS

Rob Krott is the writer of his generation whose career most closely resembles mine from the previous generation. The differences between our careers say more about history than they do about either of us.

We both served in Special Forces units as officers. We've both volunteered to fight in foreign wars for little or no money—or, indeed, at our own expense. And we've both written about a bunch of small conflicts on several continents of which the majority of our countrymen seemed entirely oblivious.

The main difference is that almost everybody I fought or wrote about was a proxy of the Soviet Union, whereas Krott has fought in or written about a bunch of wars that had no connection whatsoever.

Those differences, however, had far reaching effects.

I was about eleven or twelve when the Soviet Union set off its first atomic bomb. I remember thinking at the time, one of these days we're going to have to fight those people, and I better get ready. I spent the next forty years preparing to fight the USSR, fighting the proxies of the USSR, and writing and editing books and magazine articles that depicted that conflict as I saw it, rather than how it was portrayed in the mainstream media.

The media depicted the wars I fought in and wrote about as separate events. I never could figure out why they did that. Everywhere I went the other guys were spending the same money, using the same gear, and sending their future leaders to Patrice Lumumba University in Moscow. After covering four or five wars you'd think even a newspaper reporter could figure that out.

I remember saying to a Special Forces lieutenant colonel in El Salvador that all these wars were connected. He looked at me as though I'd just grown another head. He didn't say anything, but I could tell he thought I was mentally maladjusted. I had just stated the obvious as though it was some kind of revelation.

I also said that to Bob Brown of *Soldier of Fortune* magazine. He too dismissed what I was saying with, "Everybody knows that."

"No, Bob, they don't," I replied. "'Cause it ain't in the papers and it ain't on TV. In the past six months I've covered five of these wars on two continents. I need one more on one more continent, and then I'll do a book about it."

I was frankly beat at the time. I was thinking of taking a month to rest and work out. He said, "Great, you leave for Salvador Friday." Be careful what you wish for.

But for Krott and his generation of freelance warriors it's been a vastly different deal. They really are separate wars. There's not a lot of connection between Bosnia, Burma, and Somalia. Different folks, different strokes. Only the wounds are the same.

I have a certain envy for some aspect of Krott's military education. I don't think there is much doubt that he is more broadly educated than my generation was. He knows more about weapons, more about tactics, more medical stuff. Why is that?

Well, my generation of Special Forces spent all of our time in a revolving door, preparing to go to Vietnam, going to Vietnam, recovering from Vietnam, preparing to go again. We didn't study the weapons, tactics, terrain, techniques that weren't being used there, because we didn't have time to do that. We learned US and Soviet weapons, and we learned to fight small brown people in the jungle. Period.

In his era of Special Forces, Krott learned how to fight anybody anywhere. That's a huge difference.

Where my generation had it all over his is that we never had to fight with anybody we didn't like. At least I didn't. My SF teams were the greatest guys I ever knew. But also I fought with Montagnards. They were wonderful people, and I'm still deeply involved in helping them as best I can.

Krott had a similar experience with his fellow American soldiers. But most of the mercs he fought with were the worst collection of scumbags gathered from the lower depths of society: thugs, outlaws, perverts, murders, thieves, cutthroats, and simple assholes.

And scattered among them were a very few fully qualified, idealistic, smart, adventurous young guys who sought out the many places in the Third World where good people were being jerked around, and went there for the express purpose of kicking hell out of the people doing the bad stuff.

One thing I've noticed about mercenaries is that you can have three of them in the same place at the same time, doing pretty much the same stuff in the same way, and one will be a genuinely evil scumbag, one will be a pathetic loser, and one will be pretty much a saint. Go figure!

Actually I have a quarrel with the term "mercenary." Very few of the mercenaries I've ever met were actually mercenary. There's little or no money in mercenary work, and anybody who fights primarily for money is an idiot, because if you get killed you can't spend it.

At one time at *Soldier of Fortune* magazine the staff amused themselves by writing fortunes for "soldier of fortune cookies." The only one I remember is, "You will take over a small central African country, and make five hundred dollars."

I met a couple of guys in Burma who were on the merc circuit: Bosnia in the summertime, Burma in the winter. They were acquaintances of my friends, Don and Dave Dickinson. Don and Dave are also modern warriors, half-Thai and half-Canadian, both are veterans of both armies, both are airborne, one in the Royal Thai Army, the other in the Canadian Army, and both became the kind of journalists that the mainstream media wouldn't touch, since they actually knew something about the subject.

The two mercs were former French commandos. My understanding is that the French commandos are, or were, pretty much wall-to-wall a kind of aggressive butch. I'm looking for a non-judgmental term here: let's just say they eschewed the company of women. But they knew their stuff. They were kitted out right, and they were heading for the bush looking for trouble. But there was something about them that I really didn't like. Their auras were black holes.

They were training commandos for the Karen National Liberation Army (KNLA). They gave a picture of their idol to the Karen commander to hang in his office. The idol was Adolf Hitler. I called them the Frogs of War.

I did not pursue an acquaintance with these gentlemen.

The difference in generations has also led to a difference in approach. When Krott was in Burma he taught weapons and small-unit tactics. During my brief stay there I taught how to organize Viet Cong cadre teams. Some of those Karen villages hadn't been visited by anybody from their central government for years. But they still had their kids drafted into the KNLA. The VC cadre team would have been the best way for the central government to establish liaison with the people and actually do something for them.

The flaw of the Karen way of doing things is that it's run by old guys. They weren't about to share power or listen to new techniques.

They were better than the Burmese, though, in that they weren't actively evil.

We've lived through some eras. The Soviets were a great central threat. After the Berlin Wall came down we entered an era when everything was up for grabs. The US figured, hey, the Cold War is over. Let's disarm. So we did, and all the people who had been sat on by the Soviets for forty years started shooting at each other.

Krott wasn't about to let a chance like that go by.

Now it's all changed again. 9/11 changed it. Once more we have a central enemy, Islamic fundamentalism. Krott stuck with it, and now he's a security contractor in Iraq. The boy never could miss a good fight.

Here's a story about Krott. Our mutual friend Kenn Miller, author of *Tiger the Lurp Dog* and volume II of *Six Silent Men*, took Krott to LAX to put him on a flight for one of his tours of all the world's hellholes. The lady at the airline counter was from Japan. She'd been around and had some idea what the deal was. She took one look at Krott's itinerary and started to cry. She begged him not to go. He went.

My guess is that you won't cry when you read this book. You probably won't laugh much either. But you will be enthralled.

JIM MORRIS is author, among other works, of the bestselling *War Story: The Classic True Story of the First Generation of Green Berets*, and *The Devil's Secret Name*.

PREFACE

"If you spend more than ten years as a soldier, you'll never be worth a damn as anything else."
—Anonymous, from *Major Mike*, by L.H. "Mike" Williams

I started writing this book almost ten years ago on the day I heard that my friend, mentor, and fellow King Tomislav Brigade volunteer, Bob MacKenzie, was killed in Sierra Leone. I don't know why I started writing, I just did. I started writing about Bob and the people I knew and met in the Balkan Wars. The first draft was completed in 1995, but it was impossible to find a publisher interested in such a text. "Nobody reads books about mercenaries," I was told. It sat largely ignored until now.

I guess I should call this volume number one of my adventures as a late twentieth century soldier of fortune, as it details them only in the period between 1992 and 1993. Since then I've served in the field with the Sudanese People's Liberation Army, and twice with the Karen National Liberation Army (Burma), and have worked on contract in Latin America, Afghanistan, Angola, Cambodia, Yemen, and parts of the former Soviet Union. At this writing I have already spent nearly three years as a contracted "security specialist," trainer, or administrator in Iraq. This book is written for soldiers and adventurers. And people who wish they were.

I'm not going to whine and cry or navel gaze about my experiences. Others have done that and I'm not interested in that kind of story or in writing a book like that, regardless of how well it might sell. So why should that kind of story interest any other real soldier? I do what I do because I like it, it interests me, it beats the hell out of riding a desk all day long, and maybe because I've got a serious adrenaline jones. The only thing I've ever been addicted to is real-war soldiering. I'm not a

xiv   SAVE THE LAST BULLET FOR YOURSELF

heroin addict and I wasn't in the Balkans to make a name for myself as a journalist or anything else. I've alluded to Anthony Lloyd's *My War Gone By I Miss It So* here only because I had an agent tell me, "Your book should be more introspective, like Lloyd's." Yeah, well, a female editor at a major publishing house also told me they'd publish it if I put in a love story.

This book isn't meant to be philosophy, a "what does it all mean" screed. It's just what I saw and did and maybe a little of what I thought. I studied the American existentialists at St. Bonaventure and I ate my lunch, on occasion, at Walden Pond while commuting between Fort Devens and Harvard, and that's as close as I get to philosophical introspection. This is just my story.

SAVE THE LAST BULLET FOR YOURSELF

CHAPTER 1

HOW DID I GET HERE?

"In any war story, but especially a true one, it's difficult to separate what happened from what seemed to happen. What seems to happen becomes it own happening and has to be told that way."
—Tim O'Brien, *The Things They Carried*

Anders slammed the barrel of the Kalashnikov into my gut. I swept it aside and ripped it from his grasp. But not before he pulled the trigger. Nothing happened. The weapon was on safe and the drunken Danish mercenary hadn't taken the extra split second to slap the selector lever down to full auto. Lucky for me. The dum-dum bullets would've splattered my guts all over the walls of the cramped hotel room. As it was, the AK-47 barrel ripped a gouge up along my rib cage and knocked some of the wind from me, leaving welts and bruises.

Before the weapon hit the floor I filled his mouth with my fist, knocking him back onto one of the beds. He came up off the bunk, his eyes red with rage and spittle flying from his mouth. I hit him again, hard, and he went down. I moved in for the kill, my fists pummeling him and my mind screaming, "Stick him with your knife!" and "Finish this quick, he's at your back! Watch your back!" I wanted to kill the drunken piece of shit. He'd tried to kill me and failed. The weapon could very well have been left on full-auto by accident, or if I was a second or two slower he might've even worked the selector switch and blown me away before I disarmed him. Fortunately Pat stepped in before my own mounting rage and bloodlust got the best of me and I pulled out my knife.

The discipline problems amongst the foreign mercenaries in my unit came to a head the week before I left my job as a trainer-advisor in Tomislavgrad, Bosnia, with the King Tomislav Brigade of western

1

Bosnia's Croat Defense Force. "Pingo" Anders was in his mid-thirties, standing about 5'6" and weighing about 170 pounds. He bore a remarkable resemblance to the actor Hardy Kruger. Though slightly built, Anders was well muscled and sported a good collection of blue prison tattoos. He claimed to have been an anti-tank missile gunner in the Danish Army. The night of the fight, he told stories of spending nearly his entire term of supposed service with the Spanish Foreign Legion locked up in the stockade for a variety of offenses before they tossed him out.

Anders, along with some of the British mercenaries, got drunk one night and tore up a room in the Hotel Tomislav. The Tomislav, formerly the Duvno Hotel, in Tomislavgrad, Bosnia, was the dilapidated old Yugoslav government tourist hotel. It billeted some of the foreign mercenaries assigned to the ethnically Croatian King Tomislav Brigade of the Croatian state of Herceg-Bosna. On another occasion I had to wrestle James, an American, to the floor for the grenade he held clenched in his fist. He was going to pull the pin in a room crowded with drunken foreign mercenaries and "watch the excitement."

The night after Anders tore up the hotel room, after returning from a walk around town, I walked into the room next door to my own to see what was going on. My Talking Heads tape was playing on the boom box . . . something about finding yourself in a foreign country. David Byrne was rhetorically intoning, "How did I get here?" My thoughts exactly.

I surveyed the chaotic scene inside the cramped hotel room and it was obvious a serious party was already well underway. A dime bag of marijuana had already been smoked up and a case of half-liter beers and a couple of bottles of *rakija* (brandy) and local whiskey, most of it stolen from the hotel bar, already consumed. Anders was there along with Jeff, a British Army veteran, convict, and a real idiot; Steve Green (a *nom de guerre*), another British mercenary and Anders' best buddy; Pat Wells (a *nom de guerre*); Pat's sidekick, a French-Hungarian named Mejor; and James, the mentally deranged American, who after traveling to Bosnia with me, revealed himself as a borderline psychotic, semi-literate cretin, self-professed drug addict, and general all-around thug. Other than that he was an okay guy.

I listened to the two or three conversations going on, nursing a beer for a while. Anders, stripped to the waist, began ranting to me about something. I realized only too late that he was drunk to the point of irrationality and violence. This wasn't a drunk you could talk to. Besides that, everyone else in the room was also inebriated. Except for Green, that is. Green never drank, but if there was trouble he was usually close by, watching the show, and was usually found to be the instigator later on.

Anders started calling me names and telling me that he didn't like officers. Then he slurred, "I don't care if *Soldier of Fortune* magazine sends someone to investigate or not, I'll kill you." This assured me that the scenario of shooting me in the back had already been discussed and discounted for exactly that reason. Typical rear-area behavior for some of these "soldiers." They won't go up to the front and fight where people are shooting each other, but they'll look for enemies amongst their own when they've got their beer muscles. Green had made noises about me keeping a journal and being something of a writer.

Anders finally tired of running off at the mouth and making empty threats and threw a punch at me. I blocked it and came up off the bed I was sitting on and popped him in the face with a right jab. It knocked him back across the room. He came back and snap-kicked me in the thigh, missing my knee, but raising a bruise. I chopped him with a more accurately directed side snap-kick to the knee, pushing him back again. That's when he grabbed the Kalashnikov and I disarmed him.

After I'd punched him a few times, he landed on the same bed I'd been sitting on. Just as I got him on his back and was really preparing to do some serious damage, either with my fists or my knife, Pat, who was also drunk, got in between us and began screaming like a mad man. For his own entertainment, Pat wanted us to take our Kalashnikovs and go out into the street and shoot each other. I think Pat was envisioning some type of Wild West showdown scenario. High Noon on the Tomislavgrad main drag. Thanks, but no thanks: I have never envisioned myself as a heroic Gary Cooper type. Besides, Grace Kelly was nowhere in sight.

Pat was wound up and just wanted to see blood. Anybody's. And preferably lots of it, as long as it wasn't his own. Boredom will do that to you. I acted drunk, even though I'd only nursed one beer all night, because I was badly outnumbered. I wanted to see how things were going to go. Pat had me by the shirtfront, Jeff was holding Anders, Steve (who'd been working on Anders to get him wound up) sat in the corner, and was playing with a grenade. Again. If they thought I was drunk, they might be able to get away with more. I'd been a very light drinker around this crowd because you never knew what was going to happen.

Walking me backwards out of the room into the hallway, Pat tried to head butt me, a favorite tactic of his. The Brits called it "nutting," and I'd seen Pat do it to Croatians who mouthed off to him. I was ready. I saw it coming and, bending my knees, dropped down so that his face hit the top of my head. A nice reverse head butt. It cut his right cheek open. I broke loose and we settled things between us in my room next door while Anders tore the other room apart. Pat wanted me to shoot Anders. So much for their friendship.

I told Pat I wouldn't turn a weapon on another foreign volunteer no matter what a loser he was. I'd kill him if I had to, but only in self-defense. I didn't like the idea of sitting in a Croat jail while the wheels of justice turned. Slowly. I knew if I slotted the bastard I was through as a player in the small circle of professional soldiers for hire. Murdering one of my own troops, no matter the provocation, would taint my reputation forever. No corporation would enlist my services, and chances are someone would put a bullet in my back someday on general principle. (Something they may still do yet.)

I later heard gossip that Anders was rumored to be wanted in Denmark for the brutal murder of two senior citizens. The story, which I got from two Danish Special Forces NCOs (non-commissioned officers) a few months later at a Commando base in Latvia, was that after he committed a home invasion on the elderly couple, he bludgeoned them to death. But not before he brutally tortured, raped, and sodomized the woman. If I'd known all that at the time, I would've killed him at the first opportunity. I mean that with all my heart. Maybe someday I'll get a second chance. And even now if I saw him walk down the street, I'd shoot him in the sure knowledge that he was gunning for me. The only other thing I'd do is smile.

After Pat left, a drunk and incoherent Anders banged on my window from the window next door, where he had crawled out onto the ledge, until the others pulled him inside. I was hoping he'd slip and fall the full three stories. I stripped the bed, tossed the blankets on the floor, then threw the mattress against the window to deflect any grenade toss, jacked a round into my Kalashnikov, put it beside me, and lay down for a very long and restless night. It gave me time to ponder the circumstances of my participation in the war in Bosnia and my "arrival" as a leader of mercenary troops before I'd yet turned thirty.

I grew up in McKean County, Pennsylvania, in a little podunk town, a village actually, near the New York border about a hundred miles south of Buffalo, New York. It was a good place to be a kid, and in retrospect it was an idyllic childhood spent hunting, trapping, cross-country skiing, and fly fishing deep in the heart of the Allegheny Mountains with its hardwood forests and trout streams. When the misty fog burns off the hillsides early in the morning with the first warming rays of the sun and you descend into hidden valleys, it's like discovering some lost land like Brigadoon. It might be why these foothills are called the Enchanted Mountains over on the New York side of the border.

In 1980, right after my seventeenth birthday, I joined the Pennsylvania Army National Guard as an infantry private while still a junior in high school. I went off to Fort Benning, Georgia, for infantry training, and returned home on the first day of my senior year. I changed from my khaki Class B uniform to blue jeans and t-shirt and went back to high school. It was surreal.

In 1983, just after my twentieth birthday, I was commissioned as an infantry second lieutenant through the National Guard-ROTC (Reserve Officer Training Corps) simultaneous membership early commissioning program. I graduated from Saint Bonaventure University in 1985 with a Bachelor of Arts degree in history. Because I completed my degree requirements a semester early, I went on active duty shortly before graduation (they mailed me my diploma), and subsequently served three years in infantry and Special Forces assignments, including a tour of duty on the Korean DMZ (demilitarized zone), where I led a rifle platoon on combat reconnaissance and ambush missions. It was good duty; we had a real combat mission, and I loved leading troops, though duty as an infantry officer in Korea probably ruined me for the real, Stateside peacetime army.

While I was stationed at Fort Devens, Massachusetts, as a staff officer in Operations and Intelligence, I took advantage of the army's education programs to attend graduate school for three semesters at Harvard University on the US Army's nickel. Like I said, I took advantage. I was studying cultural anthropology and majoring in co-eds, both of which were more interesting than the boring staff work I was doing at Fort Devens. When my three-year voluntary hitch was up, I got out. I was twenty-five years old, over-educated, and unemployed. Six days later I was jumping out of airplanes in Guatemala with their paratroopers and getting drunk with Barry Sadler. His "Ballad of the Green Berets" was a number one hit in 1966.

A month after Guatemala, I was in Kenya and back to being a graduate student in my fourth semester at Harvard, working on Richard Leakey's Koobi Fora paleoanthropology research project up on Lake Turkana. I enjoyed studying fossil hominids and the origins of man, but after the first hour in a dusty hole in the ground at a dig site near Jarigole, I decided I didn't really like archaeology all that much and that I would stick to cultural anthropology. I was later adopted by some Samburu, the northern cousins of the Maasai, and went totally native, wandering about the wild and largely untamed Northern Frontier District. It was one of the best experiences of my life.

After Kenya I stopped in Paris to join the French Foreign Legion, and was told my poor eyesight would keep me out of the parachute regiment and I could quite possibly find myself chopping down trees in Madagascar as a Pioneer (engineer). I don't think so. I returned to the States via an extended pub-crawl through England (I lived with four college girls in their apartment in Wolverhampton) to find orders waiting for me to report back to Fort Devens for a short Active Reserve assignment with the 10th Special Forces Group (Airborne). Whoops. I had really screwed up by filling out some forms a bit hastily in time to get them out on the next bush plane, and now had to get my hair cut and buy a new green beret.

The next year was really weird: I finished my course work at Harvard, but never did my thesis. I was a Guard-bum living off my National Guard paychecks, partying too much, tearing up the country roads of the Pennsylvania backwoods in my semi-stock V-6 Pontiac Fiero GT, and really disliking life as a civilian. No one told me peacetime soldiers also had problems adjusting to life as civilians. In retrospect, I should have marched myself down to the nearest recruiter and signed back up as a sergeant (E-5) or any rank they'd have me at.

On my first anniversary as a PFC—proud fucking civilian—I went back to Guatemala, then to El Salvador, and then to the Dominican Republic to jump out of perfectly good military aircraft and drink beer. On my second anniversary as a civilian, I was still functionally unemployed in the real world, but enjoying the hell out myself at Fort Hood, Texas. I was on active duty again, this time as a Brigade Assistant Operations Officer in the 2d Armored Division. I also served on state active duty as part of a rural surveillance team in the Pennsylvania State

Drug Interdiction Program. The program was set up to employ guardsmen with "special skills," and it was fairly exciting and definitely interesting. Plus the active duty money was good, I stayed in a resort hotel, and they let me drive my sports car.

Somehow I had managed to get promoted to captain a week after my twenty-seventh birthday, and was commanding the same Pennsylvania Army National Guard light infantry company I had joined as a private ten years previously. Unfortunately I relinquished command of my company a week earlier than expected. This is what happens when a captain tells a major general he can go fuck himself. I have never been known for my tact.

I didn't really care all that much. I had active duty orders to report to the Infantry Officer Advanced Course (IOAC) at Fort Benning, Georgia, and after returning from Fort Hood, I had been hired by the Department of Justice as a Federal Correctional Officer. (I had interviewed successfully with the DEA (Drug Enforcement Administration) with an eye towards being a paramilitary DEA agent on Operation Snow Cap in South America, but couldn't pass the damn eye exam.) Two weeks after we started IOAC, not exactly a gentleman's course, but a little time to "smell the roses," as our brigade commander was wont to say, Sadaam Hussein's forces invaded Kuwait. So much for smelling the roses.

I spent six months at Benning learning how to fight a war from people who'd never been in one, punched my ticket, and went home. I waited in vain for orders to the Persian Gulf. Not participating in the Gulf War was a major disappointment; though later, after vets began suffering from Gulf War Syndrome, I was almost grateful I missed that one.

The next year sucked. I was not happy being a correctional officer, despite having graduated from the Federal Law Enforcement Training Center at Glynco, Georgia, with academic honors and being told I was "management material." Not all that difficult after forty-four graduate credit hours at Harvard. Stuck in limbo between the Pennsylvania National Guard and the US Army Reserves as an unwanted infantry officer, I had missed Desert Storm and was seriously pissed off at the world in general.

I felt that if I didn't do something, anything, I was going to lose my mind. That's when I decided to go to Croatia where a mean little war was just beginning to make headlines.

CHAPTER 2

MANY AND MIXED

"There have always been mercenaries, and the reasons why men become mercenaries are many and mixed . . . money, idealism, boredom, craving for adventure. It is foolish to assume you can tell what is in every mercenary's heart when he signs on."
—Reginald Maulding, British MP

We were supposed to be in a guerrilla camp in the hot, steamy jungles of Laos. Instead we were click-clacking our way on a train on a very cool spring night through newly independent Slovenia to Zagreb, capitol of its southern neighbor, Croatia.

I had met Richard Vialpando by the poolside at the Sahara Hotel in Las Vegas during the 1991 *Soldier of Fortune* magazine convention. Claiming service with 5th Special Forces Group in Vietnam, he had also once spent some time near my old haunts in Central America. It seems we both liked hot spots. Like me, Vialpando was bored with life in general and just wanted to find some action again.

We wanted to do something for the Hmong, the Montagnard hill people of Laos. The Hmong Chao Fa (sky soldiers) were fighting a war of survival against the lowland Communist Lao intent on committing genocide on the "little people" of the mountains who had made the strategically bad error of siding with the United States in the CIA-run "Secret War" in Laos. Their second mistake: trusting the United States government.

After organizing a medical training team consisting of six experienced combat medics, two former Special Forces officers who were now practicing MDs, and a five-man team of trigger-pullers for security, I got what I thought amounted to a cold shoulder from my Chao Fa contact. It was all a misunderstanding and things have since been worked out, but at that time our planned trip to Laos was a definite no-go. So I said to Pando, "How about Croatia?" He replied, "Sounds good, when do we leave?" What followed was a frenzy of gear packing, map reconnaissance, and language study.

Pando, a first-generation Spanish Basque-American, decided I could worry about communicating. "Hey, Krott, you speak German, you can learn Croatian." Just why this seemed so logical to him, I have no idea. My reply in bastard Spanish was less than polite. I had spent the last month learning survival Serbo-Croat from a Yugoslav inmate at the federal prison where I worked. I also had essential phrases written on flash cards. We worked up a quick area study from recent news items and some unclassified, open-source materials.

Neither Pando nor I was quite sure what to take with us in the way of extra equipment. Momma always told me never go to a party empty handed, and going into a war zone I always pack something for the troops. Giving away goodies helps to make friends, and it always pays to have friends when you're someplace where people are actively engaged in ventilating each other with small arms fire. We were both accustomed to military operations in Central American countries where the troopies fight over your old worn-out boot socks, and giving away your extra fatigues and jungle boots will make you friends for life. But this was a western nation that even under Tito's rule was prosperous compared to places like El Salvador. Not knowing what was seriously needed by the International Brigade (the unit we intended to join) and the regular Croatian Forces, we took things you never seem to have enough of: medical supplies and weapons cleaning kits. Both would prove extraneous.

I took leave from the Bureau of Prisons, Pando took an extended vacation from his job as a juvenile offender counselor in Albuquerque, and we left for the war in Croatia from Toronto, Canada, in March 1992. I was about to realize a life-long dream. I was going to lead foreign troops in a European land war.

We deplaned in Munich, and our train ride from there to Zagreb was fairly uneventful. The trip consisted of reading Vietnam "No shit, I was there" paperbacks, staring at the Austrian Alps (my first look at some serious mountains), and munching on a bag of trail mix. There were a few tense moments at the Slovenian border. The Slovenes were playing big shot with their border. It's a piss-ant little country, yet they made a big deal out of checking passports and issuing visas. No one in the EC was doing this anymore. Even more comical was that very few people ever got off the trains in Slovenia. It was just the route between

Germany and Zagreb. The highlight of the journey was being good-will ambassadors for our country and playing the clown for a little six-year old Croatian girl. According to her mother, who shared some food with us, we were the first Americans her daughter ever saw. I doubt if either will ever view the good old USA in the same light as they did before they met us. They probably think we're all nuts.

Our train arrived in Zagreb around 2000 hours on a rainy Saturday night. I stepped onto the platform and was nearly knocked down by a staggering Croat soldier stewed to the gills on slivovitz. Or "slivvoed," as we would be saying days later. Besides being three sheets to the wind, it seems he paid little attention to personal hygiene. You could have cultivated mushrooms in the fuzzy green-black decay of his teeth. Croatia, like many countries in the old Communist East-bloc, had poor health care and very little dental care under the old regime; hence many people in their early twenties were missing teeth. This guy, however, was way beyond the norm. He had obviously never seen a toothbrush.

He wasn't very helpful with directions to the International Brigade Headquarters, either. A note from the publisher of *Soldier of Fortune* magazine, Lieutenant Colonel Robert K. Brown, USAR (retired), in the April 1992 issue of his journal for "professional adventurers" said: "Go to Zagreb and ask the first soldier you see where the International Brigade reception center is located." Yeah, right. This became our oft-repeated "motivation check." Anytime things got a little tense or we were bummed out, we'd look at one another and repeat the phrase. It wasn't Uncle Bob's fault. He got the info from somebody else, and I'm sure that if we had arrived on a weekday during normal duty hours and found a regular Croat soldier (who was sober) he would have given us directions. He certainly would've known where the International Brigade Headquarters was, because, as we soon found out, the Croats considered the Internationals a notoriously big pain in the ass. They caused trouble and chased after the Croatian women—occasionally to good effect. Many were consistently drunk. Nobody really liked them. They were basically all considered assholes.

After we'd conversed, with some difficulty, with various taxi drivers, "*Gdje mi mojemo da nadjemo Internacionalnu Brigadu?*" a couple of the drivers said they knew where we wanted to go. They were very happy to see US greenbacks. The Croatian economy was for shit and getting worse every day. We stopped at a government building we later found to be the right place. The headquarters for the International

Brigade was at Operativna Zona Zagreb, Ulica 292, Kagarna I. The place was locked up tight. Of course it was. This being a Saturday night, there was no one around. Everybody was out partying or home with his old lady.

There was no weekend CQ (Charge of Quarters) sergeant on duty like in a US Army unit. So the taxi driver ran us out to a base outside of town. The gate had a spray-painted sign that said "Cro-Army" and the gate guard looked like something out of "The Dirty Dozen." He was wearing unlaced white leather high-top basketball sneakers with his camouflage fatigues, and was rather nonchalantly performing his guard duties. By the looks of him, if he had been in America, his first name would invariably have been Joe-Bob, Bubba, or something ending in an "-er." You know: Cooter, Goober, Skeeter, etc. He waved us through with a desultory gesture after the taxi driver explained who we were and what we wanted. No ID check, no vehicle search. Nothing. Just go right on in.

We had a brief stay at this base while a couple of staff types called around. They initially thought we were Canadians because of the prominent Canadian Air baggage tags on our duffels. For the time being that was just fine with me. On occasions since, I have found it advantageous to mangle my vowels, say "eh?" a lot, and claim my birthplace to be a hundred miles north of Buffalo. I don't think anyone in the world, other than the Russian hockey team, hates Canadians.

After much telephoning and coffee drinking, with some pointing and shouting thrown in, the staff types eventually figured something out. We got a ride back into Zagreb to a kaserne (barracks) two blocks from the International Brigade where we had just been several hours previously. We were told that a guy from Chicago would see us in the morning, and they put us up in the SDO (staff duty officer's) hut for the night. It had the last sit-down toilet we would see during our stay in Croatia.

In the morning we got up, optimistic about joining the International Brigade and looking forward to getting clued in on the situation by another American. Hey, yo, from Chicago, what could be more American than the Windy City? After a much appreciated shower and shave, Vialpando and I changed into BDUs (battle dress uniform), boots and berets, and wandered around outside. We blended in with everyone else wearing US pattern woodland camouflage uniforms, whereas we'd have stood out like sore thumbs in blue-jeans and ski jackets. Someone directed us to the mess hall and we had bread, cheese, paté, and tea for breakfast. We wandered around a little and smoked a few cigarettes. No one in the Croat Army seemed to know how to button up a field jacket. They all looked like a bunch of farmers or city-bred blue collar types thrown into uniform. No wonder. They were.

The Croatian Army, or *Hrvatska Vojnik,* had grown out of a hastily organized national militia called the *Zbor Narodne Garde* (National Guard Corps). The ZNG, also known as the Zengees, had along with the HOS (pronounced "hoss"—the paramilitary arm of the right wing Croatian Party of Rights) protected Croatia from the Serb nationalist militias and the Jugoslav Army.

As directed by the folks at the gate, we humped our gear two blocks down the street to the same building the taxi had stopped at the night before. Why we couldn't leave our duffle bags locked up with the duty officer, I don't know. It was my first indication that the Croat Army had even less common sense than most other armies. After we'd cooled our heels for an hour or so in the vestibule of the 102 Brigade headquarters housing the International Brigade, a staff type showed up and ushered us upstairs. Even though this was the capital far from "the front," everyone was carrying a pistol. They were almost as common as the *sahovnica,* the ubiquitous red- and white-checkered enamel badge of a Free Croatia that we saw everybody wearing. We had neither, and therefore felt like the ugly girl at the school dance. Upstairs we sat on two chairs in the hallway conversing in English and occasionally Spanish when we said something confidential. Some frantic phone calling took place. It appeared that two Americans volunteering to fight for Croatia on a Sunday was too much for the Croatian Army to handle.

While this was going on, a character in a mismatched camouflage uniform with foreign dog tags and several dangling crucifixes walked up to us. He was an ex-Hungarian soldier in his early twenties, Szalay Attila. It's all Pando and I could do to keep from falling on the floor with laughter. The first expatriate soldier we meet in Croatia is: Attila the Hun! Welcome to Croatia's International Brigade. Attila had recently been at the front near Vinkovci, and proved to be a wealth of information on the state of the Croatian Army and the International Brigade. As he told us, "Croat Soldier (is) shit. Drunk. Drink cognac, drink rakija, drink beer. Dirty. Don't wash. Always with AK. *Buuuuuurrrrrp!* Stupid." He then described the proper method of a three round burst. At least this guy seemed to know how to handle a weapon. Using automatic fire is stupid. As an old World War II vet told me, "There's always more air than meat."

But Attila wasn't staying. "I need money. Buy benzene for my Trabi. Go home. Hungary. Matakovic, good officer, he pay." Attila's family ran a restaurant in Budapest. Ex-paratrooper or not, he'd had enough of Croatia and was ready to go back to waiting tables for mom and dad.

Eventually an English-speaking officer came by and we were shuttled over to Ministartvo Obrane, the Croatian Defense Ministry, to see a General Russo. Damn. Everybody in town had effectively passed the buck (us) up the chain of command.

Pando and I were both a little shocked that the sum total security for the Croatian Defense Ministry consisted of one lone guard out front with an AK, and a pimply-faced teenager with a pistol manning the reception desk. The guy out front (who, by the way, was sporting a respectable beer gut, or what some rednecks would refer to as a "major life accomplishment") was busy chatting up everything in a skirt that walked by. The kid behind the desk was reading a comic book. Yep, charge of quarters for the nation's Defense Ministry, and he's reading about his favorite superhero. Wasn't even the Silver Surfer.

Across the street was a wooded park. Any Serb fifth columnist or special operations type with a deer rifle could bag himself a general or two whenever he wanted. Obtaining a weapon wouldn't be a problem: just cold cock a drunken soldier like our buddy from the train station. Hell, there were enough of them around. We just shook our heads and wondered if the Serbs had the same situation in Belgrade. We waited an hour in the Defense Ministry to no good end and then took a taxi back to the operations building.

Still waiting for Matakovic and gas money home, we found Attila the Hungarian outside in the company of an anemic, chain-smoking teenager with a skinhead haircut, wearing a really mod leather jacket, pleated dress trousers, and punkish monk buckle brogans. All dressed up for the dance clubs he was. An Irish Ranger, he said. Kevin introduced himself, and in a strong Liverpudlian accent said, "Me friend Bobby's over here makin' boodles." Great. He wanted to know where to get a uniform. Didn't he bring any gear? "Just me sass-smock (SAS smock – a coveted piece of gear of the Special Air Service, an elite British special operations unit), and I don't fancy getting any holes in it." Ha, ha. Very funny. But wait, no boots? No, no boots. What kind of soldier for hire goes to a war zone without a pair of boots? We soon found out when Kevin asked, "Where are the brothels?" He's been in country maybe two hours and it's "where are the brothels?" Oh, yay. Raise high the Union Jack.

It's at this point that Werner the Magnificent (as I've nicknamed him) enters my story. Down the street came somebody in uniform and Pando, hanging out down the block and looking like the only East LA cholo in the Balkans, initiated a conversation. "Hey, Rob, come here, this guy's an American." Werner "Vern" Ilich, was the guy from Chicago we were looking to meet. He was sporting a good Marine Corps haircut, but beyond that, his appearance became Ramboesque with a civilian scuba dive knife strapped to his leg, several crucifixes around his neck, an earring with a dangling charm of the Croatian crest, a pistol strapped to his hip, and a couple of grenades thrown in for good measure. Kevin took one look at this fearsome, war-mongering apparition on the peaceful streets of Zagreb and said, "He's got a sense of humor, doesn't he?" What the hell, I thought, maybe there's hope for this kid yet.

We received a rather chilly reception from Vern. Supposedly the International Brigade was no longer hiring. Two Englishmen had killed a taxi driver for kicks a few months previously, conjuring shades of Sammy Copeland and Costas "Col. Callan" Georgios, the two British mercenaries responsible for the massacre of eleven of their own men (all British) at Maquela, Angola, in 1976.

I suddenly had a feeling that Kevin wasn't going to get the red carpet treatment here. Concerning the unfortunate taxi driver, I would hear various versions about what really happened over the next two years. The standard version was that it was done by two Brits who both claimed the other was the triggerman. The one who didn't get caught and managed to leg it across the border and then home to the UK was supposedly the son of a British police official. The Croats said they'd release the one in prison who professed his innocence, if his buddy turned himself in and confessed. Yeah, right.

There were conflicting orders (or rumors) about getting all Internationals (or "outsiders," as Werner kept saying) out of the country. We could talk to Matakovic later, he said. He said we should just go home. I couldn't understand why this kid who claimed to be a former US Marine lieutenant wasn't greatly overjoyed to see two former US Army captains. I mean, hell, we were Americans, for crying out loud. Something smells bad here, I thought, and it ain't yesterday's fish dinner.

Meanwhile it was back to the barracks. We were getting a workout humping around our duffel bags. Werner next informed us that he had 1) spent seven years in the USMC, 2) graduated from the University of Illinois, 3) got out of the USMC in 1990 as a lieutenant, 4) then worked for the FBI for a year, 5) had already been in Croatia for close to a year (remember that this was early 1992), and 6) was now a colonel. Not bad, considering he was only twenty-five years old.

Maybe I could give him the benefit of the doubt on that chronology, but he said a few other things that didn't jibe. Part of it was that he just didn't talk the talk or walk the walk like a USMC lieutenant. We dropped our gear in a barracks room and went for lunch. A couple of troops walked in looking much too squared away to be Croat conscripts. I noticed that one had old school blue-ink tattoos on his forearms that screamed Brit Squaddie. They wandered over to the table, and that's how we hooked up with an Englishman named Howard, a comrade of Attila's from the Vinkovci front. One thing about Howie—he made it clear from the beginning that he'd been a corporal in Her Majesty's Forces, and that's all he was. "I'm no commander or great military tactician; I'm a simple soldier, that's my business, right."

Howie laughed when we recounted Werner's story. As Werner told it: "I'm in charge of the Internationals now. I came over as a lieutenant and they put me in charge of one of four desants (units) of fifty-six men. They kept giving my unit all the missions. I lost a few every time until I was down to six or eight. They made me a colonel; I was kind of surprised." Yeah, me too.

Talking to some others, I gathered that Werner had destroyed a British volunteer's hearing with the back blast from his RPG (rocket propelled grenade launcher, a weapon similar to a bazooka), had never commanded anything, and told everyone he went to West Point. West Point too—an amazing young man. I wonder why he didn't tell two US Army captains he was a ring-knocker? Howie and the boys laughed when we explained the rarity of a West Point Marine—basically, they don't exist. It's possible to achieve an inter-service transfer after commissioning or to be commissioned into the USMC from the United States Military Academy at West Point (USMA), and three cadets actually did this upon graduation in 1974. But it is extremely rare. Besides Werner's claim being total bullshit, it also demonstrated how ignorant he was of the US military.

From Howie and Attila we found out that there was no real

International Brigade per se. It was not a real physical unit, but rather just a bunch of foreigners assigned to various units, and in most cases issued a Croatian Army ID. International volunteers were farmed out to Croat Army units willy-nilly. No one was interested in forming a foreign cadre of former military professionals or a foreign special operations unit, though some sprung up in the various Croat brigades on their own. Most of the so-called special operations units in the Croat Army were organized by foreigners or by Croat veterans of the French Foreign Legion.

Most foreign volunteers were treated as cannon fodder. The Croats really screwed up. If they had organized it right, they would have had a squared away basic training program set up from all the foreign military talent running around. After the riffraff and Euro gutter-trash were sorted out and sent packing, the pros could have gotten down to business. It would have required a good chain of command, strong leadership, and draconian discipline, but it would have been productive. Croatian arrogance and the old Communist-imbued distrust of foreigners reigned supreme. Their basic attitude was, "We don't need anybody's help, we can do it ourselves." This is why a good portion of their country was, over three years later, still occupied by Serb irregular militia.

Later we walked over to meet Matakovic. He was one mean-looking dude. Long hair, tough face. He was sitting behind a desk littered with various grenades. Half a dozen automatic weapons were leaning in a corner, and a crossbow decorated the wall behind his head. His office looked like the prop room for a Rambo flick. A longhaired effeminate-looking boy, about nineteen years old, dressed in a black jump suit and wearing purple sneakers, stood by the desk. Later Howie told us he was known by his initials, TV. We had a good laugh, and had to explain that in America it was short not only for television, but also for transvestite.

TV fit right in. I assume he was good pals with Werner, because in only a year in the JNA, or Jugoslav Army, TV had been a sniper, a demo expert, etc., etc. Eric Farina, another American volunteer with the International Brigade, whom I met two years later, told me that TV spent most of his time playing with two Doberman pups. He was also supposedly Matakovic's kid brother.

Werner translated our documents to Matakovic. We both had a file containing copies of our DD-214s (discharge papers) and photocopies of various military certificates, awards and decorations. Though Werner seemed to be doing a fairly honest job of translating, we doubted that he was eager to have somebody around who could shoot his stories full of holes. He was what we call a poser and what the Brits call a wanker—your basic bullshit artist.

Kevin said, sorry, he'd left his documents in his bag. We later found out he had the British version of a Bad Conduct Discharge. By the expression on Matakovic's face, Pando and I knew not to be too optimistic. Matakovic explained that he had specific orders not to take on any more international volunteers, but transcribed our names and passport numbers into his logbook of Internationals. If I remember correctly, I was number 146. Whether that was a total count of international volunteers officially signed in through his office since the war started, I don't know. We were told to come back at 1000 hours the next morning.

After leaving the office Kevin said, repeatedly, "I might just as well go home." Pando and I were not overjoyed with his optimism. We looked at each other and shrugged. What'd the kid expect? Brass bands? We considered taking our ball and going home, but decided this might be our only chance to see an honest-to-God shooting war on the European continent in our lifetime, and damn it, we were not going to miss it. We figured if worse came to worst, we would go find the right wing paramilitary outfit known as the HOS, an armed nationalist group that was operating somewhat autonomously as an independent military organization. I'd heard they had an international company.

Back at the barracks we met another International. Milo, an Austrian of Bosnian descent, had seen action with Howie and Attila. When Howie gave him an update on the latest claims of Werner the Magnificent he had a good laugh. Seems the only people Werner fooled were the Croat officers he toadied up to. We looked at some photos of Howie, Milo, and Attila, and some other Internationals on patrol and hanging out in fortified houses and bunkers near Vinkovci. We engaged in a typical bullshit session—guns, wars, women, our national army service, women, beer, and women. We learned that Howie, like many Internationals, was romantically involved with a Croatian woman.

When the conversation finally got around to food, the six of us (two Americans, two Brits, an Austrian, and a Hungarian) decided to go across the street to the chow hall, since the one next door was closed. Before we left, Howie pulled out a Yugoslav Tokarev pistol, cocked it, and slipped it under his shirt, but not before an admiring and covetous Kevin oohed and ahhed. "Where can I nick me one of them, then?" he asked. Pando and I exchanged glances, thinking the same thing: "Let's not leave anything valuable lying around when this kid's on the loose." Howie asked if we had sidearms. No, no pistols, but fortunately we both had large bowie-style fighting knives with us. The other mercs all admired them and handled them. The others had bayonets or hunting knives. Close in, a knife is almost as good as a pistol and a hell of a lot quieter. You can also cut sausage with it.

So, armed with one Tokarev among the group and at least one knife apiece, we went across the street, only to find that the other chow hall was closed as well. We all ended up at the nearby corner bar. Which was, quite possibly, everybody's original intent anyways. A cold beer seemed to be just the ticket.

Kevin didn't have much money left, just a few British pounds, as he'd spent most of his money in Germany on—yep, you guessed it—the brothels! Kevin had pounds, no dinars, but that was okay, because good chum Howie was more than happy to exchange some dinars for pounds and help the kid out. Pando and I winked at each other and wondered how badly Kevin was about to get soaked by Corporal Howard's international banking consortium. While the others ordered up a round of Karlovacko pivo (beer) and began to drink their dinner, which was probably also their plan all along, Pando and I elected to drink Coca-Cola.

We soon noticed an older gentleman in a maroon beret with foreign jump wings attached. Introductions were made when he and his companions heard us conversing in English. Yes! Finally! Somebody who actually looked, walked, and talked like a professional military officer. With Colonel Wim "Willi" Van Noort were two other Dutchmen, Douwe Van de Bos, and a strange character named Johann Stelling, aka Crazy Joe.

Colonel Van Noort claimed he began his military career with the Waffen SS when he was captured by the Germans while attempting to cross the Austrian border into Allied Italy in 1943. After serving with them as a press-ganged "potato peeler" he escaped to British lines in France. He was taken into the British Army in 1944 as a member of the Dutch Commando contingent, and later served in India until 1950. Willi claimed he saw action again in the Korean War, then worked as an engineer in the oil fields in the Middle East for a while. He told me he then moved to Australia and served as an advisor with the Australian SAS in Vietnam in the early 1960s, although I later checked and his name doesn't appear on the roster of AATV personnel in Vietnam. If only half of what he said was true, he'd had quite the military career. Willi had been in Croatia off and on since November 1991.

Douwe struck me as very professional, but I shouldn't have been surprised. He was formerly a staff sergeant in the Dutch Army. He carried himself with the self-assuredness characterized by professional NCOs the world over, and reminded me of every good S-3 operations sergeant I ever knew. Willi introduced him to me as "my administrator, who knows all about the paperwork." That was pretty much Douwe's role in the scheme of things. He wasn't a combat arms soldier and didn't pretend to be; he was a real rarity amongst foreign mercs, a confessed rear-echelon type. He hustled funds and equipment wherever he could to keep the Croat troops under Willi's care well equipped. And, thank God, he was bloody good at it. Joe had no military experience, but saw some action in a Croat Army unit with some other Dutchmen and Attilla at the front near Vinkovci.

These three Dutchmen were the remnants of a much larger Dutch volunteer force, the First Dutch Volunteer Unit. The First Dutch Volunteers included a Dutch Moluccan NCO, whose dark skin caused quite a stir amongst the homogenously Slavic Croats. The First Dutch Volunteers were probably the first organized group of foreigners to make the trip to the Balkans. Erwin van der Mast, a former Dutch paratrooper, was KIA in Croatia within two weeks of his arrival. His death was reported in *Soldier of Fortune* shortly after my return from Croatia. From the three Dutchmen we learned that the International Brigade (about a hundred forty men, with forty more of Croatian heritage), if assembled in one place, would be a real rogues' gallery of misfits and wannabes. But there were some professionals here and there. Home to some of these guys was an army cot and a place to store their duffel bag.

After Willi and Douwe checked us out, Willi offered us a job training troops with him. He told us he had a Commando Group down south near the front. It sounded better than hanging around Zagreb until the politicians evicted us, and a lot better than traveling all the way to Vinkovci on Croatia's south eastern border just to sit in a bunker. We decided to forego our appointment with Matakovic at 1000 hours the next morning. Chances were, they were probably going to put us on a train back to Germany. We hoped he'd forget about us, or figure we left on our own. Hope in one hand, shit in the other, and see which one fills up first.

For the drive south from Zagreb all five of us (Pando, Willi, Joe, Douwe, and myself) squeezed into a battered Opel compact with all our gear. It was no easy feat. Shortly before midnight we arrived at the old JNA rocket base at Zazina, a few kilometers from Chetnik-held Petrinja. Shown to the instructors' room in the barracks, we met John Rajkovic, nineteen, from Burlington, Ontario. John had arrived with his father soon after the fighting started and chose to stay when his father returned to Canada. Johnny's 30mm anti-aircraft battery in Sisak shot down six Serb aircraft, which was a good thing because the Croats had no Air Force at the time.

John was assigned to Willi as an interpreter. His Smith and Wesson Model 696 six-inch barreled .357 Magnum "Hogleg" in a Dirty Harry shoulder holster was his constant companion. At the beginning of the war, his father Ivan, a machine shop owner, packed a duffel bag full of weapons and told his son to pack a change of clothes—they were going back to the homeland. Even though the paperwork for the weapons was all in order, the *Flughafen Bundespolizei* confiscated them in Germany and made the Rajkovics pay a fine. Cryin' shame a grown man can't ship his weapons overseas when he's about to walk into a war zone. On a subsequent trip, the .357 found its way over taped up inside an automobile dashboard.

During our stay we tried to teach Johnny as much about soldiering and light infantry tactics as we could. Since he had no prior military experience, everything about an organized military force, especially subjects like long-range patrolling and strategic reconnaissance, amazed him. It was all new to him. As he said, "Hell, a year ago I was just trying to get through high school." I envied the kid. I envied him his youth, his Croatian language skills, and his opportunity to soldier for his ethnic homeland and live history in the making. Maybe if the United States had gotten off the stick when the Chetniks invaded Croatia and sent men like Johnny Rajkovic through a shake and bake course at the Infantry School at Fort Benning or the Special Warfare Center at Fort Bragg, the war in the Balkans would have gone differently, and not have dragged on like it did, resulting in the suffering of countless civilians.

Later that night Pando said, "Hear the background music?" I then realized I hadn't consciously noticed the steady Karummmph, Karummmph, Karummmph, of artillery rounds impacting nearby. Not exactly my idea of a lullaby, but you became accustomed to it in time.

In the morning John introduced us to the troops, and I talked briefly with Pedrag Matonovic, twenty-two, the company commander, under-going training with nineteen of his troops. Pedrag proudly displayed his 5.56mm SAR-80. Chartered Industries of Singapore built the Singapore Assault Rifle-80 after producing M-16s under license from Colt Industries. It uses M-16 magazines and is very similar to the Armalite AR-18. Small arms aficionados do not think very highly of the SAR-80. Pedrag was pleased when I gave him ten M-16 magazines and a US Army cleaning kit for the M-16. I'd dragged them along, just in case. Where he was procuring adequate quantities of 5.56mm ammo, I had no idea.

A quick tour of the barracks room showed that the Commandos were armed with .308 Argentine Modelo III folding stock FN FALs, .308 German G-3s, 7.62 x 39mm Jugoslav M-70 Kalashnikovs, and an interesting assortment of pistols and knives. These guys really liked pistols and knives. As we inspected weapons to show that we knew what we were doing, the questions soon started, led off by Pedrag with, "When is America going to send us M-16s?" and "When do we get *M-sesnaest?*" I guess these guys watched too many made-in-Hollywood Rambo movies. They thought the M-16 was the weapon. No amount of discussion could persuade them that their own M-70 Kalashnikovs were superior, or at least as good as the Colt M-16. These kids had guts and motivation. Shiny new American rifles weren't what they needed. What they needed were decent boots and six weeks of basic infantry training.

But the Big Question was: "Why doesn't America recognize Croatia?" Thank god the second week we were there, the US State Department got off its ass and recognized Croatia. We heard the news on the radio in the barracks. All the Croats started cheering, as if the might of the American military was suddenly going to join their little Balkans inter-mural fracas. We got our backs slapped and cold pivos thrust into our hands. Then the question was, "Why did you wait so long? Why aren't you helping us like you helped Kuwait? Is it because we don't have any oil?" What could we say but, "Yes, you're right"? We didn't mention the fact that while allied with Nazi Germany, Croatia had declared war on the United States in 1941 and no one ever bothered to sign a peace treaty. Technically, we were still at war with these guys. Technically.

In the morning we took the troops for a run outside the small base and some guerrilla drills in a little field next to the Roman Catholic church outside of Zazina. I couldn't help but notice all the fresh tombstones in the graveyard. It was a few weeks before the outbreak of hostilities throughout Bosnia, and these people had already paid a horrendous price to preserve their freedom. During PT (physical training) we got some comments because we wore only our GI t-shirts and the troops all had their sweaters on. Vialpando and I just smiled at each other. We knew we'd be warm soon.

As we ran past the gate guard, Pando said, "Rob, don't step off the road."

"What?"

"The Colonel told me before we left that the whole perimeter is mined."

Gee, I thought, that's really nice to know, thanks.

As I led pushups, I noticed that these troops weren't much for upper body strength. Our breath misting in the frosty morning air, we circled the field doing guerrilla drills until it was churned into mud. Marching them or running them anywhere, I sang cadence. The Commandos really liked "Tiny Bubbles" for a marching tune. Don Ho would probably have sold out in Zazina.

The afternoon was spent chalk talking the standard US Army Fire Team Wedge movement formation. We moved back to our little training area near the quaint little Catholic church in the Croatian countryside along the Kupa River outside the bucolic village of Zazina, and then it was practice, practice, practice. Other than the column, this was the first movement formation these guys had ever seen. Under the watchful eye of some former JNA officers, I explained techniques for exiting what the US Army calls the FEBA (Forward Edge of the Battle Area) or Front, as the Croats and everyone else in the world calls it, and how to establish a hasty cigar-shaped perimeter from a "Ranger file," or single line in column, thus executing a listening security halt.

The guys were eager to learn some real tactics, and after practicing some more patrol movements, we quickly moved into the proper techniques for establishing an ambush position. The concept of left, right, and rear security for a unit set up in an ambush position was new to them. But when the concept of *sigurnost* (security) and stop-groups was explained, they quickly grasped the common sense reasoning behind it. I didn't know enough Croatian to translate, "A well-executed ambush is murder—now let's go commit murder," or "Ambushes mean killing, and killing is fun." Just as well. That kind of rah-rah stuff never impressed me much when I heard if from my instructors at Fort

Benning. It would mean even less to blooded combat veterans.

After we completed the instruction and walked the troops through it a few times, the unit leaders drilled their people. In keeping with standard US Army Special Forces doctrine, we trained the trainers. The Commandos executed some ambush drills and looked expectantly at me for my approval. I just nodded my head and said, "Good, do it again." Repetition would drill it into them until it became second nature to react that way in combat.

Later that afternoon Willi handed us two brand spankin' new Romanian AKM rifles. They were still wrapped in plastic shrink-wrap. We were very happy campers. We really didn't like the idea of being a few klicks from Serb-controlled territory without a weapon. No pistols, though. To get one, you took it off the body of a dead Serb, and since these teenagers we trained were all combat vets, they packed Tokarevs, CZ-52s, CZ-50s, and the occasional Spanish Army surplus Star 9mm. It would take me almost two weeks before I could score a Tokarev.

We each had four magazines, but only about sixty rounds of ammo for our fine examples of factory-fresh Romanian "farm tools," but the troops kicked in some more ammo, including some green Combloc tracers and some lovely armor-piercing rounds. That made Pando mucho happy. We both wanted more than a hundred rounds, obviously, but the Croats just didn't have much ammo to spread around.

We wiped the Cosmoline off the rifles and did a detailed field strip. The only drawback of the Romanian AKM, according to the troops, is the tendency for its barrel to "melt" after several magazines' worth of sustained automatic fire. I know from experience that the vertical foregrip, peculiar only to the Romanian version of the Kalashnikov assault rifle, causes some problems with speedy magazine changes. I had always liked the Romanian Kalashnikov's foregrip, but that was before I'd actually carried one for long periods of time and had to make magazine changes while under fire. Throughout my three tours of duty in the Balkans, I saw several Rumanian AKMs with the vertical foregrip chopped off, and the remaining forearm sanded smooth and revarnished.

The Croats supposedly had all these Romanian rifles because of some dirty deals in Zagreb. The story, which may very well be apocryphal, was that the Croats bought a large shipment of Argentine FN-FAL .308-caliber assault rifles on the international arms market: enough to equip their army. As the story goes, most of the shipment was sold off to one Lebanese faction or another in Beirut. The middlemen, Zagreb generals and politicians, pocketed most of the cash. They replaced the FNs with Romanian AKs bought for a fraction of the cost of the Argentine rifles. How much truth there is to this, I don't know, but there were quite a few dirty arms deals done dirt cheap in the Balkans arms market over the course of the war, especially after the UN embargo went into effect.

After PT that first day, Douwe left for Zagreb to scrounge equipment. According to Willi, he was pretty good at shaking supplies out of the military and getting Zagreb businessmen and various international groups to cough up special items and cold hard cash. We were not quite sure what Joe's purpose was. Willi said he was a survival expert and would teach survival. Great, that would cover about one day of the training schedule. If we had a training schedule, that is. Survival didn't seem like it would be much of a problem. In a land dotted with family farms and orchards, there was plenty to eat if a soldier had to forage. Joe seemed to devote much of his time to teaching English to Sonya, a good-looking and very shapely little brunette who worked in the kitchen. War is hell.

The next morning, a Tuesday, we rode a small bus through the local village, Zazina, which borders the Kupa River, towards the front for some live fire training or combat, whichever came first. The houses were pockmarked by small arms fire and artillery fragments. Here and there windows had been blown out by incoming artillery shell concussion. At the time I thought the post-war building contractors were going to do well in this area. The pontoon bridge across the river was a major target. Six kilometers due south down Highway 12-2 and just across the winding Kupa, is a well-known little town, Petrinja. Willi told us the war story I still call "The Saga of the Petrinja Swim Team."

Petrinja was the scene of fierce house-to-house fighting in the fall of 1991. A Serb armored force overran the little farm village in October just as the leaves were beginning to fall. Shoulder-fired light anti-tank weapons like RPGs don't do much against the T-84 (the Yugoslav version of the Soviet T-72 tank). Many of the Croat defenders, uncomfortable in their new US Army surplus BDUs and old style steel helmets, were armed only with bolt-action hunting rifles, which don't do anything against tanks other than annoy the tankers with the *ping, ping, ping* of rounds hitting the armor.

A battalion of Croat troops operating south of the Kupa was

pushed back to the river and forced to swim for it. Many were shot while entering the water. Non-swimmers and those who turned back after attempting to swim the river were captured and later executed. The survivors are still known as "the Swimmers." A Croatian general asked Willi what should be done with them. Willi shrugged and replied, "Send them home, they're finished."

I have a videotape of the Croat troops manning hasty defensive positions in Petrinja. Many of them were from the hastily organized Sisak infantry unit. These were friends, neighbors, and even brothers of the men I was working with. Somebody had come up with stocks of US Army surplus BDUs, field jackets, and old style steel pot helmets. By the way they wore this military gear, it was obvious that the bulk of the fighters were civilians, plain and simple.

One guy was running around wearing a black fedora. Some of the Croats were armed with FN FALs, but the bulk seemed to be using captured Kalashnikovs and a wide variety of sporting arms. In the video they were using a stack of beer crates packed full of bottles as a parapet/barricade, popping up over the top like the inexperienced troops they were, rather than shooting around cover, to loose off a few rounds. The video ends with a long line of Serb/JNA T-72s rolling into town. Without their own tanks or any decent anti-tank weapons, the Croats never had a chance.

After making our way through the town, the bus dropped us off south of Zazina. We were still in one of the landlocked curves formed by the Kupa River, but a bit nearer no-man's-land and Serb-occupied Croatia. We'd heard that other Internationals at the front had wandered through the large gaps in the largely undefended lines, only to be waved back frantically by Croatians. The war here along the border of the Krajina was fought neighbor versus neighbor. Everyone seemed to know everyone, and the locals knew the terrain intimately. Not a good place to be a stranger.

We locked and loaded full magazines, jacked a round up the spout, and checking our gear one last time, moved out. Spreading out in staggered files, we patrolled the graveled country lane. Houses and farms in the immediate area were abandoned, their occupants no doubt having fled the Chetnik marauders backed by Serbian tanks for safer havens in Sisak, Zagreb, or abroad. Other homes may have been owned by Serbs forced to flee Croat retaliation. We were on our guard for ambushes or Chetnik patrols. This area was still hotly contested. There was no fixed line and small units actions were frequent with ambushes and raids occurring daily.

Being very wary of booby traps we took a look around, immediatel noticing that the small cottage-like homes were stripped clean. No loot or war souvenirs to be found here. The troops moved up the road in patrol formation while we observed their technique. Mindful of possible booby traps, tripwires, and mines, we cleared the houses without incident. We critiqued them a little and the Commandos' performance improved. This training was as near to being in actual combat as you get without becoming engaged. In fact we were in combat because locked and loaded with live ammo, we were conducting a security sweep—reconnaissance patrol in a contested and very hot area. The threat of ambush, snipers, or just getting a foot blown off by a "toe-popper" was very real. The last two days of tactical training was the only real training this ad hoc Commando unit had received. Though they were mostly all JNA veterans, their training as conscripts hadn't contained much in the way of small unit infantry tactics. Some of the group were previously tank drivers or missile crewmen during their national service. Cleaning Kalashnikovs and sweeping floors they knew.

For two weeks Willi had concentrated on getting them into shape, pushing them on ever increasing long-distance marches. Unfortunately the troops developed some bad blisters from their poor quality boots. We spent the day patrolling the area and setting up a few ambushes on likely avenues of approach and known routes used by local Serb forces. Not making any contact except for encountering the day-old boot prints of an eight- to ten-man enemy patrol, we packed up at last light and moved back to our pickup point. Back at Zazina, I explained the principles of zasjeda—the ambush: Organization, Coordination, Communication, Security, Surprise, and Violence of Action. The only way we could translate "violence of action" was "to go *ludite*" (crazy). From the way it was explained to me, I guess *ludite* is the Croat version of "mad minute."

Breakfast the next day was fatty sausage. Again. For some reason the troops didn't drink anything with their meals, not even water. They looked dumbfounded when we put a canteen on the table or walked into the mess hall with a liter carton of Tok brand *naranca*, the processed orange juice that was part of our rations issue. Pando and I loved that stuff. By that time we had gotten the Commandos in the habit of wearing their LBE (load-bearing equipment) and carrying rucks every time they left garrison. Prior to an operation, our "Commando trainees" were all cammied up and were wearing black watch caps. Well, at least they looked like a special operations unit. A far cry from the shirt open, no headgear, in-need-of-a-shave Croatian soldiers most people were accustomed to.

True, appearances don't make a good soldier, but they're usually indicative of a well-trained professional. It was easy to see how differently the local people responded to our unit moving through town on its way to a combat operation as opposed to some others, who looked like gypsies running away from home. Everyday as we passed by on patrol, the local people shouted greetings and waved from doorways and windows. Others left their work momentarily to stand by the road and watch when we trooped past. Just seeing a uniformed and well-equipped unit moving out on a combat operation imbued them with confidence. To the average civilian, the Commandos looked rather forbidding with their painted faces, black watch caps, and full combat gear, and their foreign trainers shouting commands in a mix mash of Croatian, German, Dutch and English.

While we would have been much more comfortable in boonies or watch caps ourselves, Willi, who always wore his maroon paratrooper's beret, asked that we wear some sort of beret so that we might "stand out." Pando and I were both a little uneasy about "standing out," especially in an area inhabited by Chetnik snipers. I had a bad feeling that if we got hit by an ambush, the two guys wearing berets were going to take a lot of rounds. Bullet magnets. Maybe that was the idea. We tried to explain to Willi that American soldiers don't wear berets in the field. But we understood that part of our *raison d'être* was to be a morale builder and a visible reminder of foreign support. The unit, also, received a certain cachet by having foreign advisors.

On one mission we led, as the Commandos moved out through Zazina, the surrounding countryside, and into the hills, we passed small groups of indolent reservists. It seemed that when the fighting broke out, every yahoo in the country was issued a uniform and a Kalashnikov. Pando found it all hilarious. "It's just like Zagreb, Rob, none of these guys do anything but hang around." That was to be a major problem. If they weren't actively engaged in combat, there was also no organized training or equipment maintenance program to occupy the troops. Without training it was an army of cannon fodder; more an unorganized mob than a disciplined military formation. Even daily enforced PT would have been an improvement.

Most of the physiques we saw were indicative of a high-fat diet and too much pivo. We passed one group in maroon berets. Nothing special. In the Croatian Army in those days, if you had some extra dinars, you just bought some berets and called yourselves Special Forces, Rangers, whatever. These guys even had matching shoulder patches that translated as "Street People." Pando and I kept walking, lest our giggling got us shot by an inebriated "Reservist." There were a lot of strange characters wandering around their hometowns loaded down with their new Kalashnikovs and, uh oh, *hand grenades.* Yeah. Just imagine some of the gooners loitering down at your local body shop or the wannabe rock stars working at the record shop in the mall suddenly being handed automatic weapons and fragmentation grenades. Scary thought, huh?

Another day we moved up to the front to conduct some more immediate action drills—IADs (with live ammo) such as "react to contact" and "react to sniper fire," followed by some instruction and critique. The biggest problem was communication. These guys, even the leaders, didn't like to shout at each other. Maybe, culturally, they felt it impolite or disrespectful. Their technique was for the scout, i.e., the point man (if he was still alive) to run back down the formation and try to find Pedrag. Right. While under fire. Sure. By the time he managed to accomplish that small feat, their point element could be overrun and the flanks pinned down.

Because we weren't confident yet in the skills of our point man, Pando and I scouted ahead and out on the flanks on these combat patrols. The last thing we wanted was for one of our nineteen-year-old soldiers to lead us into a Serb ambush. The local Chetniks were noted bandits and I assumed at least some of them were woodsmen. We were really hanging it out there.

If we got hit—wounded—we were dependent on the Croat trainees to get us out. We tried not to split up very often, so that one of us could help the other if everything went tits up. On one patrol we stopped by an isolated farmhouse for a minute to snap a few snapshots of the truly charming rural scene. The farmer came out to join us on the dirt road, offering us *rakija* and inviting us inside for lunch. Since there were no lissome farmer's daughters in evidence, and we were supposed to be on a combat operation, we begged off. Almost forgot there was a war on.

During that same patrol, we broke the Commandos for lunch on a grapevine-covered hilltop with a beautiful vista. The area reminded me of the wine country in western New York near where I grew up, especially the scenery up along Keuka Lake, one of the Empire State's Finger Lakes. I looked around at some of the little cottages and fantasized about buying myself one, finding a good woman (or a bad one) and growing grapes and making babies. Or maybe I could just stay there part of the year, up on the side of one of those hills, away from television, phones, and all the other bullshit. I would drink wine, read good books, and maybe write one. Oh, to live a life of leisure as a country squire. That was back in 1992, but I still think of that idyllic hillside now and again. More and more so it seems as time passes.

After lunch we resumed our patrol. As we moved out in a staggered column, it quickly became obvious that Willi was interested in the PT element, while Pando and I saw the need for further live fire tactical training. I thought we were moving a little too fast for an area where we could make imminent contact with Chetnik units. Our security was for shit and forget stealth. The possibility of stumbling into an ambush or bumping into a Chetnik patrol was very real. We had over twenty men moving on patrol—too many to be truly stealthy on a recon mission, and not enough to maneuver against a large enemy force. Worse yet, if we hit a main force Serb unit, we were too many to die and not enough to win.

We moved down a ridgeline for a klick or so until Willi changed our direction of movement a full 180 degrees. I was quickly confronted by a very irate Spanish-Basque American. What the hell was going on? Willi had no map. "Oh shit, this is not good," I thought. I finally got a map of Zazina and the surrounding countryside from his large stack after we left the AO (area of operations). Typical. What he was saving the damn things for I don't know. Willi had shot his compass azimuth from the wrong hilltop. We were lost in the wine country.

Pando was up front with the lead element and felt that the Colonel's momentary "mis-orientation" caused him to lose face. Willi learned something the hard way: don't piss Pando off. I was moderately concerned and hoped we hadn't strayed too far into Chetnik-held Croatia. It wasn't very comforting to know that we were off azimuth in the middle of enemy territory. Thanks to lessons drilled into my thick skull at (Fort) Benning's School for Boys, I was periodically shooting azimuths and keeping a rough pace count, just in case. I knew I could find my way back to Zazina, and it was a nice day in some beautiful countryside, even if we were in a war zone. What the hell.

I tried to keep from daydreaming and ditty-bopping in the warm spring sunshine as we conducted our combat patrol through the picturesque countryside. It was definitely too nice a day for stepping on a landmine or walking into an ambush. Stuff like that just tends to ruin your whole fucking day.

Moving back towards our own lines, we stopped after a while, secured the area, and I did the rucksack flop. Even though it was March, the weather was warm enough that we worked up a sweat. We'd conducted a good sweep of the area and failed to make enemy contact, so we decided to use the open terrain for some training. There just wasn't any place in the rear where we could live fire, so after a ten-minute water break we conducted more IADs.

With a couple of troops out for local security, Pando played OPFOR (Opposing Force) on an L-shaped bend in a dirt road. As the first burst of AK fire shattered the afternoon silence, Pedrag issued commands, decisively this time, and the Commandos executed their react to ambush immediate action drill rapidly and violently. Kalashnikov, FN, and G-3 rounds snapped through the air. As I moved up and down the road to observe their fire and maneuver, I caught a burst of AK fire over my head. The tracers turned into little green footballs as they floated out over the valley. Somebody had decided that instructor or not, Krott needed to be in the dirt with everybody else. I really hate it when that happens.

After a brief critique, I explained by using a hastily made sand table how to execute an L-shaped ambush. Points stressed were use of Claymores, personnel mines, security, and searching the kill zone. We discussed how to react to both far and near ambushes. The unit was split into two ten-man groups to go force on force. With live ammo, of course. It's important to train with live ammo for combat, I can't stress that enough. In this case we weren't confined by the usual peacetime army safety regulations. But it's possible to fire live ammo to enhance realism in training with a modicum of safety, especially when experienced troops are doing it. You fire into the ground, a tree next to you, or the air above the "enemy's" head—closely, if you don't particularly like the guy. Yes, I know, the Post Safety Officer, US Army Infantry School, Fort Benning, Georgia, would have conniptions.

Once each group had established and conducted an ambush on the other, we reconsolidated for a quick AAR (After Action Review). Typical of troops the world over, they were all hot, sweaty, pumped up, and talking at once. I calmed them down and talked them through their actions so they could learn from their mistakes. With the AAR completed and fresh magazines in our weapons, we moved out and resumed the patrol into Chetnik territory.

Because there'd been enemy activity in this area recently, everyone had their weapon at combat port arms, pointing out toward possible enemy contact. Everyone, that is, except Joe. Joe, sans rucksack, was at sling arms. The guy had to be nuts, this was a hot area, Chetnik patrols had been through there and part of our mission was both to recon for evidence of their incursions into the area as well as to "interdict" them (the current politically correct US Army speak for "ambush and kill the bastards"). We regularly took fire in the Zazina AO or heard small arms fire nearby. Plus we'd just fired up the area a few klicks south. When I tried to explain "setting the example" to him, he got pissed. During the patrol Pando and I snacked on cattail roots plucked from the marsh, something I'd learned while muskrat trapping as a boy with my grandfather, but we passed on a large salamander. Hey, let's not take the Special Forces hard corps bullshit too far, okay?

Joe, whom we secretly nicknamed "Mr. Survival," was nowhere to be seen while we were partaking of nature's bounty. The dumbshit was off wandering around alone somewhere. If he ran into a Chetnik patrol, he was going to be in deep shit. I slowed down and grabbed my buddy as he passed by and whispered in his ear, "Pando, I have dibs on Joe's coffee maker back at the barracks." He looked at me, shook his head, and then his eyes lit up and he grinned, "Okay, Rob, but I get Sonya, amigo." Damn, outdone again. The bastard.

A kilometer later and where the hell was Joe? Perhaps he was off communing with nature and thinking of Sonya. Just as well, the guy was basically worthless. He came out on patrol without his rucksack, just an AK with one magazine. Shit like that gets people killed. "Crazy Joe" was either certifiably nuts or just plain stupid—maybe both.

Near sunset we rendezvoused with our vehicle pickup and returned to Zazina. Joe soon reappeared. He must have been off discovering himself or something. The troops were beat. Too bad. We gave them thirty minutes to be in the classroom. After a review of all they'd learned on ambushes and patrolling, we chalk talked some more tactics concentrating on combat patrolling techniques: point and area recons, rally points, establishing an Objective Rally Point (ORP), cloverleaf and box recon techniques, and surveillance of a target area.

Later that night while we were in our quarters cleaning weapons and sucking down some orange drink, John walked in and announced that the troops were packing up to go to Sisak per Pedrag's decision. Sisak was the regional center some ten kilometers to the southeast and home of Pedrag's battalion headquarters. While Pando and I exchanged raised eyebrow glances, Joe whined, "Sisak? But I can't leave Zazina, I have a girlfriend!"

CHAPTER 3

LOOKING FOR WAR IN ALL THE WRONG PLACES

"I won't describe the operation because it was one of the most frustrating experiences of my military career, a compendium of tactical errors and blown chances grotesque enough to break the heart of anybody who likes to kill people."

—Jim Morris, *War Story*

We were moving because Pedrag thought the living conditions at the old missile base were lousy and the food sucked. He was correct on both counts. Pedrag's older brother, Drago, twenty-seven, was the Sisak Battalion commander. When Pedrag issued an order it got obeyed and it was backed up by the battalion CO. Big brother was sending the trucks to get the troops at O'dark-thirty in the morning. In the morning we packed it up in about fifteen minutes. Joe didn't move. After a little while he got up and wandered off to disappear again. He wasn't going with us. Sonya's allure was compelling. I was going to miss his Mr. Coffee machine.

We loaded up with the troops. Willi was despondent. He liked Zazina because we were the only game in town. Despite it being an easy target for Serb artillery and rocket fire, we liked the barracks at Zazina because we could walk easily to the front, and good ambush patrol sites were only a half an hour away. We were on the sharp end of the spear there. It was where the action was. But we were also a speed bump for Serb tanks. If a major Serb offensive kicked off to take the Kupa River Valley, we'd be rolled over. But until then we were practically operating behind enemy lines.

While I liked and admired the Colonel, I began to get the idea that Willi and I might have problems. He was too quick to stop all training with the evening meal. If he wasn't up to it, he didn't want any one else doing it. Also, he took umbrage when I just shrugged off the fact that the troops were moving to Sisak. He was upset and wanted to bitch and moan. He couldn't, or wouldn't, order the boys to stay in Zazina, so why cry over spilt milk? Maybe it was the realization that he was not really in charge.

I fully understood that as foreigners we were "outsiders" (as Werner Ilich said) and we should always be cognizant of that fact, no matter how much authority we were handed. I always tried to relay any "advice" through the unit commanders, and pushed Pedrag in his leadership role. It was up to us to develop their leadership potential. I knew I was going back home someday, but there was no rotation home or R and R for these guys; they were in the shit for the duration. This was their country, their war. Their friends and relatives were dying every day.

Willi was angry that I was going along with Pedrag's orders. On the subject of the troops deploying back to Sisak, I wasn't going to fight a battle I couldn't win. I respected Pedrag's ability and I thought the Commandos had a lot of potential, so I was going to stick with them and not go wandering around Croatia from unit to unit like a lot of gypsy mercs I met later.

Vialpando was in agreement with me. We had discussed our options and decided to go with Pedrag. I can't stress how important and how valuable it was to have a loyal, trustworthy friend like Pando. We watched each other's back. My attitude toward Willi and his disagreement with the move to Sisak was—what the hell, roll with it, baby. He went off on me a little when he saw me packing my gear. My reply was, "Hey, Colonel, if you want to train the troops, you got to go where the troops are. I'm not going to sit on my ass down here and make goo-goo eyes at Sonja." Joe was sitting there listening when I said this. He glared at me, but said nothing in response. Here I go again, I thought, Mr. Tact, making friends and influencing people wherever I go. I oughta read that Dale Carnegie book someday.

I couldn't blame the troops for wanting better living conditions or wanting to be nearer to home. They pulled some rough duty patrolling the hills and in the bunkers on the frontline. If they got some downtime for "training," well, they should get a little bit of a break, too. The problem in Sisak was that there were no decent areas for live fire training. And the troops preferred Sisak where their battalion was quartered. It meant a three-story *kaserne*, TV with VCR, and beer and women in the town's bars just across the old stone bridge.

No problem there, as long as they trained hard the next day. I've always had that attitude. When I was a mechanized infantry platoon leader in Korea, my company's motor sergeant was an old Ranger with bad knees. He got soused almost every night on Jim Beam, but at 0530 in the morning he was down in the motor pool, clear-eyed, standing tall, and ready to soldier. Others drank a six of beers and weren't worth a damn the next day. Some were always sober and likewise not worth a damn.

The highlight of the ride north to Sisak bouncing in the cab of an old Yugo Army truck was listening to a Sinead O'Connor tape. The troops liked their rock n' roll, which was fine by me. After arriving in Sisak we dumped our gear in an empty room at the *kaserne* and then went downstairs and inspected the arms room. We were in heaven: Yugoslav SKSs, Mannlicher-Steyr sniper rifles, racks of Yugo M70 Kalashnikovs, old MG34s, Yugo Mausers, you name it. The multitude of obsolete, arcane, and sometimes innovative weaponry was enough to give any smalls arms nut a nocturnal emission. A tour of the ammo supply point (ASP) revealed rockets and more rockets. I didn't feel particularly happy about sleeping two stories above this ammo dump, especially after I saw the NCOIC (non-commissioned officer in charge) smoking a cigarette. So we had lots of weapons and plenty of ammo. No pistols though. Vialpando and I still felt like the ugly girl at the school dance.

Pedrag noticed our interest in all the weapons and took us up to his room where he opened a wall locker and began pulling out weapons. In addition to the Singapore-made SAR-80 he'd been carrying, he showed us his Czech copy of an AM 180 .22-caliber submachine gun with sound suppressor—what some people call a silencer. He told us he liked to carry it on point to hose down any targets he "surprised," while his SAR-80 remained slung across his back. He had several Kalashnikovs of various national origins, a Yugo version of the Czech Skorpion machine pistol, a Zastava bolt-action hunting rifle, and an M76 sniper rifle, the Jugoslav derivative of the Soviet SVD.

The M76 *Poluatomatska Snajperska Puska* uses the old German 7.92 x 57mm Mauser round rather than the Soviet 7.62 x 54mm, although a variant exists for that caliber as well as the NATO 7.62 x 51mm cartridge (.308-caliber). The 4-power ON M76 scope on it was similar to the Soviet PSO-1, but it uses tritium illumination rather than a battery operated light to illuminate the scope. Nice rifle for targets

under six hundred meters. I'd fired the Soviet SVD (aka Dragunov) at
Fort Devens while training with one of 10th Special Forces Group's A-
Teams. I found the Dragunov to be a nice weapon for short range snip-
ing, but I could only get really comfortable with it in the sitting position.

We used Pedrag's M76 to check out downtown Sisak, placing the
cross hairs on unsuspecting pedestrians. Pedrag had quite an impressive
collection of weapons, and I was sure he wasn't planning on giving any
of them up after the war was over. This was before the Dayton
Agreement. I thought that there was so much military hardware scattered over the Balkans that even if they finally settled things and drew
up some new borders there would be loony-tunes and bank robbers
punching holes in innocent civilians for years to come. It was good
knowing Pedrag had a stash of specialized weapons in case we needed
anything exotic for a mission.

While I like weapons a lot, you can really only use one at a time.
My plain old Romanian Kalashnikov was good enough for the job at
hand. Then again, I would have liked a CAR-15, about 20 magazines,
and a good stash of 5.56mm. But that wasn't going to happen unless the
gun fairy miraculously appeared.

The *kaserne* was a three-story brick barracks facing the Kupa River
just across the waterfront street. It had a quadrangle or inner courtyard
with the mess hall in a separate building on the other side. Off to one
side by the vehicle entrance was an auto junkyard. The junked cars were
courtesy of the battalion officers. The lieutenants could be counted on
to pile up an Audi a week. There was also an abandoned armored car
with its unlocked troop compartment full of .50-caliber machine gun
ammo. We took a few belts as souvenirs.

In the battalion's training room we found stacks and stacks of JNA
field manuals on the dusty bookshelves. I flipped through them. They
were in Serbo-Croat, but printed in Roman script for the Croats rather
than Cyrillic for the Serbs. I picked one up and read the cover. My
Croatian language skills having improved considerably in the past few
weeks, I said, "Hey, wait a minute, this says *Infantry Tactics*."I opened
it up. I recognized the diagrams as depictions of standard Soviet-type
infantry tactics and field fortification plans. When I asked why the officers weren't using these to train with, they replied that the books were
"Serb manuals" and they didn't want anything to do with them! My
attitude is that any organized tactics and scheme of maneuver is better
than none. The opposing Serb militia forces were more or less just

mobs. Many were illiterate pig famers down from the mountains or weekenders up from Sarajevo and Belgrade looking to score some loot. JNA tactics employed by this well-equipped Croat light infantry battalion would have kicked some serious butt.

I picked up a few of the manuals for further perusal (I still have them to this day) and walked back to our quarters to settle in. Besides the conspicuous absence of our very own personal Dutch annoyance and occasional amusement (Crazy Joe), our new living quarters were a vast improvement over the crowded and drafty little room in Zazina. The room that I shared with Vialpando and Johnny was spacious, airy and clean, with beautiful parquet wood floors. It was on the third floor and we had several windows affording a nice view of the Kupa River and the main settlement of Sisak across the river. From our window we could see the old stone bridge spanning the river into the city center. Nice digs.

Later we took a tour around the city with Willie, Johnny, and Pedrag to scout out routes for Willi's forced marches. This made Willi happy to no end. He was always talking about the Nijmegen marches in Holland. I prefer rucksack runs for strengthening the legs and toughening the feet, with some time off to heal blisters. Rucksack runs do more to develop dynamic strength than plain old road marches. Rucksack runs also work the back and upper body, especially if you carry your weapon at port arms.

With the wealth of motorized transport in the country these guys weren't going to do much walking, unless it was a long-range penetration into the Krajina Republic of occupied Croatia. And they had a long ways to go before they were ready for that. While traipsing around the countryside my buddy Vialpando, the first-generation New Mexico-born Basque-American cowboy, got excited when he spied a horse, but soon turned to me and said, "This has got to be a fucked up country. That's the first time I've ever seen a horse with a bell around its neck."

As I've mentioned before, though the Commandos were all former JNA, their conscript training didn't contain much small unit infantry tactics. So we went over some of the basics with them after I drafted a nine-day training schedule. After a couple of days of tactical training combined with actual combat patrols, we spent two days of "light training," teaching rappelling and unarmed combatives with some knife fighting drills and sentry removal techniques as a break from the strenuous patrolling exercises.

I decided to include some knife fighting and unarmed combatives because I observed some of the men practicing their knife throwing behind the *kaserne* during a lunch break. I was amazed that they hit their mark every time, using Kalashnikov bayonets as throwing knives. I'd always thought knife throwing was something best left to Hollywood and the Ringling Brothers. I was wrong. The target, a good ten meters away, was a head-sized oval marked on a large hardwood tree. I was watching the troops make good on their bets. I was also the schmuck losing a pocketful of dinars. One of the Commandos, Gypsy, as we called him, was deadly accurate. He could throw AK bayonets in tandem, striking a head-sized target from nearly twenty meters away. I gave him my SOG brand combat knife to try. He really liked that and immediately tried to buy it.

When we first got in country, we had met Werner the bull-shit artist with the big dive knife strapped to his leg, so we thought maybe all the big knives we saw later with the Commandos were just for show. Yes, these guys really liked pistols and knives. Lots of knives. Before the war Croatians had no legal access to handguns, so many carried knives as a sidearm. Most of the Commandos had a variety of Soviet, Yugoslav, and Romanian bayonets, though we also encountered some very large homemade Bowie knives as well as that universal symbol of latent anti-social tendencies and juvenile delinquency, the switchblade. The owner invariably picked his teeth with it.

Every one of the troopies had his own favorite combat knife war story, and it seems more than one Chetnik failed to wake up from a guard duty nap. One of the bigger Commandos (most were around 225 and 6' 3"), Boris, told me how his combat knife saved his life. A cartridge stove-piped in his overused Kalashnikov during some urban fighting. (Of course it helps if you clean the gas piston once in a while and make sure your magazines are clean and well maintained.) He was trying to clear the jam when a Chetnik raced around the corner of the building and literally ran him over. Boris jumped on the surprised Serb and dispatched him neatly with a mean-looking Bowie knife. He showed the crude but serviceable weapon to me, and told me he had made it himself in the government-run steel mill where he worked before the war.

The Commandos did well with both the unarmed combatives and the knife fighting, incurring a few minor training injuries. They were a little leery, however, of bayonet drills, but they got the basics down despite slightly wounding their instructor. I got cracked across the bridge of the nose with an FN. The flash suppressor opened up a nice gash on the old proboscis. Oh, just dandy, that's all I needed: one more skid mark on an already badly scarred visage. I saw stars for a minute but no real damage was done. Blood ran freely down my face, but the only thing really hurt was my pride.

I wasn't upset or angry, just disgusted with myself for getting too close to one of the Commandos who was demonstrating a technique for me while I was trying to show and tell at the same time. He misunderstood a command and turned abruptly and swung the barrel into my face. The Commando was almost in tears that he'd hurt me, and the troops were surprised that I just wiped away the blood and continued instructing. I think they were a little unhappy that I didn't wimp out and call it day so they could hit the town. The whole incident reminded me of the Special Forces sergeant from 7th Special Forces Group on the El Salvadoran MILGROUP training team who handed a troopie a knife and said, "C'mon hombre, stick me." Whereupon the troopie did exactly that and sent one very embarrassed gringo Green Beret trainer back to Fort Bragg and Womack Army Hospital.

The unarmed combatives, bayonet drills, and knife fighting instruction were done without Johnny, who had the day off and was visiting relatives. I managed to communicate to the troops by speaking in German, which two or three of the men understood and then translated into Croatian. We had also identified at least one "clandestine" English speaker, whom the Commandos called Blondie. He liked to eavesdrop on our conversations, so Pando and I sometimes switched to Spanish. The hodgepodge of occasionally misunderstood Croatian, English, German, and rudimentary sign language combined with the flashing of a lot of razor-sharp combat knives made for an interesting training day.

Pando demonstrated sentry removal techniques. I actually let him garrote me with a piece of 550 parachute cord (in place of the wire which would actually be used). For demonstrations the trick is to pad your throat with a towel and have the "garrotter" grab your shirt collar as he turns and throws you. The best technique to garrote somebody is to spin back to back and execute a shoulder throw while pulling tight on the handles of your garrote.

You don't just strangle the bastard; when you spin around back to back and flip him over your head, you ensure a broken neck, and/or a slashed windpipe. A strong man can nearly sever a sentry's neck.

Of course in combat a piece of wire or thinner cord, even a few strands of high-test monofilament, is what you want to use. I'd learned this as a teenager at RECONDO School at Fort Bragg a decade previously. This was back in the day before soldiers had to carry a "Warrior Ethos" aide memoire card in their pocket. We may not have been familiar with the term "Warrior Ethos," but we lived it. We were trained to kill and looked forward to an opportunity to do so. Unapologetically. We were conditioned and indoctrinated to be infantrymen. That was the army I knew, the army of the 1980s before the Clinton administration watered down the military and futher feminized it into a "kinder, gentler," organization, turning it into a social-welfare experiment.

The troops had nicknamed Vialpando both "Pancho Villa" and "Dr. Death." Pancho Villa because of his mustache and beard, as well as his colorful Spanish phrases and expletives when one of the troops was really screwing up. He would often deliver his best Frito-Bandito routine to me: "Chico like a beeg ka-nyfe, Señor, you geeve Chico beeg ka-nyfe, por favor. Hey gringo, Chico no keel yoo becuz you are my fren'. Chico lahk yoo, besides gringo, yoo owe Chico moneeey." It never failed to crack me up. Then again I'm quite easily amused. The Dr. Death moniker he got for his habit of carrying about three or four edged weapons on his body at all times. Pando was schooled in knife fighting not at Fort Bragg, but in the back alleys and Tex-Mex honky-tonks and cantinas of Albuquerque, New Mexico.

The remainder of the day was spent on crossing danger areas. We drilled them again and again. Later that evening I stopped by the barracks room for sick call. The troops were watching videos, "training films," like *Attack Force Z*, *The Dogs of War*, and a very instructive Traci Lords feature. The troops loved the war movies and anything of a *Rambo* nature. The *Rambo* Syndrome (as I call it) was prevalent throughout the Balkans. David Rieff discusses it in his excellent book on the early days of the war, *Slaughterhouse* (p. 130):

> Whether it was in Sarajevo, or Tuzla, or Mostar, young men dressed in Rambo-like gear could be found lounging in cafes. . . . The degree to which they had styled themselves on characters they had seen in films like *Rambo* and *Road Warrior* led the Sarajevan film director Haris Pasovic to once confide to me that after peace returned, he hoped there could be a war crimes

trial. When I told him that he should not imagine the UN was really serious about this . . . Karadzic and General Mladic . . . he shook his head impatiently. 'No, no,' he said laughing. 'I don't mean them. I mean Sylvester Stallone. He's responsible for a lot that has gone on here!' On the Bosnian side, so many of the fighters tended to be young men raised on violent Hollywood films, who dressed and acted as if they really did think they were Stallone or Mel Gibson . . . pure Hollywood. Of course, on the Serb and Bosnian Croat side, it was far more extreme.

Yeah, what he said.

I didn't know what the boys were up to until one evening they all burst out into the hallway after viewing *The Dogs of War*, my all-time favorite movie (I can quote most of the dialogue verbatim), to find me drinking *kava* (coffee) with the battalion secretary. They interrupted my conversation with the pretty brunette and all began asking me how much Croatia was paying me and would I take them with me the next time I went to a war. I think they believed that shit about million dollar contracts to plan coups and knock off places like the movie's fictional African nation of Zengaro.

Leading the pack were Blondie and two of his friends. Blondie could be a real smart-ass at times. His English was pretty much American idioms picked up from movies. Blondie left a good paying job in Switzerland as a plumber (yeah, they make almost as much there as they do in Manhattan) to come home and fight for Croatia. He told me about his apartment and the Swiss girlfriend he'd left behind. His buddies were Angel Damiano, aka Italiano, and Cerni (Blackie). These were the Commandos who became my closest friends. Italiano was one of the smallest Croats in the unit, but he made up for it with a big heart. He loved the ladies and he really loved money. I expected this guy to make a mint in the postwar economy, probably as a booking agent for topless dancers. He was excited by the glamorous Hollywood portrayal of the life of the high-paid international mercenary. Italiano was also the kid who whacked me in the face with his FN barrel during bayonet drills. I usually had Italiano and Blondie or Blackie, if not all three, with me on combat patrols in the river valley as well as on our nighttime forays down town.

One day Pando and I stopped by the Di Di Bar's outdoor terrace, the Commandos' favorite hangout, to talk over an upcoming operation with some HOS troopers. (Well, I was there for that, Pando was there for *"una cerveza, muy fria."*)During our chat with the rightwing militiamen, I was introduced to a couple of young ladies. One of them, according to the HOS troopers, had spotted me around the *kaserne* and really wanted to talk to me. She didn't speak English and the HOS weren't interested in playing interpreter, so I switched to German. Her German, like mine, was grammatically incorrect as hell. But obviously it was good enough to converse coherently, because when I looked at my watch later I realized we'd been speaking German for an hour. That became my yardstick for foreign language proficiency: if I could talk to a pretty girl for an hour and then teach troops to kill people—all in a foreign language—then I was doing okay. I'm not sure Charles Berlitz would consider this an effective measurement of foreign language proficiency, but, hey, it worked for me.

While all this multi-lingual verbal lovemaking was going on, Pando was keeping my female companion's very attractive young friend entertained. Then in walked Blackie, the unit's jester. He immediately homed in on the girl sitting next to Pando and decided all's fair in love and war. He told the girl Pando's real age. Vialpando didn't look forty-three at the time and just as well, as no eighteen-year-old Croatian beauty was going to hang around a forty-three-year-old. She left the table, but that was okay because Pando was just killing time talking to her. But Pando thought about what Blackie had done, dwelling on it for a while. Then he got up and walked over to Blackie's girlfriend and told her that Blackie was married. Blackie wasn't married, and Pando bloody well knew it, but that didn't matter—she threw her drink at Blackie and left anyways. I nearly fell out of my chair laughing. Cross Vialpando and he played real dirty. Take no prisoners.

My extracurricular activities in Sisak weren't exclusively limited to cafes or party girls though. During one of my trips into the city center I stumbled upon a quaint little art gallery. I wandered inside and soon found myself buying an oil painting. Art gallery shopping in the middle of a war zone. It was surreal walking around a well-appointed gallery sipping a cappuccino while wearing my dirty BDUs and trying not to track in mud from my jungle boots. Two lovely young lasses in fashionable clothes hovered over me waiting on me hand and foot (hence the cappuccino) as if I was a millionaire there to buy a Picasso.

I bought a painting by Ivan Marekovic, who was born at Sela near Sisak in 1954, and graduated from the Academy of Fine Arts in Zagreb in 1980. He taught visual arts at several primary and secondary schools and starting in 1991, fought in the war. He lives at Sela, near Sisak. His paintings currently are sold in a couple of Croatian galleries. The Marekovic I have is a very nice scene of a canoe beached along the river-bank. The hues of purple and blue were very evocative of the Kupa River at that time of year. I think it may have cost me two hundred dollars on my AMEX. Before the war you could have doubled it just due to the better exchange rate. I also took home a beautiful wool blanket I pilfered from the barracks. Like my painting, it was appropriated from me by an angry girlfriend a year later.

One evening while hanging out with Pedrag and some others in the battalion armory, I noticed a Yugoslav Mauser with a sporting tele-scopic sight attached. The Yugoslavs made a 7.92mm Mauser, the Model 1948, which was a slightly modified copy of the World War II German 98K. It's a good rifle and the 8mm cartridge, as it's known to most people, pushes a 150-grain bullet at about 2,600 feet per second. Varmint shooters in the US have loaded this cartridge with a 115-grain bullet and worked it up to a velocity of 3,000 feet per second. It com-pares well with the .270 Winchester that I grew up shooting in the Pennsylvania woods and the military .308 Winchester. It is low recoil, flat shooting, and most importantly, accurate. The Germans had great success with the Mauser as a sniping rifle. An Austrian *gefreiter* (pri-vate), Matthäus Hetzenauer, was the most successful sniper in the Wehrmacht. From 1943 to the end of the war, he scored 345 confirmed kills on the Eastern Front. He used a ZF 39 sniping rifle—an accurized Mauser 98K with a 6-power scope.

I picked up the Yugo Mauser and looked at it lovingly as the con-versation ebbed and Pedrag looked at me quizzically. The rifle was in excellent condition. The scope was mounted expertly. It was a civilian manufactured 4- to 9-power variable scope. I put it down and we began talking about sniping. Pedrag said he preferred his M76 Yugo Dragunov. I thought it impolitic to tell him the Model 1948 I'd just inspected was probably more accurate.

I'm no Carlos Hathcock. I don't consider myself a sniper, although I've had the training and have found myself in situations where I was using a sniping rifle. Thanks to my boyhood experience with bolt-action deer rifles, my grandfather's handloads, and shooting on the high school rifle team and with the Boy Scouts, I learned the basic skills at an early age. I would consider myself a marksman. I always scored Expert with an M-16, I shot well with an Army Marksmanship Training Unit at Fort Devens, and I've trained with snipers of foreign armies and even assisted in their training, such as with a Karen guerrilla sniper unit in Burma. In Korea I equipped myself with an M-21 sniping rifle, which is basically an M-14 rifle with ART and Lake City Arsenal match grade ammunition.

In subsequent adventures after the Balkans, I assisted in training KNLA snipers in Burma and trained tactical team shooters in Europe. I also dropped a few *jellaba* at intermediate ranges in the southern Sudan with a captured .308 G-3 with open sights, and won shooting contests with a World War II Mauser among Yemeni Bedouin. So you can say I'm a better than average shot, but in combat situations I will happily defer to people who make long-range shooting their avocation and their passion.

In Korea I had a young private in my platoon. His last name was Carol, and to add to that unfortunate moniker he was boyish, quiet, and shy. He wasn't a partier and a carouser like most of the seventeen- to twenty-year-old infantrymen in my platoon. But he could shoot. When the division sent out a memo asking for qualified volunteers for the 2d Infantry Division Sniper School, PV2 Carol came to me quietly and begged for a chance to go. Unfortunately he didn't have enough rank, but I'd seen the kid shoot expert with an M-16 with ease. I went to our company commander, pled Carol's case, and then wrote a letter to the school OIC requesting a waiver on the rank requirement. Private Carol went to the sniper school assessment and selection and was one of the few volunteers who could fire expert again during the initial try out. He came back from that okay but another part of the screening process was a psychiatric evaluation. I was initially worried that the shy, almost meek, eighteen-year old didn't have the killer instinct required for a sniper. He told me he had talked to the sniper school shrink already.

I asked him, "So how did it go?"

Carol replied, "He asked me why I wanted to be a sniper."

"So what did you tell him?"

"Sir, I said I wanted to see people's heads explode."

He was a good student, passed the course, and was one of my assigned snipers on the DMZ in Korea. He was an asset to me and the platoon. His improved fieldcraft and stalking skills were invaluable. In the US Army this is called "developing subordinates." And in Carol's case I was a success at it. I had taken a nice, all-American boy and turned him into a beady-eyed killer consumed with blood lust. I'll probably burn in hell.

Pedrag and I hatched a plan for me to borrow the rifle and head down to a section of the front with some of the boys and get in some shooting. I took the rifle and three boxes of ammo with me to the empty barracks room next to our sleeping quarters. I had the next few hours before I had to turn in to go through the cartridges and check head-stamps in order to select identical rounds for accuracy. Vialpando was going to scout out the enemy positions across sections of the river from some vantage points around town. There was actually an observation post atop the Sisak Hospital. If I remember correctly, it had some pedestal-mounted naval binoculars. We had looked through them one day with one of our troops who said, "Look at those Serb bastards in my grandmother's house! The *papki* are throwing garbage right out the window."

At about O'dark-thirty, after a quick breakfast, I jumped in the back of a truck with four soldiers heading down to the bunker line. With them was Petar, whom I'd gotten to know fairly well in the armory. He spoke a little English and was fairly fluent in German. He'd learned to shoot in the Yugoslav sports program and was a competitive shooter. During his two years in the JNA he'd been, naturally, a sniper. He was carrying a Yugo Zastava hunting rifle: a copy of my Winchester Model 70 deer rifle at home in Pennsylvania—only his was chambered for .308 NATO. Petar had wrapped parts of it in burlap and tape for camouflage. I had used one of my GI brown t-shirts and some sandbag burlap on my Mauser and rubbed camo stick on parts of the barrel. I had cleaned the weapon the night before and experimented with the scope. It appeared sound. Besides my camouflage BDUs, I had a British Army scrim or camo netting to use as a sniper's face veil. After I camouflaged my face and hands with cam cream and US Army camo stick, I would drape this over my head and face to further break up my outline. I didn't have a ghillie suit so I would have to improvise with sticking foliage in my uniform and gear. I would soon find out that this wouldn't be necessary.

We sat in the back of the truck and nervously fiddled with our equipment and weapons. I was told that the situation where we were going was basically a *sitzkrieg*—pot shotting and some limited sniping across no-man's-land and the occasional artillery barrage.

Willi was adamant that we not go down to the front to the "boom-boom" on our own. It was tough enough to maintain anything resembling discipline in the unit without everyone running down to the front-lines to get in some "bang-bang" whenever they felt like it. It was almost a social thing. If one of your buddies or, as was usually the case, a cousin or brother-in-law, was sent down to the bunkers for a rotation, the guys felt themselves almost honor-bound to go along with them, regardless of their orders or assignment. It wasn't uncommon for a few of the troops to get liquored up and just pay a visit, pop off some rounds, and nearly start an offensive.

After about a two-hour ride we unassed the truck behind a small hill. From here on out we would follow Vlado, a tall blond-haired ex-JNA soldier with an ugly red scar on his chin. I didn't ask if he got it in combat or a fight, as he could just as easily have got it from a car accident or falling in the gutter, but I would guess he'd been nicked by shrapnel.

Following a well-worn footpath, we came to the bunker line and moved up a communication trench. Some of the bunkers were well built, whereas others were just piles of logs, dirt, and a few sandbags positioned without any real tactical foresight. I looked inside a partially destroyed bunker and immediately recoiled from the rancid stench and the sight of what I recognized as hunks of meat splattered on walls dark with dried blood, along with a few recognizable body parts and bits of clothing. Petar nodded and said "artillery." Somebody should have torched what was left of the bunker. This was typical of the laxity of discipline and field sanitation (or lack thereof) in the fledgling Croat Army of early 1992.

The plan was for Petar and myself to join Vlado's platoon. His friends had been sniped at ineffectively over the last week, and had pinpointed some Serb positions where the Chetniks could be seen briefly as they moved about. We attracted a little bit of attention from some of the soldiers sitting in their positions. It was an uncommon sight to see two heavily camouflaged guys with camouflaged, scoped-out, bolt-action rifles. Of course as soon as word got out that I was one of the Americans with the Commandos everyone wanted to get a look-see. It was mid-morning and there were still a few small fires smoldering for coffee and rations. No one seemed to be doing anything much. Most of the soldiers slept farther to the rear in fortified houses. A few slept in the better bunkers where there was a sleeping space. Petar told me that the bunkers filled up when they thought there might be some action, or if someone was laying into the line with machine gun fire or a lot of rifle fire. I was introduced to the troops as "the American Commando."

The first thing I needed to do was sight-in the rifle. Petar took me to a bunker where we could fire across no-man's-land at a tree stump. We estimated the range at five hundred meters. I wanted to sight-in at a closer range and then adjust for range. Petar said we should shoot at about five hundred meters and then work in closer if we could find targets. Whatever. While he shot with his Zastava (which was already dialled in pretty well), I spotted his shots as best I could with my scope. We really needed a spotting scope or at least some binoculars, but this would have to do. He was on, definitely, in five rounds as I saw a chip fly off the stump. I was worried that the Chetniks would pick up our position and lay in some mortars or send one of their snipers after us. I didn't think it was such a good idea to sight-in here. We might as well hang up a neon sign saying "snipers now visiting the front." Petar said not to worry, as they would just think it was a couple of bored soldiers banging away. Fine by me.

I now had to show Petar, and the seven or eight soldiers who'd gathered in the lee of the bunker behind us, that I could actually hit something. Time to make some money. I picked out a clump of dirt about a hundred meters out and slightly to our right and directed Petar's attention to it. I centered the cross hairs on it, center of mass not holding under: I would aim where I wanted to put the round. I took up the slack on the trigger—it wasn't a bad pull, but definitely not what I'd want for a real sniping rifle. I hadn't had the time, the tools, or the experience to properly tune a stock Mauser trigger. I'd thought about it the night before, but considered that butchering the only decent rifle available the night before I went down to the line wasn't a good idea.

I also had no idea how well or poorly this rifle might group and what minute of angle (MOA) accuracy I could expect from it. I had a good stock-to-cheek weld on the t-shirt-wrapped stock and was resting the rifle on a sandbag. My body leaned into the wall of the bunker and my elbows were resting comfortably in the dirt. Okay, I thought, now relax, breathe normally, relax, exhale, inhale, start the squeeze, exhale, and continue squeezing through…. *Bang!* I sent a round downrange. Petar called it low and right. I was on 4-power, which was fine for now, and I made the necessary windage and elevation adjustments to the scope. I fired twice more to confirm a zero, sending up little puffs of dust from the dirt clump. I was on for a hundred meters and could now just make my elevation adjustments to five hundred meters.

Now, five hundred meters might sound like a long shot to some people, but I have always been able to knock down the three hundred-meter silhouette target on the M-16 qualification range using just the open sights. I can even do it wearing a protective (gas) mask and shooting the rifle off my bicep. As long as I'm shooting from the prone supported position, it's a fairly easy shot. Even today, with waning eyesight, I can still shoot a tight group on the three hundred-meter pop-up target with one of the new M-4 rifles, and in Iraq I consistently fire three-round shot groups in the same hole on a twenty-five-meter zero target. That translates as three headshots at two hundred fifty meters. This rifle had a much better performance envelope than an abused M-16 firing a .223 cartridge. And I would be firing from a supported position from inside a bunker while someone called my shot if necessary. Petar and I had agreed to act as each other's spotter/observer and take any follow-up shots that were required.

But I didn't know what increment of MOA the scope adjustment target knobs would give me. I knew that most riflescopes gave _ MOA per "click" on the target knobs. I used the flat-head screwdriver blade on my US Army issue demo knife to make adjustments and give it a try, incrementally, until I could hit the stump. I was making notes in my notebook. Petar looked at me quizzically and then just shrugged. We weren't in any hurry.

Having carried a .308 M21 sniping rifle with ART-II on my hilltop "guardpost" (read firebase) in the Korean DMZ, I vaguely remembered my trajectory tables for M118 7.62mm NATO MATCH ammunition. Zeroed at one hundred meters, I would lose trajectory and have to hold over about a foot at five hundred meters. I remembered that the holdover for .308 Match ammo from a one hundred-meter zero to three hundred meters was about sixteen inches. I knew on my rifle scopes at home (all standard _ MOA clicks) that I would have to adjust for a holdover of about three feet or go up nine clicks of elevation from a three hundred-meter zero to five hundred meters. I guesstimated that the Mauser ammo might perform comparatively. At the very least it would give me a place to start. There wasn't time for me to work with the rifle in the rear someplace where I could practice, check my shot groups, and work out my holdover for various ranges.

As the day's action would prove, I needn't have worried.

I decided to adjust my zero to three hundred meters and work from there. I fired three more rounds at a small grassy spot on the edge of a shell crater at the approximate range. I was a bit nervous about firing so much, but Petar said not to worry, as we'd move before we went looking for targets further down the line. Shooting conditions looked good. Fortunately it was a mild spring day with negligible wind. I wouldn't have to worry about bullet drift. We would be shooting between three hundred and five hundred meters, and with any luck, I would get some "large" targets--something more than a headshot. I was wondering how much the scope would wander if I flipped it from 4-power to 6-power.

Petar, whose Zastava was already sighted-in, was beginning to show his impatience. Few of these guys were known for their patience--hell, they were young. At twenty-nine, I felt like everyone's big brother. (Admittedly, in Iraq these past five years it has gotten worse, as I could now be the father of some of my fellow operators.) I nodded okay after my last shot and we moved back to the trench, following a guide. Petar knew most of these guys and exchanged greetings and wisecracks as we moved along the defensive line. I was surprised when we left the few bunkers and began cutting through yards and even a house. We would actually get to shoot from the boarded up and sandbagged ground floor window of a fortified house and a nearby loophole.

This was an excellent position, as it offered a good field of fire and superior shooting rests for both of us. An old bookcase lay behind my loophole with two sandbags and a musty old blanket. This was great. I could get comfortable in a prone supported position. Petar actually had a small wooden table for a bench rest and part of a couch at his window position. He was going to sit sideways on the couch arm with his rifle resting on a sandbag on the table. Perfect. And he was back far enough that his rifle wouldn't stick out the window. Petar told me he'd had this set up by friends in anticipation of coming down to shoot. The position hadn't been compromised by sniping from it yet, nor had there been any heavy weapons fire directed from this house.

The top floor was mostly demolished by shellfire, but a handful of troops had positioned themselves up there to watch and add AK fire to our shooting on Petar's command. No one really seemed to be in charge; at least I didn't see anyone resembling an officer or senior NCO. This kind of warfare resembled a pickup ball game more than any military operation I was accustomed to. As we were getting into position, Petar yelled something to the troops upstairs and movement and conversation above slackened.

Some possible targets were already identified for us. A Chetnik machine gun crew had set up a light machine gun in a position not quite four hundred meters away. I was still fiddling with my scope when Petar asked if I was ready. I hoped he was accurate, as patience sure the hell wasn't one of his virtues. I was finally set and could distinctly make out the upper torso and head of one soldier sitting next to a shell hole just to the rear of the machine gun position. It looked like he was brewing coffee or cooking, as I could see thin tendrils of smoke.

I was experiencing just a hint of the pre-combat jitters I sometimes get. Not really butterflies, but something akin to slight anxiety. The first *bang!* settles me down and then I'm in my bubble. After I'd killed my first two men in hand-to-hand combat (albeit I had a knife and a stick) I nearly threw up pure adrenaline—it burned like battery acid in my mouth and tasted as bad. Having eaten no food for two days, I had an empty stomach so that didn't help any. Plus I'd run about ten blocks through downtown Nairobi with a rucksack—exercise that would make me throw up on a good day. As the outsider here I was under a bit of pressure to perform, and I certainly didn't want to get pumped up and get the nervous shakes that would screw up my shooting. There's definitely a high associated with making a good shot, a difficult shot—just ask any big game hunter or competitive long-range rifle shooter.

I asked Petar if he had the shot. I thought it best to wait until we had multiple targets if possible, or I would let him shoot first and follow-up on the same target. Nearly as soon as I spoke, another soldier, having exited the machine gun bunker, walked over to join the first. Petar merely said, "Rob, *llevo*," telling me to take the target on the left who was already sitting down, as I was to Petar's left. This would give him the one standing. It was a bigger target, but one that could also stoop or turn at the decisive moment. I was taking up the slack when Petar fired and even though expecting it, I flinched just the slightest. But I let out my breath, and in the respiratory pause before I sucked in another breath, I took up the rest of the trigger slack before my target could react. It seemed like a long time, but wasn't even a second. *BAM!* I worked the bolt immediately after I fired and looked for movement: a skill learned as a teenager hunting whitetail deer in Pennsylvania's Allegheny Mountains.

Somebody upstairs was yelling down to us. Petar told me we'd both scored hits. According to one of our observers upstairs, Petar's shot had spun his target around, and he disappeared from sight. Obviously a confirmed kill. The second Chetnik just fell over to his left rear when I fired. I'm certain my bullet took him in the top of the chest, as he almost faced me dead on. Petar put two more follow-up shots into the position. I wasn't sure what he was shooting at, but he later told me he thought he saw someone peeking over the logs and sandbags.

I picked up a third target, got a good sight picture, and started to take up the slack on the Mauser trigger. He was actually standing up on a step or something in the trench to the right of the machine gun position to look over towards the bunker where we'd just dropped the two machine gunners. The idiot was curious! Obviously a new soldier, not a veteran of the fighting here, he probably couldn't see as the line curved there and the bunker was in the way. I had him nearly from the waist up and then he turned away from me in a three-quarter profile. It looked like he was yelling something to someone behind him. I was practically looking at his back, but I didn't care about that and made the shot. He dropped back into the trench. Again I worked the bolt automatically. It was a weird feeling, I'd just killed two enemy soldiers, and I was watching for another target just like I was waiting for the next pop-up target on the qualification range at Fort Benning. It was years of conditioning at work. I had the urge to turn around and ask my grader, "Did you see that one?"

People have asked me how many people I've killed. It seems to be a frequent question especially among civilians, whose sum total experience with terminal violence is what they see on TV in action movies or playing a video game. Men actually seem to get worked up when they ask the question. They're frequently drunk, belligerent, and trying to belittle me. Women ask it most often, like they get some kind of thrill just thinking about it. I don't know what's in their heads. Maybe they're just naïve. I never answer the question, though I'd like to say, "I don't count and why do you want to know?"

And of course the other question I get asked is, "So what's it like to kill somebody?" Now, really, if you have to ask, you wouldn't understand the answer. I will say that it doesn't bother me. I've never had any guilt for shooting someone. I've never hurt a non-combatant or an innocent person. If you wear a uniform and tote a rifle you're fair game. To quote an old cop saying, "There are no victims, just volunteers."

As for numbers, it would have to be a guess. Almost two years to the day after this sniping expedition with Petar I would find myself manning a 12.7mm Soviet heavy machine gun in the southern Sudan and gunning down the better part of a human wave attack of two hundred to two hundred fifty Islamic *mujahideen*. How many I personally accounted for on that day alone is anyone's guess, but every burst I put into the valley was dropping them. And it was really sweet purposefully ricocheting rounds off the hull of T-55 tank and watching about a dozen guys hiding around it fall down. I figure we killed or fatally wounded one hundred to one hundred fifty that day.

After we'd fired our shots there was some excitement in the Serb positions. They opened up with everything they had—AKs, RPKs, two machine guns and even some RPGs. It almost made me feel special. I could hear a few rounds slapping into the face of our house. They obviously hadn't located our exact firing position, but were laying into the entire line in our general direction. This is why regular infantry grunts sometimes hate snipers. They heat things up in your sector, possibly draw heavy fire, and may even attract the attention of enemy snipers. Then the friendly sniper leaves and the grunts have to deal with the fallout.

Since we weren't pinpointed we spent the next two hours in our cozy house. While Petar cranked off two rounds, I only fired once more. I'm certain I missed, but Petar thought I hit somebody. I only observed one of Petar's shots as a probable (he was shooting at someone running down the trench line) and definitely called the second a miss. We'd shot enough from this position. Petar wanted to stay all day and we nearly got into an argument. Maybe I was being a nervous Nellie, but I was really worried about catching mortar or artillery fire on the house.

We finally left the house, crossed two yards, and cut through another house to reach an observation bunker. From there we ran around a low knoll and entered the trench line. Walking along the trench, we stopped to eat some paté and bread with one of Petar's friends. I wolfed down the bread and goose liver and swigged *kaserne* water from my canteen. I mentally kicked myself for not throwing a liter carton of that orange drink into my buttpack.

After a while Petar used his scope to observe the line across from us. I was getting up to spot for new targets as well when he fired. Someone to our right opened up with a few short bursts from a machine gun and we soon heard firing from the other side. Great, now we'd just started some shit at lunchtime. The bunker occupants wanted to get in on the fun and started popping away with an AK and an FN from their firing ports. Since we were no longer wanted, we decided to go else-where.

Dropping low out the rear of the bunker, we ducked back into the trench and scuttled further down the line to a point where we could move back to the low hill. From there we were directed to another van-tage point where we could snipe some more. Petar had a discussion with a pimply-faced kid in the line as we squatted in the lee of an unoccupied bunker. He was talking a mile a minute as he sucked on a cigarette. Even though I don't normally smoke I wanted one myself, but knew the nico-tine would probably hurt my shooting. (I sometimes smoke in the field, or chew if it's a tactical situation. I really enjoy a cigar and I had some cheap coronas with me during this adventure in Croatia as well as a year later in Bosnia.)

Petar gave me the gist of what the kid had to say. There were two particularly obnoxious Chetniks in the line opposite. They liked to shout taunts from one of the bunkers. It had an open viewing port about the size of a shoebox right in the center. Not a very good design feature. According to the kid, using some cheap Japanese binoculars, they could detect movement at the aperture when the Chetniks yelled their insults. It was close to four hundred meters away and they couldn't hit the small target—certainly not with their Romanian AKs. The bunker itself looked pretty substantial. It had been taken under fire with light machine guns in the past with little, if any, effect.

Petar and I decided we would set up where we could both put fire directly into the bunker window. At the very least we'd shake the bas-tards up. The kid, I never learned his name, would yell some obscenities at the Chetniks. When the Chetniks moved to the window to reply, we would take our shots. We should get at least one of them, possibly both, if we could get both our rounds through the small hole. With our plan made, we both settled into good foxhole-supported firing positions. I actually kicked out a step in the side of the bunker to wedge my left foot, and my non-firing side was wedged tight against a log support, my right elbow on an earth shelf dug out of the front of the hole. After brushing some trash and ration tins onto the floor, Petar used his knap-sack to build up a firing position on the unoccupied machine gun firing table. The kid yelled some insults across the line and we soon heard a reply.

Bang! Bang! Our shots were almost simultaneous. Three of the troops nearby were also firing away with their Kalashnikovs. This was good, as maybe it would mask our presence in the area. The Chetniks might think one of our pot shotters was just lucky. After I shot, I continued observing the bunker with my scope. There was no movement. I was certain one or both of our rounds had found their target. A few seconds later there was some shouting. It was obvious they'd found the Chetnik either dead or wounded. The kid was all smiles. He offered a bottle or rakija to Petar and me, but we declined. We weren't done for the day.

For the next six hours or so we searched for more targets, and I would say we scored three probables. One for me and two for Petar. He'd made a good follow-up shot, almost as fast as a semi-automatic M76. We had a good half-dozen misses between us. We obviously overstayed our welcome, but had definitely given the Chetniks opposite us something to think about, which was the entire objective of the exercise, not to just rack up a bodycount. I wanted to rest for a few hours and wait for last light. Let them start moving around a little. There was a good chance we could get a couple more at twilight. As the sun began to set they would get confident and we would still be able to shoot, thanks to the light-gathering ability of our scopes.

Petar said no. We had to catch the truck back as it was leaving soon. He had no permission to be there and I wasn't exactly sure of the reception I would get back at the *kaserne* if I stayed down there overnight. We both thought we'd have plenty of other opportunities to come down and shoot. Both of us were mistaken.

I had no inkling of the strange turn of events that was about to occur.

The next morning came too early for me. The stress and excitement of the previous day had taken a lot out of me. Even though I was exhausted, my nerves were too jangly to sleep well. Plus I was worried Colonel Willi would find out I was out fucking around at the front when I was supposed to be recharging my batteries with a day off, and chew my ass royally. I woke up at the usual time, about 0500, took a hasty cold shower, and got my ass in gear. Our training schedule called for an introduction to patrol base operations. It was fairly straightforward stuff and Vialpando, who'd been off into the city center on his own "mission," and I had an easy day of instructing. I felt a little guilty that he didn't get to play down at the line, but I figured there would be plenty of opportunities.

Another day when we were training the troops on how to run patrol base operations, Willi drove down to Zazina and brought back Joe that night. We didn't know this, and the next morning they moved out the troops on one of their little ruck marches without telling us. So much for our training schedule. Someone told me what was going on as I walked down the hall to the troop barracks which I found empty. Actually, I found out later that Willi had formed the troops up a half an hour earlier than the normally scheduled morning formation (as posted on the approved training schedule), and told them there was a change in the training schedule and I wasn't going. Hell, of course I wasn't going—I hadn't been told! I had to run two klicks to catch up to a twenty-kilometer road march with Willi and Joe. Willi and Joe—I never did fill them in on Bill Mauldin's World War II cartoons. Pando didn't come along. He had a badly infected toe and his foot was in bad shape. I had filled him in on what had happened and told him to stay behind. There was no way he could run or force-march down a macadam road. We were shooting his foot up with Lidocaine from my med kit just so he could go on patrols.

Willi and Joe were marching without rucksacks of course. Willi was wearing high-top sneakers, but the troops minced along in their shoddy old Yugo Army boots while favoring blisters the size of half dollars. They had some very good Adidas hikers, quite suitable for special operations, but Willi wouldn't let the Commandos wear them because they were gray in color and didn't look military. Joe had a weapon with one magazine, but Willi never carried one. I think he secretly wanted to carry a swagger stick, but was afraid of somebody laughing at him. Joe always carried a folding stock Yugo AK that he had picked up as a war trophy and planned on taking home to the Netherlands. He didn't carry it as a soldier normally carries a weapon, for training or at the ready to fight the enemy, but slung on his shoulder because he was afraid somebody would steal it.

Willi liked this guy who was always giggling and laughing like a lunatic. At first I thought he was coming off as an idiot because of his poor English. Then I realized he was mentally deficient. Willi and Douwe had made a few comments, but I didn't think they'd really keep a mental deficient around. I found out later that the guy couldn't pass the Dutch Army's mental aptitude test for enlistment. The refugee from windmill land wasn't exactly all right in the tulips, so to speak, but the wooden shoe crowd in the Balkans tolerated him. Pando and I tried to avoid him. I realized later that real professional soldiers would be a rarity in the Balkans War. Instead there was an abundance of Joes, Werners, and Kevins.

On the march Joe made one too many mean insults about Americans. "That's it, that does it," I thought. Willi had tasked me with setting up a two-week training program for these kids and running it. He screwed it around as much as he wanted, fine, he was the colonel, but I couldn't deal with his mascot, the village idiot, any longer. After the march I cornered Joe in the room and went off on him. I don't remember what the particular issue was, but at the time it really set me off. I snapped. Pando was a bit taken aback. Actually he was shocked. He had never seen me like that. I went totally off my nut, yelling at Joe that we were going to fight, fists, knives, broken Karlovacko bottles, whatever the hell he wanted.

He said okay, he'd meet me *later* down in the troop barracks. Right. He was going straight to Willi's room and I was tired of the Colonel letting his pet monkey both off the leash and off the hook. I've never needed a court jester in my unit. I really wanted a piece of him—later in the barracks, my ass. I wanted to deck him right then so I pushed him towards the empty barracks room next door, "C'mon Joe, just you and me, and only one of us walks out." He backed down, grabbed his bags and returned to Zazina. To Sonja. Then again, maybe he wasn't so crazy!

In the morning there was another road march and Pando went on this one after numbing his foot, shooting it up again with Lidocaine. I tried to prepare some training and draft a new nine-day training schedule for Willi. Poncho raft construction, rucksack packing, and basic rappelling techniques filled the afternoon schedule. We included the rappelling training more as a confidence builder than as an idea that the Commandos would have a chance to put the skill to use, at least in the immediate future. Pando and I both demonstrated rappels from the third story of the *kaserne*. I then demonstrated Australian and slack techniques. We taught the Commandos to tie a Swiss-seat harness and about 80 percent of the unit actually rappelled down the side of the *kaserne*.

Unfortunately the second in command of the Commandos backed out. Though he was fearless in combat, he couldn't summon up the courage to rappel down the building. He was fit, but just didn't have the intestinal fortitude: a killer but not a stayer, something I noticed on the morning runs. The troops called him *"Ustasha"* (Nazi) because he was formerly a HOS trooper and still thought to be underground HOS. Without a doubt there were HOS members and hardcore HOS sympathizers in the *Hrvatski Vojnik*. I tried to coax him into rappelling, but no dice. The battalion "comfort girl" (as I was later informed), who looked pretty damn good in a pair of fatigue pants, wrapped a Swiss seat around her very shapely butt. Tossing her blonde hair out of the way, she executed one of the best rappels of the day. "Hmm, now if only she could cook," I thought.

After we put away the ropes, I treated some more blisters in the barracks and passed out aspirin for tendonitis and shin splints. I put two of the worst blister cases on a limited profile. They could have done those beaten feet ads for Danner Boots. Back upstairs in our quarters, Pando injected some more Lidocaine into his foot. I pulled out a scalpel and offered to remove the toe. He was not amused.

One Sunday morning we were up and out to the local church for Mass since Pando and I were both lukewarm Roman Catholics. We figured that as long as we were in a war zone, it might not hurt to dip our fingers and eat a wafer. There's definitely truth to the old saying, "There's no atheist in a foxhole." Crucifixes weren't bulletproof, but neither was my GI t-shirt. The church was full of the little old *babushkas* that kept the faith alive during Communism. The old women lit a lot of candles and everyone brought bouquets of flowers to lie around the altar. The Orthodox Serb artillerymen liked to use the Roman Catholic Croatian churches as target registration points. Blown away by an artillery round, part of the large, ornately carved wooden frieze behind the altar was missing. In the roof above the damaged frieze was a boarded-up shell hole. The windows were all boarded up. We wondered if the centuries-old stained glass would survive the indiscriminate Serb artillery.

Sunday afternoon was still training time. Back at the *kaserne* after Mass, we went over some basic military symbols as we chalk talked reconnaissance patrol techniques. We taught reorganization and consolidation using the clock method, and developed a status report format in Croatian: *ROM-Raniti* (wounded), *Oprema* (equipment), *Municija* (ammo). The troops all laughed: *rom* is Croatian for "gypsy." We had just devised the Gypsy Report Format. Hooah. There was no provision made in the reporting format for POWs. It was rare for either side to take any prisoners. The Serbs were known to cut off ears, noses, fingers, and "other" body parts of captives before they executed them. The best you could hope for was a quick bullet. The general consensus, at least amongst foreign volunteers, was that if you were about to be captured you were better off committing suicide. Just like fighting the Plains Indians. *Save the last bullet for yourself.*

We were out that Sunday night with the boys. We bumped into a few of the schoolgirls from the sewing school that was next to the barracks. What more could a soldier ask for? No wonder these guys wanted to re-locate from Zazina. I usually had good reason to drop the unit into the front leaning rest position for pushups right outside the school windows. It taught the boys a lesson. Shoot off your mouth or screw up, and Rob would have you groaning in pain and looking like a real wuss in front of the womenfolk.

One of the girls, Claudia, had lived in Canada for a year, shipped off to her two uncles in Mississauga and Kensington when the war broke out. Many of the buildings in Sisak had been hit by artillery and rocket fire. Hell, if I had daughter living there, I would have shipped her off to Canada too. Another Croatian girl who'd spent some time in Mississauga was Mya, whom we visited at the grocery store where she worked, whenever we were in town. Her boyfriend, a HOS trooper and just a kid of about twenty, was recovering from a very nasty knee wound. They were nice kids who suddenly found their hometown in the middle of a war zone. I felt for them; they deserved much better. They hadn't asked for this war. They could care less about the geo-politics and the Balkan power plays that had precipitated the war.

Johnny, of course, knew these girls and scads more and would introduce us to them when we were out. However, one night I saw him talking to a very attractive, très chic blonde in the Rhino Bar. I walked over and asked him, "Johnny, what's her name?" She obviously spoke no English because he wrapped his arm around her, smiled at me, and said, "Mine." It was nice to come in out of the field once in awhile, scrub off the camouflage face cream, shower, shave, put on a clean uniform, and head downtown for an espresso and some attractive female companionship. What a way to fight a war.

I did feel funny talking to these girls in a bar, since I was pushing thirty at the time. Yes, they were still in high school, but this was Europe. As far as chasing girls was concerned, I preferred to talk to someone, if not more mature, then at least born in the same decade. Fitting the bill in town was a good-looking and sophisticated honey-blonde whose acquaintance I'd made, Mirijana Zugaj. She was about twenty-six, spoke good English, and was a very attractive young lady. She liked me but had a boyfriend problem. He was a crew-cutted ass-hole I nicknamed "Butch the MP" because of his flattop haircut and the obvious fact that the only thing he ever did was swagger around in his military police (MP) uniform. He had a sidekick who was very similar in appearance. Of course we nicknamed him "Butch Two." They both looked like the kind of guys who practice glowers in front of the mirror every morning and think pulling the wings off of flies is the epitome of entertainment.

The Commando troops ridiculed these rear-echelon types constant-ly. Barney Fifes with steroid muscles and extra bullets. Butch knew Mirijana liked me and it really irked him. One night he plopped himself (followed closely by Butch Two) down next to me in our booth in the DiDi Bar. Although he spoke practically zero English he kept trying to converse directly, rudely shushing Mirijana whenever she tried to trans-late. He pulled out his pistol and started rambling on about it. I think he was trying to intimidate me. It would've worked except under the table I was holding a cocked 7.62mm Tokarev semi-automatic pistol (they don't have safeties, by the way), pointed at his balls about two feet away.

I was wondering if I could hit such a small target when Butch pulled out an interesting conversation piece, a homemade single-shot pistol fabricated by cutting down a .16 gauge shotgun. Sweet. He could blow away Pando, Italiano, Johnny, and me with one shot if he got enough stand-off distance. Well, okay, maybe he couldn't blow us *all* away, but he'd sure as shit ruin our evening. I took up the slack on the Tokarev's trigger. Just in case. If he did shoot us, I hoped my nerve reflex or flinch would snap off at least one shot into him.

Things were going from tense to bad when we eventually got the guy to leave us alone. I felt bad for Mirijana. Butch was the type who'd grow a beer gut in about five more years and would go from telling her to shut up to slapping her around. After the bar closed and we were walking down the street, Butch followed us out onto the sidewalk and discharged his shotgun-pistol over our heads. Vialpando and I and a handful of other combat veterans hit the pavement. At least two guys pulled out their own pistols. Butch and Butch Two thought it was absolutely hilarious. A few of the Commandos, a HOS trooper or two, and a couple of regular infantry types gave Butchie a look that foretold Mirijana being up for grabs, soon, if her boyfriend wandered too close to the frontlines.

Butch and his buddy equaled trouble I didn't need, and Mirijana was just looking for extraneous attention and a chance to practice her English. Besides I've never understood why women put up with guys like that. My reasoning is that it's because they must be as screwed up as the guy. So I moved on and found companionship elsewhere, though I did name my Kalashnikov Mirijana, kind of like "old Betsy."

Valentina was another beautiful blonde Croatian girl whose acquaintance I'd made in Sisak, and I enjoyed talking to her. She could only be described as saucy. I met Valentina because Pando was always joking around with Valentina's best friend, Durdica, aka "Georgia," a little redhead young enough to be his daughter. The relationship was strictly platonic, but it was funny to see him teasing her.

On the few nights when we were free and not too beat from a mission or a training day, I would go see Valentina. She was a quiet, almost moody, girl with curly blonde hair that fell to her shoulders. Valentina had an enigmatic smile and a shy way about her. She was the type of girl you fell in love with and married. When everybody's favorite hangout, the Di Di Bar, closed, I would walk her to her bus. I had a new girl friend (and a job) at home at the time, but I couldn't keep from thinking how easy it would be to just say the hell with it, stay there in Croatia, soldier, get married, make babies, and grow grapes on the side of that hill down near Zazina. I'm sure there's some American GIs from our peacekeeping force in the Balkans who have made that fantasy a reality. Sometimes I think about that vineyard on the hill where I issued patrol orders to guys who are now long dead and forever nineteen, and it's tough not to choke up.

Monday was a training day and we busted the Commandos out of their bunks at O'dark-thirty. PT was guerrilla drills on the quad followed by a run. There were a few Sunday night hangovers in evidence. The Commandos didn't understand how the two Americans could drink Karlovacko with them all night and then do this bullshit with a smile in the morning. Pando and I smiled at each other and whispered one word. *Practice.*

Tactical training commenced rather late in the morning, late for us anyways, at 0800. Prior to moving them out, Willi started lecturing me:

"Don't break them. You are trying to break them." I was confused and a little put out by this interruption, especially in front of the troops. We had no idea what he was talking about. Maybe somebody complained about our brisk two mile run. These guys hadn't begun to see killer PT yet. Willi continued to march them until their feet were raw while we just made the eighteen-, nineteen- and twenty-year-old soldiers do a few pushups which we, the two old guys (me at twenty-nine and Pando at forty-three), did right along with them, and then walked them through some tactics. I wondered what was going on. We usually just shrugged off Colonel Willi's goofiness and got down to business. We thought the world of the distinguished old soldier, but at times dealing with him was very taxing—kind of like putting up with your favorite uncle when he's drunk.

We were attempting to run a regularly scheduled training day with rather mixed results since somebody always wanted to stand around and discuss what was going on. The first time they attempted to form a 360-degree defensive perimeter it was a comedy. Monty Python's Flying Circus meets Rambo IV— "Goat Rope in the Balkans." Leaders kept standing up and exposing themselves and troops kept wandering over in the usual Croat impatience to look over their leaders' shoulders until no one was left on the perimeter. A couple of hefty rocks thrown in their direction got the message across, after an initial amazement at the distance and accuracy of the throw. Baseball is not a popular sport in Croatia. It especially got a guy's attention when a fist-sized rock smacked off a tree near his head.

We had them practice establishing a patrol base, setting up ambushes, and crossing a danger area. Hand and arm signals improved and the leaders were getting their "gypsy reports." After some more practice the Commandos could finally organize a 360-degree defensive perimeter without forming a committee. I showed them how to use the "Panama Triangle" patrol base technique to employ their light machine guns to best advantage. For squad automatic weapons they were equipped with RPKs (actually M72 light machine guns, the Yugo version of the Soviet RPK), which is nothing more than a heavy-barreled Kalashnikov with a folding bipod. One of the gunners, also a squad leader in the battalion, toted the 11.4-pound machine gun around like most troops carried a rifle. He was formerly a national kickboxing champion. Occasionally we spent some free time together in an old storage barn next to the *kaserne* kicking a heavy bag.

Later that day I stopped by Willi's room to talk to him about our little confrontation that morning. He quickly got going on a tirade. "You Americans are just in it for the show." Show? What show? I didn't understand Willi and tried to get him to explain what he meant, and it soon became glaringly obvious that he, like many other Europeans, harbored a deep-seated and hidden resentment towards Americans. My attitude towards this is, well, too bad. These has-been world powers (France, to name just one of my favorites) colonized continents and raped and plundered all over the world and are now pissed off because they have to take a back seat to a bunch of crude, obnoxious, and technologically superior Americans. Well, screw them.

By this time I was on a low simmer. This guy wanted me to train this unit for him and then he became jealous and began to stick his fingers in to make me look bad to keep his own ego going. I thought it was all a bunch of garbage and went back to my quarters to clean up my gear. I mulled over the possibility of packing up and signing on with another unit, maybe near Osijiek, but the Commandos were probably going to be one of the best units in the region once we completed their training. Besides that, Vialpando and I were getting bored and weren't planning to stay in the *kaserne* much longer.

The next day, the troops were on another road march and unfortunately Willi was in foul spirits. There was a serious communication glitch about Pando and me going back down south and to the front for a few days. We had our rucks packed and were getting ready to move out for a few days. We just decided we'd go down to the frontline since there wasn't anything scheduled for the day after Colonel Willi's impromptu road march and we could get in some more "bang-bang" in our off time. We were combat soldiers, and that's why we had gone to the Balkans. Sure, we were training the troops and leading them on combat patrols, but with some down time we wanted to get in on some more action.

We hadn't been on what we considered a real combat operation together since our last combat patrol near Zazina. Back down south a few klicks there was the occasional firefight between bunkers along the frontline. It was more like World War I warfare. Pedrag said we could ride the resupply truck over to the frontline and play with his unit. We were pumped and had drawn extra ammo from the ASP and bummed some grenades. For some reason the whole thing pissed Willi off. He thought we were grandstanding or something by wanting to go back down to the front on our free time and see "the boom-boom" as he called it. We were really just bored because it'd been awhile since we'd killed somebody.

Fortunately I hadn't related anything of my day with Petar to Willi. I think Willi also realized he couldn't really command us to do anything without a rubber stamp from the battalion commander. We all took our orders from Drago; it was his unit, not Willi's. The chain of command was quite clear to Vialpando and me; all foreigners, including Colonel Willi, were just advisors. And Drago, the battalion commander, was okay with us going down to the line with his boys, as it was his kid brother who'd come up with the idea. For the rest of the day the Commandos practiced assembling two rubber assault boats. They had motors, but no one knew where they were. I'd have been happy just to have the damn paddles. We were literally up the creek, or the Kupa River, without a paddle.

Douwe returned from Zagreb via Zazina and brought Joe with him. The goofball got out of the car in full combat gear. Joe was looking very smug. Something was in the wind amongst the Dutchmen, but Pando and I would have to bide our time. In the *kaserne* everyone just wore their uniforms. Weapons and web gear were stored in the barracks. We dragged our gear down the stairs and then jocked up in the quadrangle in formation just before we moved out. But here was Joe strutting around with his web gear on like some kid dressed up to play GI Joe. It was the first time we'd ever seen him wear it, and in a rear area yet.

A group of us were talking about the day's training when Joe waltzed all over in full harness, including ammo pouches and canteens. Everybody was amused at watching him wander around all day in full combat gear. Even his magazine pouches were full. Joe told us that an officer down in Zazina had offered him the opportunity to set up his own training unit. Pando and I turned around and walked away snickering. We just couldn't help ourselves. I straightened up, turned around, put on my best poker face and walked back to Joe to ask him if he brought his Mr. Coffee machine with him. Pando laughed so hard he broke into tears.

Training continued. The Commandos wanted more exotic training than basic light infantry tactics and patrolling techniques, so like the rappelling training, we spiced things up a little. We practiced using ropes to scale a bridge abutment and gave impromptu classes on bridge demolition and improvised munitions. While we were on the subject, I showed them how to make fougasse and tie it in to their defensive perimeter or line. We also showed them how to properly employ Claymore-type AP mines, something we both had a lot of real world experience doing. The troopies called the Combloc version of our M18A1 Claymore mine "the TV mine," because of its square shape and steel mounting stakes that look like a television's rabbit ears. From then on Vialpando and I began to refer to setting up ambushes as "watching television."

Later that night we got the word from Douwe that the "politicians" in Zagreb were unhappy that some Americans were training troops in Sisak. They had supposedly been making the stereotypical demagogic remarks about American imperialism and the CIA. At the time I thought that the recycled Communist party hacks in Zagreb really needed to come up with some new material for their little stand-up routines. I wondered just where they'd received the information about American mercs in Sisak. According to Willi (but more likely with some help from Willi), Matakovic had tracked us down. Basically we were now supposed to get the hell out. We were going to be thrown out of yet another country.

This was, respectively, the second and third country "expulsion" for Vialpando and me. At the very least we had to disassociate ourselves from Willi, who had tenuous approval for his operation. Whether this was all actually going down the way Willi was presenting it to us, I'm still not sure. He may have wanted to get rid of us out of fear and jealousy and not had the guts to order us out. It didn't matter, because we were becoming bored with what was effectively a sitzkrieg bunker war along the Kupa River and Willi's inaction, indecisiveness, and generally maudlin behavior were wearing a little thin. I wasn't going to get a chance to go sniping with Petar again and Vialpando had been unlucky in love. A change of scenery was required.

We had considered going to Osijek or even Vinkovci to find a unit there, but were put off the idea by reports from our troops of little or no action. We were also worried that someone would inform on us and have us arrested or detained for not having official Croatian Army ID cards or permission from the International Brigade. There was also the problem of travel orders or authorization if our papers were checked on the train to Osijek. Since the Easter vacation was near we decided to boogie. We weren't really all that upset: if we hustled our asses to Zagreb and made the night train connection to Munich, our departure would coincide nicely with the date on our plane tickets. Although we initially planned to extend our tickets, we certainly hadn't planned to stay in Croatia forever. We guessed correctly that the war would slow down over the holiday.

Wearing civvies and sunglasses to fit our new image as CIA agents, we observed boat drills on the Kupa. The troops had found the paddles. Too bad the battalion didn't have some of this stuff when it had to pull out of Petrinja and swim the Kupa. Pando and I spent the day wandering about the city acting like tourists. We hung out with our friends Italiano and Blondie and stopped at our favorite French fry stand and bought our lunch. With extra mayonnaise. Wandering about, we watched a twenty-one vehicle United Nations convoy roll into town. Dressed in our wool Commando sweaters and green berets, we had been mistaken previously for UN peacekeepers from the Swiss Army, though my atrocious German may have helped. At the International Hotel where we did our money changing, we met a Nigerian Army officer with the peacekeepers. Major Sam Folorunsho knew Major Vincent Akpokoro, one of my good friends and classmates from the Infantry Officer's Advanced Course at Fort Benning a year previously. We wished Major Sam well with his mission in Croatia.

Back at the *kaserne* we packed our gear, cleaned our weapons one last time, and went back downtown to get some train tickets at the station before it closed and maybe have a drink at dinner. We didn't have much luck with finding dinner, though as it turned out we were lucky in the extreme. That night after we went to sleep in our barracks room there was a loud explosion that rattled the windows. Actually there was a loud explosion immediately followed by the racket of both of us tumbling out of our bunks and onto the floor with our rifles, yelling something along the lines of, "Oh, shit, what was that?" There'd been no whistling scream, so it didn't seem to be artillery, but it was much too big a blast to be a hand grenade. I prayed it wasn't a marker round, because a "fire for effect" on the *kaserne* would definitely mess up my evening.

Pando and I both took up positions by our window, peering over the sill, our freshly cleaned and oiled Kalashnikovs gripped in our hands. We soon learned that the Restaurant Korablja just around the block had been bombed in some of the curious in-fighting amongst Croatians and the Serb fifth column in town. We had noticed the restaurant before and had always planned to stop by and have a nice sit-down dinner of real

Croat food. To mark our departure from Croatia, we had gone to the restaurant for a farewell feast, but the place was closed so we just went home to the *kaserne* to sleep. Lucky for us.

The next day was Holy Thursday. The troops were on pass and the Dutchmen departed for Zagreb. Willi wanted to know if we were going to Vinkovci. We didn't think it was a great idea to travel across the country without papers when we supposedly had some people in Zagreb pissed off at us. Vialpando and I somewhat reluctantly turned in our Kalashnikovs to the arms room, grabbed our rucksacks, and organized a vehicle to take us to the train station. Johnny loaded up his Volkswagen Jetta, said his goodbyes and left for his relatives' house. As we stood saying our good-byes one of the troops told me the latest joke making the rounds:

Q: "Why has the fighting in the Krajina not spread to the south (Bosnia)?"

A: "Because after this game we're going straight to the playoffs in Bosnia."

I had no idea how horrifyingly prescient the black humor would prove to be.

Our train ride to Germany was uneventful. At the Munich airport Vialpando got busted for having a belt of .50-caliber armor-piercing incendiary machine gun ammunition and some souvenir armor-piercing Kalashnikov rounds in his bag. I passed straight through the X-ray (twice) and was cursorily searched. I could have got on the plane, but that would have meant leaving Vialpando, who spoke no German and had no money. By hanging around waiting for him, I attracted attention to myself. My bags were X-rayed and searched again. They found a belt of ammo like Vialpando's (how'd that get there?) and a new Yugo hand grenade (it was on my list of "items of interest" provided by a friend in the US Intelligence community) that Johnny gave me as a going away present. Hey, what can I say except, what a great paperweight.

The Germans were looking for people like us because they'd recently busted a merc trying to smuggle an RPG and they had also caught a Danish trooper taking his M76 sniper rifle home. One of the German customs officials, a former *Fallschirmjaeger*, or paratrooper, who happened to be from my family's ancestral home in the tiny village of Monch-Krottendorf, recognized both my name and the German World War II-type paratrooper helmet I had been issued in Croatia, which he informed me was 1950s East German Army production.

The rest is a long and very funny story in itself involving a female US Army military police investigator, a matinee idol German cop, and *Bundespolizei* gun nuts. In short, we made our plane after I paid a reduced fine. The Munich airport police chief personally loaned me the money: four brand-new crisp hundred Deutschmark notes from his own wallet with which to pay the fine. All on the trust of a handshake and a smile. To my surprise, the money was repaid to me in 1997. I received a check for four hundred Deutschmarks and a letter from the German court stating that it was a security deposit. I actually made a few dollars on the fluctuating exchange rate. All in all an interesting little incident, and I could now add "international arms smuggler" to my resume right after "professional mercenary."

As troops were going home on their last leave before joining troop movements south, we witnessed the start of the war in Bosnia. April 6, 1992 is considered the start of the Bosnian War. It was on that date that Bosnian-Serb forces opened fire on a peace demonstration in Sarajevo. I watched the news reports of this on TV. Milosevic appeared on Sarajevo TV to say, "It only takes a few bodies to start a war. That's the tragedy of the Balkans." The very next day his bodyguards opened up on the Muslim peace demonstration and the whole Bosnian War began.

CHAPTER 4

GOOD INTENTIONS GONE BAD: VACATIONS IN HELL, PART I

"If you liked Beirut, you'll love Mogadishu."
—Smith Hempstone, US Ambassador to Kenya, in a State Department
cable to Deputy Secretary of State Frank Wisner

*"The first things the Somalis will do is find out your weaknesses and
then exploit them. You have to admire them for that. They are
the world's greatest entrepreneurs."*
—German aid worker Willi Huber, from Chris Cassidy's
The Road to Hell

After leaving the International Brigade and the Croatian Commando
unit in Sisak, I returned home to Olean, New York, and spent another
three months with the Bureau of Prisons as a Federal Corrections
Officer. To be blunt, it sucked. It was early summer and I was talking to
a friend, Colonel Buck Swannack, USMC (retired), when he convinced
me to come to work for his company, ITS. ITS provided airport security, baggage handling, courtesy services, airplane cleaning, etc., for airlines in the United States and was expanding worldwide. I was offered
a job as a district manager with the responsibility to oversee security
operations in six airports throughout upstate New York.

I walked into my captain's office and said, "Sir, I've got a job offer
at twice what the Bureau of Prisons is paying me, I'm unhappy here, this
job is only a job, not a career for me, so I'm quitting." I shot down any
attempts to keep me there, and asked if I could out-process in the next
two days, as my job started with OJT (On the Job Training) in Detroit
on Monday. I wasn't going to be at work on Monday no matter what
he said, and my captain was smart enough to know it. What were they
going to do, have me arrested for not showing up?

The jerks in admin actually whined that they needed more than two days to out-process me when they could ship out a thug (inmate) in a matter of hours. My response to them was less than polite. I worked for ITS for the next few months. Unfortunately the guy I was supposed to replace got a reprieve, and the company tried to bait and switch jobs with me. Even though I was on track to be a VP with a six-figure income in a year or two, I wasn't happy. So I quit. A week later I was packing my go-to-war gear for Somalia.

A few weeks earlier my live-in girlfriend, a nineteen-year-old blonde and sometime exotic dancer, left to go back to college for a semester. So I was kicking around the apartment alone. No job, no girlfriend. After almost six months of being strangled by a necktie, I figured I'd spend some time working on the great American novel and wait for something to come up or, failing that, earn an honest living. I also could return to the Balkans and get back in on the war.

I was thinking that Bosnia would be an interesting place to spend the winter when I received a phone call about the job in Somalia. President Bush made the announcement of our pending involvement in Somalia on a Wednesday, Thursday I got a heads up from a friend at the Pentagon, and Friday my phone rang again. I was asked if I could come down to Washington DC that weekend and possibly deploy to Somalia on the following Monday. I'd been unemployed for barely a week.

As it turned out I didn't have to get on a plane for Somalia quite that soon. I was contracted by BDM Inc., a defense contractor, at the nice round sum of ten thousand dollars a month as a Department of the Army consultant with a bonus of another ten thousand dollars at the end of each quarter. The initial deployment of US troops to Somalia in December 1992 was seen as a humanitarian effort. Ordered by President George H.W. Bush, the mission was to help the relief effort in the war-torn country. Feed the children.

Because of my special operations background, my experience on the ground in Kenya and Somalia while a Harvard graduate student in anthropology, and my working knowledge of Somali and Swahili, I was hired at the onset of the US troop deployment. My job was as the Assistant Team Chief of the Somali Linguist Team, a hundred-person unit of native Somali speakers recruited in the US. Basically BDM, Inc. recruited one hundred Somalis off the streets of Washington, DC. Some were college students at Northern Virginia (NOVA) but most were in typical third-world immigrant jobs: taxi drivers, security guards, and convenience store clerks. A standard joke was that the Southland Corporation was going to sue because they didn't have anybody left to work at their 7-11 stores. Some, including one engineer branch lieutenant colonel, were formerly Somali Army officers, who never went home following courses in the US, but the best of the bunch were the college students and the kids raised in the US.

After I got the call I threw a change of clothes, a suit, my Colt Officer's .45 pistol with a box of new ammo, and my GI field gear into the car and drove to Washington DC—McLean, Virginia, actually. As was my habit before going overseas, I visited my family before I left. When I tried to explain to Florence, my paternal grandmother whose grandfather had been a wildcat oilman, rumrunner, and notorious justice of the peace, what kind of a job this was, she interrupted me and said, "Oh, you're going to be a mercenary! Well, be careful. We'll see you when you get home." That's the kind of people I'm from.

Six hours later I was inside the beltway and being interviewed for the job. The guy running the show was a roly-poly asshole named Mosely. A former submarine officer, he was one of those guys who can't look you in the eye when he talks to you, shakes hands like a limp fish, and can never give you a straight answer. In other words, a slimy fucker. There should be one day a year where we cull the herd just by whacking, for sport, all the Moselys we can find, thus greatly improving the human race's gene pool and life on earth in general. And no bag limits. That's a program I'd sign up for. So I guess you could say I didn't like the guy very much.

After some handshakes and an interview, I found myself sitting across the table from some geek in contracts. He asked if I had any questions or concerns with the contract. Being the irreverent smartass that I am (and considerably more so when I was in my twenties), I deadpanned, "As a civilian contractor I won't be eligible for any medals." He didn't get the humor and appeared confused, the poor dear. While he was still trying to figure out what was going on, I grabbed his Mont Blanc and flipped the contract to the signature page. So, 160 K a year to wear BDUs and go play great white *bwana* in East Africa? No problem. I couldn't sign that fucker fast enough.

In country my duties required me to travel widely throughout the Operation Restore Hope area of operations with a variety of US and UNISOM units, and coordinate the individualized missions of the team's hundred members. In Virginia my job was to ride heard on

BDM's motley collection of Somalis, and to get them prepped in some way for entering a war zone. I sat in on the interviews the company conducted with the prospective interpreters. Not too many were passed up. There were several I thought were trouble, but BDM wanted to fill the contract immediately and collect their money. They weren't interested in my opinion. Most of the people came in from the immediate area around the beltway. Later we would get queries from Somalis in other parts of the US and even Toronto who were much better qualified, but by then it was too late. BDM needed to fill the roster ASAP and get boots on the ground.

A couple of people from the State Department showed up. Their job was to vet our people, but how the hell do you do that? Somalia was in turmoil. There was no infrastructure left and no way to access any records if any existed. They (not we, don't sign me up for this) had to take what these folks were telling us at face value. Did I mention that being a skilled liar is a common Somali cultural trait? Hell, a lot of them were in the US illegally, so how trustworthy could they be? During the interviews the applicants were asked for personal information and this was recorded in a personnel file.

Unfortunately, and despite my objections, we were not recording their clan affiliation. One kid had to call home and ask his mother, because he'd come to the states as a toddler. Mosely said tracking our translators' and interpreters' clan affiliation wasn't necessary and we weren't to differentiate—a native Somali-speaker was a native Somali-speaker—just interchangeable units like pieces of equipment we could use in Somalia. This attitude and oversight would bite us in the ass later. In country it would become a major deal.

Since I was the cultural expert, you would think Mosely and his boy wonder, a kid only two years out of college, would have listened to my counsel. Wrong. Regardless of the Harvard education and my experience in East Africa, to them I was just a knuckle-dragging gun for hire.

Mosely knew absolutely nothing about Somalia or Somali culture and society, so of course he was right. I'd cautioned him to clear with me any "promises" he made the Somalis. He had no idea how skilled the Somalis were at flim-flam. Over the next few weeks he would get set up and then flap his mouth and goggle his eyes like a fish out of water, wondering, "How did this happen?" I hate to think what kind of a naval officer he was. He'd let a half-dozen or more Somalis berate him over some nonsense, then he'd do his fish out of water imitation and come and complain to me about a mess he'd perpetuated. Then I would have to try and repair the damage. A perfect example was the taxi scam.

One day some Somalis approached Mosely about reimbursement for taxi fares. They cannily did this while I was occupied elsewhere. Mosely, being the big man and still not getting it said, "Sure, we'll reimburse you up to fifty dollars. Just bring a receipt." Idiot. Half the Somalis we hired were current or former taxi drivers. The next morning a taxi pulled up in front of the office. As Mosely watched in interest, six Somalis clambered out and waved goodbye to their taxi driver buddy—probably a relative. They promptly marched up to Mosely and each presented him with a receipt for fifty dollars. When he started his lip flapping and eye avoidance routine, the Somalis became very irate. He hadn't produced a wad of crisp fifty-dollar bills from his own pocket immediately. He said he'd reimburse them fifty dollars, right? Mosely said they'd all arrived in the same cab. The Somalis, bold-faced liars all, were adamant that they'd arrived in separate cabs. Mosely must be hallucinating. I had long since washed my hands of bailing him out of his fuckups. By the time I walked away shaking my head, they had him half believing their version of the events.

I was on the Somalia job with two other vets, both retired USAF. Neil, the colonel, had worked for BDM before, but he'd never been to Africa. He was a do-nothing the whole time. He hated to make contact visits and treated every personal interface with our interpreters as a chore. Because he was a corporate employee, BDM just wanted to get their money's worth out of him.

Carl, an NCO, was just an asshole. A smarmy, weasel-faced, ex-clerk also with zero experience in Africa, he'd just retired from the Air Force. Carl admitted he was just taking the job so he could move into a desk job with BDM back in DC. He didn't want to go to the field at all. In Somalia he liked to talk about his "Intel experience," which was never anything specific or verifiable. He started bragging about spy school "grade skills" to the Army Intel guys we worked with in Somalia, and they immediately shot him down. If you've done that stuff you don't talk about it. He also couldn't fight his way out of a paper sack, but proved to be an accomplished back stabber. The one time he was handed an M-16 he threw it to me as if it would burn his hands. He was what the Brits call a wanker.

You couldn't have recruited two guys more ill-suited to a civilian contracted special operations support task in an East African counter-insurgency/OOTW (operation other than war). But the BDM office pogues loved them.

One really bright spot in the whole business was one of the civilians from the Pentagon. Lane Aldrich was working with Colonel Lipky, the Pentagon's action officer for the project. I knew Lane from Fort Devens where he'd retired as a warrant officer with the Intelligence school. I had dated his youngest daughter and nearly become engaged to her. Lori was working at both the Officer's Club and the Post Clothing Sales Store when we met. Years later I became her daughter's godfather and a Dutch uncle to all three of her children.

At the time I took the Somalia job, Lane, a Russian linguist, was a Department of the Army civilian working with the Army Language Program Office in the Pentagon. As is common in defense contracting, there was a slightly adversarial relationship between BDM, the contractor, and the Pentagon, the client. Basically, like most civilian contractors, BDM was trying to screw the army, and with a weasel like Mosely in charge it got interesting. Because Lane and I were friends we had to pretend we didn't know each other, even though, unknown to BDM, I was staying at his house in the guest room. Mosely never did figure out how his lies and obfuscations were always trumped by Colonel Lipky. Maybe I'm not a very good contractor, as I refuse to lie to my government or fuck over the US Army.

When I was introduced to Lane it was, "Hello, Mr. Aldrich, it's a pleasure to meet you, sir." During the day we would work on the project together and in the evening compare notes over a good bottle of wine and an even better dinner prepared by his wife, Linda. Good living for a bachelor like me.

We took all the Somalis on buses to Aberdeen Proving Grounds for in-processing, shots, and equipment draw. During the equipment draw I got in line first. I wanted to draw gear and stow it, so I could check the procedure and then get to work on making sure everyone else got the right stuff and get on with coordinating the day's activities. Some of the more vocal sharpies in the front of the line thought they were getting short shrift: basically they were a couple of assholes.

Next stop was lunch, and as the Somalis were Muslims, I marched right up to the mess sergeant (the grousing that I was up front had already started) and asked him if there was any pork on the menu. "No, sir," he said. I stepped back and went to the back of the line. The Somali problem children thought they'd won a victory when, like any US Army infantry officer, I waited for everyone in the unit to eat before I got in line. After about twenty had gone through the lunch line, I saw about a half-dozen coming back to the line with their plates. They didn't look happy. They had bowls of what looked to be spinach. Uh, oh, I thought, they've got collard greens on the menu! Yep, good ole southern collard greens (traditionally cooked with ham hocks), seasoned with pieces of freshly cooked bacon! Sorry about that guys. I made an announcement quickly and then let the mess sergeant know I thought he was an idiot. He couldn't understand what the fuss was about. The whole Muslims-don't-eat-pork thing was news to him. I don't think he thought much of fellow blacks being Muslims, let alone forgoing good soul food like chittlins, barbecued pork ribs, pig's knuckles, and collard greens.

We had a few Somali girls who were absolute hotties. After all, super model Imam is from Somalia. Two or three of the girls were damn near drop-dead gorgeous. One was Suad, a classic Somali beauty. When we got in line for shots at the hospital, we were informed that the gamma globulin injection would be given in the top of the ass cheek and we'd have to step behind a screen and lower our pants. Carl shouted out, "Suad, make sure he buys you dinner first!"

Before the immunizations started, I did a head count and knew we were missing some bodies. If they didn't have their shot cards, they couldn't proceed to Somalia. I found about six jokers hiding on a fire escape and smoking cigarettes. I booted them in the ass and told them to get inside. They didn't like being told what to do and said as much. Too damn bad. What did they think was going to happen in Somalia? As soon as I told them off, they went inside to besiege Mosley. They were the same crew who had mouthed off at the equipment draw.

Funny thing was, they didn't want to be in the front of the line this time. I'd already seen the head of immunology with my shot cards and had a note ordering just one or two shots. I was still pretty current from immunizations for my trip to Kenya and from my last stint at Fort Benning.

I went right to the front of the line and got the shots I needed. Nobody complained about me cutting to the front of the line this time. The Somalis were all dreading the immunizations. What the Somalis didn't know was that the first few people getting shots would get more delicate immunizing from the male physician's assistant (a warrant officer) and the nurses than the last guy in line after they'd already jabbed a hundred other people. By that time they'd be tired and not as concerned about administering a painless shot. I made doubly sure the problem children were in the back of the line.

They thought I was doing them a favor.

Right after I arrived in Virginia, I got a Dear John letter from my old girlfriend, who had come home from college in Rochester, thrown a party, drunk all my booze, trashed my apartment, and moved out. So I guess that meant we were through. A month previously, while working for the airline security company, I'd found myself in Kansas City. While catching a ride in a hotel security van, I'd met a United Airlines flight attendant. The attraction was mutual and we'd exchanged phone numbers.

She was from Alexandria and living just down the road in Reston, so I gave her a call. Judy and I were soon effectively living together in her apartment. Her mother thought I slept on the couch. I went to Christmas Mass with the family and slept over at the family house for Christmas morning. Momma made shit on a shingle (corned beef on toast) for breakfast. Things were going well between us and obviously getting fairly serious.

The night before I was due to leave for Somalia, we shared a room at the Tyson's Corner Hilton. We'd completed in-processing for the trip that day. BDM used the Hilton, as it was just around the corner from their office buildings. In the morning I was informed that there was a problem with flight scheduling and we were to stand down. It would be another few days or a week before we made movement. I had to make a quick trip over to the BDM office building for some paperwork. I caught a ride over with one of the office pukes, some smart-ass about my age with a PhD. We didn't have much of a conversation. He was looking down his nose at me and being very condescending, until he learned I'd gone to Harvard. Then he just shut up. He'd asked me where I'd gone to school, but didn't volunteer that info about himself. I didn't care for his attitude. Who did these guys think made all the money for the company? The guys like me at the sharp end wearing boonie hats and dirty boots, not the academics passing around memos and think-tank analysis.

I was in desert "chocolate chip" BDUs and desert boots. Man, the looks I got as I walked through the office building. It was the same place I'd worked for the last few weeks in a suit and tie without a stare or a comment. The girls in the office were so far removed from what the company actually did to make its money on this contract that they didn't know what to think.

So I was stuck in northern Virginia for a few more weeks until we got another set of travel orders. Then I was off to see the elephant. Again. I was packing both my civilian Colt Officer's .45 and a 9mm Beretta. To hell with BDM's policies. In Somalia we would be told that we couldn't carry weapons because BDM's lawyers were afraid that we would shoot a Somali who would then sue the company. The US Army major in charge of ensuring our support went on a tirade, shouting, "You can't carry a weapon!" Actually, we weren't authorized to draw a US Army weapon from him, but there were no regulations against a civilian contractor or DA Civilian carrying a weapon. Neil, the former Air Force colonel, had actually come to me and informed me that I was in charge of getting us some weaponry. How nice. How utterly plausibly deniable for him if I got caught with some hardware. The key word there being "I."

When everyone showed up in uniform for the bus ride to Dover Air Force Base, I encountered another Mosely-induced situation. A Somali woman we all called the Beauty Queen showed up with a piece of luggage that took four men to carry for her. (Her looks were anything but attractive—she earned her moniker because of all her make-up, perfume, jewelry, and haughty airs.) When Mosely was asked how much personal gear they could take, rather than specify weight and size, he told them "one bag." The idiot. I'd advised BDM to spend a few bucks and issue everyone the same bag, either a gym bag, an overnight bag (what we called an AWOL bag in basic training), or a cheap rucksack. But once again, Mosely the submariner knew better!

Neil, Carl, and about twenty-five Somalis had preceded my group of thirty. After taking over the second lift, I would return from Somalia to Dover AFB in a few days and pick up the remainder. At Dover I had to teach everyone how to assemble their Kevlar helmet and their load-bearing equipment, and how to put the desert camouflage cover on their green woodland flak jacket. Not as easy a task as it might seem. Anything resembling work would cause some of them to mutiny. In effect, I rigged about half their gear for them myself. When some Somalis were trying on their boots, I had to show them how to lace them up. They'd never worn shoes with laces before, just sandals or loafers.

The Somalis could drive you crazy. They would ask you a question and then argue about the answer. As a group they just wanted to be told what they wanted to hear. I lost my temper in a PX annex so badly I think I had a small stroke. I experienced a rushing in my ears, pounding in my head, and dizziness. I went outside and sat on the curb. The pain was intense. It was definitely a burst blood vessel. I resolved not to give too much of a fuck about any of the Somalis, theirs or ours.

A few years later I was quizzed by a project officer in the Pentagon about the conduct of the contract. When I was asked what it was like to work with the Somalis, I replied: "The Somalis are the liars, cheats, thugs, and murdering scumbags of East Africa." The colonel who was interviewing me said, "Sounds like you don't like them very much!" I told him that he had obviously misunderstood me. "Oh no, don't get me wrong," I said, "I admire them! That's what it takes to survive where they're from. They live in one of the world's most inhospitable regions and they adapt to their niche very well. You can't look at them with our cultural biases."

I still believe that. BDM had painted a glowing picture of how the contract was run. They didn't mention any of the problems we had encountered in Somalia, or in recruiting and administering the Somalis, hence there were no lessons learned. So regarding my opinion on how well they executed the contract, I really stuck it to BDM. I wasn't going to go on the record supporting the lies they'd put on paper. Personally I took great satisfaction in it, as they'd cheated me out of a bonus by bringing me home a week early and not sending me back. Then they interviewed me at Fort Chaffee for a high-speed job at Fort Polk, gave me the job, and then notified me later I was no longer qualified. Meanwhile, the colonel from the Pentagon who oversaw the Somali contract conveniently got a job with BDM right after he retired. Hmmm.

The plane ride over was largely uneventful. I passed out the Dramamine to everyone when somebody started acting queasy. It wouldn't do any good, except to act as a placebo; which was my intent. I had to calm one of the guys down and make him promise to keep quiet when he realized the windowless passenger compartment upstairs in the cargo plane had the seats positioned so we were all facing backwards. Nearing arrival over Mogadishu, after a day-long flight and a stop at Taif airbase in Saudi Arabia, I made an announcement in Somali: "Welcome home to Somalia." Everybody clapped and cheered. Even on the ground that night everyone was still in high spirits. They really had no idea what was going on in Mogadishu.

We had to bunk at the airport, the old Mogadishu International terminal, for the night. The place was a disaster. Despite the USAF being in control, it was dirty and littered with trash. The whole operation was poorly organized. I was directed to a pile of cots that I had to show the Somalis how to assemble so they would have something to sleep on. Most just stood around acting helpless, and a few were looking outraged that there weren't plush accommodations awaiting them. They were all in for a big shock. In typical Somali fashion, everyone grabbed for the cot I assembled as a demonstration. Uh, no, assholes, that's mine. I rummaged around in the old duty free shop looking for souvenirs, but found only an American Express credit card machine marked Mogadishu International Airport.

Pakistani soldiers were guarding the airfield as part of the UN mission. I use the words "guarding" and "soldiers" loosely. What a sorry bunch of losers. A group of them were bunking on cots on the veranda in front of the terminal building and bordering the airfield. They simply swept all their trash, dirt, and uneaten rations through the knee-high iron grille fence that separated it from the airfield. Every time a plane landed, it blew all the dirt and rotting garbage back onto them. Unbelievable. They'd been there for several months and still didn't have indoor sleeping quarters or a decent latrine. The toilets in the terminal building were a lost cause and a serious biohazard, so the USAF built a wooden latrine around the corner. I watched an airman get into an argument with two Pakis who wanted to cross into the USAF area to use that latrine. Build one yourselves, you lazy bastards.

In the morning I had the linguists stack some of the cots with our gear. I knew they'd make good barter material in the future. While they were doing this, two guys from the first bunch to fly over (both were problem children at Aberdeen) met me. They were attached to the Marines and had been involved in a firefight with Somali militia just the day before. A Cobra gunship had flown overhead for fire support, and they told me they'd been hit with the hot shell casings from the Cobra's nose-mounted cannon. Both had been handed M-16s and had fired back during the firefight.

They looked like a couple of Marines; an amazing transformation in a few weeks. They were studs now. Both thanked me effusively for the preparation I'd given them. The help with their gear, the lectures on combat and tactics, and my general ass chewings were much appreciated. "We had no idea it would be like this, Mr. Krott, thanks for getting us squared away." Their attitudes had done an abrupt about face. When I asked them how they felt about firing on their fellow countrymen they replied, "What? Fuck that, we're Americans, we're not Somalis!" Funny how things change when you're thousands of miles from home and on the other end of incoming automatic weapons fire!

With only six hours in country and all of that stuck in the old terminal building, my group had yet to learn this lesson. I had the two studs speak with them and try to prep them for what they would encounter outside the wire and on their job. I don't think it did much good. We loaded up some deuce-and-a-half trucks for a ride through the war zone to our office in the US Embassy compound. I had a good idea of what we were getting into. The Somalis, especially the ones who hadn't been back in many years, or had been born abroad and never visited the country before, were in for a shock.

Former *Washington Times* editor Smith Hempstone was appointed President Bush's ambassador to Kenya shortly after the fall of the Berlin Wall. Just days before President Bush's announcement of our intended intervention, Hempstone sent a cautionary (and confidential) cable to his State Department superiors that the United States should think "once, twice, and three times" before getting involved in Somalia. He warned that the Somalis were "natural-born guerrillas" who would engage American soldiers in ambushes and hit-and-run attacks: "They will not be able to stop the convoys from getting through. But they will inflict—and take—casualties."

Referring to the ill-fated US intervention in Lebanon in 1982–1983 that ultimately cost the lives of more than two hundred and sixty Marines, Hempstone's cable concluded, "If you liked Beirut, you'll love Mogadishu."

As the truck pulled out of the airfield gate, I surreptitiously pulled my Colt .45 auto from my bag, an Israeli Paratrooper's map case, and press checked it. Locked and cocked, condition one. I wasn't about to ride through this shit with my dick in my hand. I didn't know how much good a pistol would do in a firefight, but I was ready to stand and deliver if I had to. If it got hot there would be a spare rifle or two lying around soon enough.

As we drove through Mogadishu, many of the linguists in the back of the truck with me became visibly terrified. Others just burst into tears and became nearly hysterical. I don't know if that was because of how bombed-out and destroyed Mogadishu looked, or because they suddenly knew this would be no picnic and they were certainly going to earn their two thousand dollars a month.

Mogadishu was a shithole. And fourteen years later it's still a shithole. My journal entry for my first trip through Mogadishu after getting off the C-5 at the airfield says, "The faces of the Somali people lining the streets stared back impassively at us as we drove through the desolate city. Their overall expressions were grim, miserable, and yet not really hateful. They were the expressions of people who've seen so much misery and human suffering that they just don't give a damn anymore. The troops (who have been fired upon by Somali bandits, stoned by teenagers, and harassed by children) riding shotgun on the convoy darted their eyes uneasily around the crowds and up to the rooftops. No one said much until we reached the embassy, where amidst the rubble of destroyed buildings, the stinking refuse heaps, the general hustle and bustle of a major military operation, and wedged between GP medium tents, generators, commo vans, and Humvees, I was surprised to see East African wildflowers blooming under the harsh heat of the equatorial Somalia sun."

That one bunch of African violets was the only truly beautiful thing I saw in the entire pestilential country.

The day after I arrived I was presented with two dirtbags that had gone over the fence. They had walked out past the gate guard in pursuit of pussy. Idiots. Of course they were barred entry and taken into custody by their unit. The immediate decision was they were to be sent home. *Pour l'encouragement des autres*—to set an example. Neil and Carl wanted me to go talk to them and handle their dismissal and shipment back to the US. They were too busy with paperwork. Ah, yeah, paperwork, I get it. That pretty much set the tone for who did what for the rest of the mission.

The two problem children were a couple of the whiners from Aberdeen and their plea was also immediate, "Please, Mr. Krott." Whine, snivel and whine. Yeah, right, now I'm their buddy. I put a polite face on it like I cared and acted as if I'd like to help them, "Gee, guys, my hands are tied." Actually what I thought was, "Hey, go fuck yourselves." Payback's a motherfucker.

We had other problems. Remember what I said about Somalis being consummate con artists? One of the women, the Beauty Queen, had shown up at her unit and promptly informed the leadership she was due leave. She'd only been in country for three days. But she led the unit NCOIC to believe otherwise. So some deserving American soldier got bumped from R&R, and she took his slot on a recreation flight to Mombasa. It didn't take me long to find out about that.

In marked contrast to these losers was "Sam H." He and his wife were both hired by BDM and deployed to Somalia with the Linguist Team. Young, twenty-something Somali-Americans, they were both well-educated, polite, and hard working. They were great people to be around. I would happily call them friends and associate with them any-time, anywhere. Sam had already done an outstanding job in his detail to a special operations unit. I liaised with the commander on Sam's spe-cial assignment. He was heading north, to Somaliland. We weren't sup-posed to be operating up there, but we were. Sam had impressed the green beanies with his physical fitness (he could hump his own ruck) and his attitude. He had the aptitude and potential for further service, either in US Army Special Forces, if he cared to join up, or maybe with the CIA. I've often wondered whether he went on to a career in Intelligence or black operations. It's guys like "Sam" that our govern-ment agencies and our military needs to recruit from our ethnic com-munities at home in the US for deployment overseas in HUMINT (Human Intelligence) and Special Operations assignments.

It wasn't long before I started to get heat seekers from that idiot Mosely in Virginia. The first complaint was I was refusing to pay the Somalis in hundred dollar bills rather than twenties. I knew they want-ed the hundreds, as they brought a higher exchange rate on the black market. I had absolutely nothing to do with it. The reason we weren't paying them in hundreds is that the US Army finance office didn't have any hundreds. The finance office, where I was drawing about 250,000 dollars every payday, said that the US State Department didn't want hundred dollar bills floating around on the black market. Hundreds make transport for illicit deals—drug transactions, money-laundering, *and terrorism*—all the easier. Despite my explanation that there weren't any hundred dollar bills in Somalia and the State Department would not allow them, Mosely couldn't get his head around it. Mosely was unbe-lievable. But what an expert at passing the buck. I found out from the Somalis he just told them they couldn't have hundred dollar bills because it was my fault! I spent days on this issue, just one example of the penny ante bullshit that I had to deal with.

Besides hitching rides back and forth to the Mogadishu Airport to catch flights to other areas of operations such as Bali Dogle, Baidoa, Bardera, and Kismayo, I had the opportunity to ride around Mogadishu a few times with the Psyops (Psychological Operations) unit that produced *Rajo* (*Hope*). *Rajo* was the Somali-language newspaper, and the same unit that cranked it out also made the distribution runs around the city, passing out the only newspaper in Somalia. In the back of one of the Humvees where I elected to ride with the troops rather than up in the cab, was the Beauty Queen, who had found her true calling as an announcer for the *Rajo* deliveries. While the Pysops vehicles drove around town and black American soldiers (by design or coincidence) alighted from the vehicles to pass out stacks of the newspaper, she stood triumphantly and flamboyantly in the back of the vehicle greeting the city with a microphone: "*Rajo, Rajo. Suba Wanaxsed.*" She so loved herself. She was a star!

On one run, about half way through the day's deliveries, we started taking fire. Our driver punched it and we squealed around a corner as several green tracer rounds from a Soviet .51-caliber machine gun flashed overhead. At the same time the two Pysops NCOs and I immediately ducked down in the back of vehicle and scanned the receding rooftops, trying to spot the machine gun, and looking for targets as we prepared to return fire. The Beauty Queen was a bit put out—she had lost her grip on the cab of the Humvee and almost fallen out of the vehicle. How dare the driver upset her composure.

She actually turned around and glared at us in rebuke, unmindful that we were obviously hunkered down and trying to shoot somebody, before she continued her announcing, smiling and waving like a Rose Bowl parade queen, as the driver took evasive action and the machine gun fire continued to narrowly miss our vehicle. I looked at one of the guys in the back with me, and he shrugged back and gave me a look like, "Hell, I won't tell her if you don't." I was almost hoping she'd take a round for having cheated some poor soldier out of his well-deserved and hard-earned R&R.

I also rode with a Military Intelligence unit that had set up some "meets" in the city and was looking for arms caches and "technicals." One trip turned up a disabled Panhard AML-90 armored car with a working turret and 90mm gun sitting only about a hundred fifty meters from a small Italian compound and just a few blocks from the embassy compound. A locked Conex near the armored car yielded a large cache of ordnance. Another day I spent way too much time outside in the street while a meeting went on in a nearby house. Eventually a group of kids arrived begging for candy. I ended up entertaining them. We were really hanging our asses out there in that neighborhood with nothing more than a couple of MI (Military Intelligence) kids lightly armed with just their M-16s. I knew how quickly things could go sideways in situations like that and wasn't enjoying myself. I don't think the MI team had any idea of the risks they were taking or how hairy things could get in Mogadishu.

The streets in Mogadishu were sometimes desolate, other times crammed with beat-up vehicles belching blue-black smoke and teeming with loud throngs of Somalis. It all depended on the neighborhood or the time of day. Often we'd pass vehicle convoys or patrols of coalition forces; Italians (not particularly well-liked by Somalis, as they were the former colonial oppressors), Moroccans, Botswanans, Canadians, and Australians. Other times you could drive for a half-hour without seeing another sign of military presence in the city.

Riding in open Hummers presented a problem because both driver and shotgun were exposed from the side. Goggles and gloves were worn while riding in the open, doorless Hummers, for protection from the hands of thieves and to guard against injuries from thrown rocks. Tailgates were left down so grenades could be kicked out. It seems like everybody was fired at. The first time some Somali thug sent some rounds my way, it was three short bursts of automatic and nobody could locate the sonofabitch. Very seldom were shots actually exchanged, and it was anybody's guess if the fire was even directed at us as we drove past.

Besides the possibility of being perforated with some of the habitual—and at times somewhat desultory—gunfire, riding around Mogadishu was not without its other perils. Rocks and other objects were commonly thrown at US troops, causing more than a few to require stitches in the face. In one case I was nearly hit by a floor tile flung from a second story building. It hit the doorframe and shattered, showering my face and neck with stinging fragments. Except for a few bloody nicks, I was fine. I was lucky it didn't hit me. Because thieves regularly swarmed around slowed or halted vehicles and stripped them of equipment, the troops armed themselves with "people beaters"—axe handles, homemade clubs, and whips—anything to beat people off the damn vehicles. Well, hell, it was better than *shooting* them. On February 4, 1993, Marines shot and killed a thirteen-year-old Somali youth who rushed their vehicle with what appeared to be a grenade.

Yankee ingenuity went to work trying to protect the troops, and at the same time accomplish the mission. In the way of defensive measures GIs taped and wired MRE (meals ready to eat) box cardboard on the back slats of seats in the backs of the unarmored pickups and Hummers and to keep out groping hands and block prying eyes. The Canadians, who were serious players, attached lengths of concertina wire to the sides of their vehicles. Some vehicles had benches of wood or piles of sandbags in the center of the bed, so that the shooters sat back to back and faced outboard to monitor the crowds in the streets, search rooftops for snipers, and respond to attacks. The sandbags also provided some protection from possible mine blasts. Shooters rode high in the back of vehicles, standing erect behind the vehicle cab and remaining alert—their weapons locked and loaded. To maintain communications between vehicles and between passengers in the cab and passengers in the back, drivers removed the tarps that separated the cab. Many units equipped their personnel with Motorola walkie-talkies.

But even taking all precautions, it was still a bad situation. I was riding in a CUCV (the military version of the Chevy Blazer) down near the port one day, when the vehicle driver slowed to maneuver around a large road crater and had his sunglasses ripped off his face. Two blocks down the road, it almost happened again. While I beat three of the scumbags off the tailgate and out of the back with a club, they went for the passenger's prescription lenses. Some units kept a count of sunglasses and eyeglasses lost. The thieves got ingenious, using long poles with wire hooks on the end to fish items out of the cabs and beds of moving vehicles. A lot of the victims were joy riders or tourists—curious people who just had to see Mogadishu, when they should have been at their desks in the embassy compound or back at their home station.

The frigging tourists were starting to get annoying. There were several navy ships parked off shore, and their officers were always finding some excuse to visit the embassy compound, probably so they could qualify for an award and hazardous duty pay while sightseeing and taking photos. I was in the back of a US Army deuce-and-a-half truck one day, getting ready to roll out of the embassy compound, when a grossly fat US Navy captain (the same grade as an army colonel) had her fat ass hoisted into the back of the truck. It took two soldiers to boost her up there. With her was another fat squid, this one a man (and I use that term loosely). I mean, really, if you can't climb into the back of a truck without help, especially when not wearing combat equipment and a rucksack, what business do you have being in the military, let alone in a war zone?

As we were locking and loading on the roll out through the gate, neither of the naval officers could figure out how to load and make safe the Beretta 92F 9mm pistols strapped on their belts. I chambered a round for the navy captain, showed her how to flick the de-cocker lever off and on safe, and instructed her to point and shoot only if everyone else was shooting. How she got the thing unloaded back at the port I can only guess.

When I first arrived in Mogadishu one of the Marines showed me a packet of post cards. They were recent shots of people around the city, including gunmen. The photographer was Danny Eldon, a white Kenyan in his early twenties. Eldon's mother Kathy was an American and the Reuters bureau chief in Nairobi. One day while traveling down near the Old Port, I crossed Eldon's path. We chatted briefly about Nairobi and acquaintances in common and discussed linking up together sometime. Unfortunately, on Dan's last day in Somalia, July 12, 1993, he and three other journalists were beaten to death by a Somali mob.

Just a year after my Somalia contract (March 1994), I met Dan's father, Mike Eldon, in Nairobi. I'd just come out of Sudan, where I'd spent several months with the guerrillas of the Sudanese People's Liberation Army. In Sudan, near Nimule, I had met Marc Dominic Cunningham-Reid, a freelance photojournalist and a friend of Eldon's. Dom was also a white Kenyan and he wanted me to talk to Mike about Dan's death. I had to explain to Mike why US helicopters flying above the mob and reporting the situation were unable to fire on the Somalis and save Dan's life. It was not a pleasant conversation.

I still have the set of Danny's postcards that he gave me. They are not only one of my most prized keepsakes, they're my only souvenir from my time in Somalia.

I'd been in country about a month or so when I was ordered to fly back to Dover AFB to pick up another load of interpreters. At the Mogadishu airfield, I was directed to a tent where I could wait. It was nighttime, and I walked into the tent blinking under the harsh light of the fluorescent bulbs. Then I shivered. It was friggin' cold. The damn air force had air-conditioned tents! A zipper head (an air force zoomie with his hair parted in the middle) walked up to me. His hair was as long as mine, he was wearing an earring, and, I shit you not, his brown GI t-shirt was cut off above the navel. Christ on a crutch, welcome to blue-suit air force land.

He said, "Hey man, what's up?" and immediately clocked my Colt Officer's .45 in the leather DeSantis shoulder rig. I was taking it back to Dover with me so I could leave it. It was jamming up. The heat or humidity was affecting the ammo. I'd shot the same lot of ammo in the States and had no problem, but in the sandbox, no matter how clean it was, the casings would jam. So I decided I'd leave that back in the US and go to my Beretta 9mm when I returned. At least with the nine, I wouldn't have to worry about ammo resupply–though if I'd run through a hundred rounds of .45-caliber ammunition in Somalia that would have been some serious shit.

The zoomie was eating a bag of popcorn. Holy kernel, Batman, where do I get some of that? I offered to buy a bag, and the kid said, "No problem, it's free." I was stunned. I sat down at a table and looked at the wide screen TV at the other end of the tent. They were all watching a movie. It was rec time for the USAF. I looked around the room and saw just about everyone was looking at me, including some very cute young females. Wearing t-shirts. Braless. In a cold, air-conditioned tent. Damn. It was two tickets to Titsburg, please, and give me the change in nipples.

The USAF had it beat. When the zoomie came back from the microwave with my popcorn he also handed me a bottle of water that I almost dropped. It was like ice. I couldn't believe it. "Shit, this is cold!" He looked at me and said, "Man, where you been livin'–-in a cave?" Er, no, but pretty damn close some days! Next he asked me if I wanted some Campbell's soup. Shit, yeah, bring it on.

On the way out of Somalia we laid over at Taif, Saudi Arabia. Well, at least I thought it was Taif. They told us when we got on the flight that our destination was Dover AFB and we would stop to refuel at Taif, Saudi Arabia. As soon as it was wheels up, I zonked out. Knowing that the scorched earth of Somalia was receding below me lifted a great weight of exhaustion and ache from my sorely stressed body. I was just grateful to be out of my vest and helmet for the next day or two. I slept soundly until we landed to refuel. Some soldier woke my ass up and I got off to see that there was the usual Arab in khaki pawing through my carry-on, searching for whiskey and porn and looking very dejected he didn't find any. Then some sand and palm trees and the Quonset huts where I crashed on a cot for a while. When I woke up I was thirsty and asked one of the soldiers on my flight if I could bum a buck's worth of local money from him so I could buy a soda. He handed me some money I'd never seen before.

"What's this?"

"Egyptian pounds."

"Egyptian? They ain't gonna take this. I wanna buy a Pepsi."

"Yeah, they'll take it."

"They're not gonna take Egyptian money in Saudi Arabia, man!"

"Er, excuse me, sir, *we are in Egypt, sir.*"

"Uh, yeah, sorry, thanks..."

Our flight had diverted to an air base at Cairo West. I'd been in Egypt for five hours and didn't know it. Hell, it all looked the same to me—Arabs, palm trees, sand ... lots of sand. Fuck me.

Before I left Mogadishu I was able to call Judy on our sat phone link. She drove up to Dover to meet my flight. We checked into a nearby hotel. Her airline ID got her a better discount rate than my military ID. So much for the patriotism of major hotel chains. We spent the whole night in bed, but obviously didn't get any sleep. I took her to the champagne brunch at the Officer's Club the next morning and kissed her goodbye in a teary farewell at the terminal before I boarded my flight back to Mogadishu. The whole rendezvous was bittersweet: I knew what I was leaving behind just like before, only now I knew what a screwed up mission I was going back to. Operation Restore Hope was considered doomed to failure by even the most uninformed on-the-ground observers. The country and the people were just too damn fucked up. It all looked good on CNN but we were just spinning our wheels. The tar baby was sticking but good.

Arriving back at Mogadishu Airport in the early evening, I made a call to the unit and told them where I was. Since it was beginning to get dark, there wouldn't be any travel into the city. I knew I'd have to find a place to crash for the night. I was wandering about the airfield near the terminal building looking for a spare cot when I saw about a dozen Green Berets frantically loading M-16 magazines. Oh, shit! Were Somalis coming through the wire? I had to wonder why these guys hadn't shipped over pre-loaded mags in a locked footlocker. The NCO in charge seemed to be a bit hyper, what with all the shouting of orders, scurrying to and fro, and much attendant humping of ammunition crates. You'd think this was Custer's Last Stand or the Alamo.

I wandered over and said hello. I got the brush off. Ooh, secret squirrel time, Omigod, there are US Army Special Forces soldiers in Somalia! I picked up on the attitude that "they" were here now and would get everything sorted out in Somalia. I told them about the travel policy. "Hey, you guys can ease up. You won't be going anywhere until daybreak. You should get some sleep." I was politely told to fuck off by the NCO in charge. "They" were *Special Forces* and "they" were certain they were going into Mogadishu that night. I didn't bother to tell them I had time with JFKSWC and 10th Special Forces Group, nor how tight I was with their new CO. I went back to my search for a cot to sleep on and some chow. When I was leaving in the morning, I shouted over to their confused and now tired little gaggle and asked them if they'd like a ride in the back of my truck to the embassy compound.

A few days before I had flown back to Dover, I had been wandering around the embassy compound and met some Botswanans. They invited me over to their living area and I joined them for lunch. They were cooking caterpillars—yeah, no kidding. They had tins and tins of these large caterpillars, larger than my thumb, packed in oil like sardines. Fried up, they tasted like beef. I expected they'd "taste like chicken." After a month of MREs, they were damned good. I got to be pretty good friends with the Bots, so the day before I was due to fly back to the US for thirty-six hours to pick up some more translators and rendezvous with Judy, I asked them if they needed anything.

"Yes, Mister Rob! Porn!"

Unfortunately I didn't have an opportunity to hit an adult bookstore for some really raunchy stuff, but I bought *Penthouse, Playboy,* and whatever else was available at the Dover AFB base exchange on my way out. When I got back to Somalia they were *beaucoup* happy with the glossy pages of airbrushed big-titted American blondes. They told me I could go out on a mission with them some time and we made arrangements to do just that. A few days later I went over with all my go-to-war gear. I loaded up with a squad of the hearty Botswanans and my new-found buddy, their lieutenant. They were going out on patrol and I was no longer bored as hell.

I was going to fire up some Skinnies with the Botswanans and it felt *good.*

We started off by driving up to Armed Forces Road and then on to the K4 traffic circle. First we stopped outside Mogadishu Airport and then went up to Bakara Market. This was a bad, bad neighborhood. It was only a few blocks from the Olympic Hotel that would become famous in "Black Hawk Down" and west of the areas where Durant and Wolcott crashed their helicopters after they were shot out of the sky by volleys of RPGs. I had an AK and extra mags stuffed into my one-quart canteen pouches, with my Beretta 9mm tucked into the back of my pants (a tad uncomfortable with web gear and flak vest), and was squeezed into the front of a pickup with the Botswanan el-tee. When we'd left the embassy everybody had jacked rounds into their rifles and the machine gunners charged their guns. I think having me along gave them some added impetus for a fight. It didn't take much to pick one in Mogadishu. I was just happy to have a Kalashnikov locked and loaded in my lap.

We were sniped at once, but the patrol through the city was largely uneventful for the first few hours—that is, until we drove into Aideed territory near Bakara Market, just as the afternoon *khat* chew was winding down. How propitious! As we started around a corner, I saw that there was an impromptu roadblock at the far end of the block and three or four Skinnies running out of a building. Oh shit!

One of them turned and loosed off a burst from his Kalashnikov. The Botswanans immediately opened up. Hot casings bounced around inside the cab of our vehicle. I cursed myself for not having enough fore-thought to put in my earplugs. My ears would ring for hours.

The lead vehicle was committed to the turn already and had gone partially crosswise in the street. The Bots in the back were giving the roadblock hell with all weapons whapping away on full-auto. I was in the cab of the next truck. Our truck was halfway through the turn and there was another truck behind us. The troops in our truck and the one behind us were deploying when I saw a Skinny with a RPG—empty, thank god—pop up.

Damn! The dumb fucker actually ran across the alley in front of me. I already had a good firing position against the front fender and over the hood, so I put the front post on him and gave him the good news. Fire was continuing to come from the building on the corner, and I fired off three or four more sustained bursts at those jazbos. Needing to reload, I dropped to a knee behind the cover of the front bumper. Not really much in the way of cover, but at least I had some concealment. I snapped out the empty mag and hurriedly reloaded a full mag. Jacked the bolt back and released. Back in business. This shit was good. Talk about stress management!

I looked for more targets or incoming fire. Nothing. It was over that fast. There were two more gunmen lying dead in the street, shot down by the Botswanans. We searched the bodies for documents, but found nothing except for a few shillings and some scraps of paper. The dirty shillings were divvied up as souvenirs, the weapons were tossed in the back of the truck, and the bodies left to be dragged off or to rot.

Just another day in Mogadishu for the Botswanan Army . . . but a damn good day for a bored assistant team chief of interpreters!

You didn't have to go looking for trouble, like I had with the Botswanans, to find it in Somalia. It usually came looking for you. One day, a one-vehicle road accident occurred right in front of our three-vehicle convoy while we were coming back from the 10th Mountain Division's outpost at Ceel Jaalle, near Merca along the coast, eighty miles south of Mogadishu. Part of the "mission" there was a much-appreciated swim in the ocean. We paid some Somali boys hunting octopus a few bucks for the use of their masks and snorkels, then stripped naked and spent the afternoon snorkeling. The war was all but forgotten for a few stress-free hours. It was good just to be out of boots, uniform, helmet, and flak vest as well as away from the embassy compound. Although part of the afternoon was later spent in vehicle recovery operations (in other words, digging a five-quarter-ton pickup out of the sand while doing a lot of cussing), this was about all the downtime I experienced in Somalia. So, despite the absence of bikini-clad beauties, we were returning from a very delightful day at the beach.

We were making fairly good time in order to get back into the embassy compound in Mogadishu before dark when a Land Rover flying a German flag passed us. It was going like a bat out of hell and obviously driven by an idiot. About a klick further down the road the driver swerved to avoid a coil of concertina wire on the left side of the road, and he lost control of the car. The Sammies who were in the process of setting up the "checkpoint" before the Germans hit it were already running through the scrub as they saw our dust cloud approaching. I was standing in the back of the five-quarter Dodge pickup and looking forward over the cab, my normal position while riding the roads, as we watched the Land Rover slide down the road on its side and then flip over onto its roof. Before we could stop, I saw the oily rag serving as a gas cap shoot out onto the roadway and several gallons of gasoline pour out of the gas tank. Fortunately no one in the vehicle was smoking.

We quickly piled out of our vehicles, ran over to the Land Rover, which was carrying three relief workers and a driver, and got them all out of the wreck. My "homie," Corporal Pat Cooper, Buffalo, New York, rendered initial first aid to one of them, a German woman, while I slung another woman, a Somali, over my shoulder and carried her away from the accident. Gas was pouring out of the Land Rover and I beat feet back up onto the roadway before it could catch fire or explode.

Darkness was less than an hour away, and no one knew where that concertina wire had come from. It was probable that some nighttime bandits were setting up a roadblock a little early, but we couldn't be certain. Were they locals setting up a checkpoint for protection, or bandits extorting money, or Somali militia organizing an ambush for us? Captain Dan Dobrolowski, 513th MI Brigade, quickly organized a perimeter.

Although he was now a Military Intelligence officer, Ski was formerly an infantryman. He and I had both been rifle platoon leaders in sister battalions of the 2d Infantry Division on the Korean DMZ back in '86, and he quickly slipped back into the infantry small unit leader mode. I was beaucoup happy to be serving with Ski in Somalia. He was one squared-away soldier: a real professional. Commandeering an M60 machine gun for our hasty perimeter from another passing vehicle, he began organizing vehicle shakedowns of civilian traffic entering our perimeter that crowned the highway.

Within five minutes there must have been a crowd of seventy to a hundred civilians from the nearby village lining the road. Many were men, and it was easy for them to hide weapons amongst the crowd. They didn't seem exactly friendly towards us. Malcontented grumbling translates the same in every language. This was not good. We were prime targets. Crowned on the roadway with a wide expanse of bush on each side harboring who knew how many bad guys, it was only a matter of time before some clown hopped up on *khat* decided to send some rounds our way. I was worried about a technical making the scene and Momma Krott's little boy catching the business from a 12.7mm heavy machine gun. We had to get this goat rope moving, get everyone patched up and a Medevac organized before our little band got hit and we had to pull an Alamo out in the middle of nowhere.

The German woman was becoming a real pain in the ass. I knew we were in trouble when I saw her Birkenstock sandals. Great, I thought, another friggin' tree-hugger. I'd grabbed a first aid kit from one of our vehicles and made myself useful by bandaging her up. I had her hold a piece of gauze to the gash on her face while I worked on the worse wound on her forehead. We'd cleaned the worst of the blood off her and now she was alternately worried about a) her knapsack, b) her passport, c) the driver losing his job (as well he should), and d) the state of world peace. She kept yelling at Nigel, the young geeky Brit who was with her. She was really getting on everybody's nerves. In both English and my bastard German, I was trying to get her to stay calm. She didn't seem to be in shock. I was seriously considering stuffing some gauze into her gob and telling her she had a mouth injury. Then "Brigitte" started asking about her camera (add item e). She wanted to take pictures. I couldn't believe it. Maybe she did suffer some brain damage. While we were on the subject of photos, I took Coop's photo and then gave Coop my camera and struck a pose. It was so ridiculous I couldn't help but laugh despite the seriousness of the situation.

Luckily no one was critically injured, because the MPs on the scene couldn't establish good radio commo with a Medevac. All we had was the GI-issue vehicle first aid kit until a combat lifesaver showed up. He took one look at the work I was already doing, gave me his bag, and left to take up a position on our hasty perimeter. Thanks fella. With some better gear, I got to work doing a better job of patching up Brigitte and the cuts and scrapes on the other passengers. When I get in situations like this, I always joke that my mother always wanted me to become a doctor. When a medic did show up he had to leave to check out another vehicle accident nearby with multiple victims and a gunshot victim. Things were heating up on our little stretch of roadway in the middle of nowhere. It looked like our bad guys had set up down the road and hit someone not as prepared as we had been. We could hear sporadic small arms fire up ahead in the distance. Just another day in Somalia.

Before we pulled out to Medevac the relief workers ourselves, I wandered back over to the trashed Land Rover where one of the aid workers asked me what should be done with the weapon. Weapon? Sure enough, with all these *khat*-chewing Skinnies milling around, there was a loaded .308 G-3 assault rifle lying out in plain sight on top of the flipped-over vehicle's underside. I appropriated the weapon for some added personal firepower. Yeah, now this was a *rifle*—not one of those .22-caliber poodle-shooter M-16s. I dropped the magazine, push-checked the rounds and got some give. I found it was short about six rounds, and checked the chamber to make sure there was a round up the spout. It was comforting to have a battle rifle in my hands, although Ski was worried the major (as in Major Dickhead) would find out. That really pissed me off. If some shit came our way, at least I could defend myself with something besides a pistol.

As we were leaving I hastily cleared the rifle, placed it on safe, and shoved it at Nigel, telling him, "Here, take this, sling it muzzle down, and fer Chrissakes don't play with the damn thing," then ran back to our vehicles.

Nigel looked at the rifle like he might abruptly piss himself, prompt-ly handed the weapon to their Somali guard, already whining and cry-ing, and climbed into our pickup asking for a ride. What were we gonna do, say no? We left their "good" Somali out in Indian country alone to guard the Land Rover with his G-3, one partially charged magazine, and a bottle of water. Better you than me, pal.

The ride back into Mogadishu was uneventful, although it was balls to the wall dust flying everywhere on a white-knuckle drive to beat sun-down. We pulled into the Swedish hospital and the nurses and medics came out to meet us and take care of the wounded. One of the nurses was a forty-something blue-eyed blonde in a tight green army t-shirt, hair in a bun, and Swedish accent. Yowza! Hot Lips Hoolihan take a back seat. I was smitten. So were about twenty other guys. I think we were all wondering how we could get ourselves wounded—nothing too serious though.

After we dropped the relief workers at the hospital we continued on to our compound. Pretty well wrung out from our day at the beach and our evacuation of the relief workers, I walked into the office with Ski right behind me. David Davis, the unit's asshole clerk, tried to toss a Willy Peter (white phosphorus) grenade to Ski as in "Here, catch! Isn't this neat!" Everybody scrambled to get out of the room through the nar-row doorway, bumping into other soldiers in the hallway trying to get into the office. If it hadn't been so serious, it would've been comical in a Keystone Kops kind of way.

The manufacture lot date on the damn grenade was 1954. Davis' excuse was he'd taped the spoon down. He knew just enough to make him dangerous. Taping the spoon or safety lever down wouldn't have done any good, as the "mouse trap" firing mechanism of the M206 fuse was undoubtedly long corroded, making the grenade dangerous and unstable. The chemical composition of the detonator and the tetryl burster were old, crystallized, and unstable. Contrary to standard operating procedures and current standing orders—there was a blanket order in Somalia not to pickup any ordnance—this idiot had picked up dangerous ordnance, an M-34 white phosphorous grenade of all things, and then walked into a small concrete-walled room where as many as a dozen people would gather.

Perfectly illustrating how screwed up his priorities were, the major disregarded the whole incident of his clerk and the grenade, but got his panties in a knot when he found out we'd been skinny-dipping. Something about cultural sensitivity. His complaint was absolutely ridiculous. The boys on the beach didn't care about our white penises flopping around, and as for cultural sensitivity I'd about had enough from the chairborne warriors at the embassy compound. It's no wonder the mission in Somalia turned to shit, with careerists like this guy, albeit three ranks higher, calling the shots. The major of course brushed off my complaint that his clerk was playing with unstable and deadly ordnance in the office. Some people never get their priorities straight. Cultural sensitivities, shit.

After the grenade incident, Ski and I talked about the Swedish hospital guards armed with 9mm Swedish K submachine guns. US Special Forces had used them in Vietnam, and I was surprised the Swedes still had this World War II-era weapon in their armory. Ski and I were both gun nuts and were having a good time in Somalia: there were weapons all over the country. Everywhere I went, there was an arms room filled with the same hodge-podge assortment of small arms captured from the local thugs. While AKs, M-16s, Thompsons, and PPSH-41s were the most common weapons I saw, there was a wide assortment of weapons lying about, including at least one of just about every European and American military small arm made in this century.

While I was in Kismayo I inspected a conex full of captured weaponry. I almost burst into tears at the sight of badly rusted Thompson .45-caliber submachine guns destined for the demolitions pit, knowing that even in their ill-maintained condition, the venerable Chicago Pianos were a collector's dream. Sgt. Jako from the 10th Mountain Division S-2 shop down in Kismayo showed me a very pristine M-14. No doubt there were a few USMC vets of the Southeast Asia

War Games back at MARFOR headquarters who would've appreciated this robust weapon. I considered the idea of scrounging for ammo and spare magazines and taking it back with me, but knew I'd catch shit from somebody in the embassy compound. Who's the long-haired civilian with the M-14?

A really interesting find was a Smith and Wesson 1917 service revolver, the one chambered for .45 Long Colt, but used with .45 ACP cartridges and half moon clips. Strangely enough it had a short snub-nosed barrel. The finish was 100 percent and the grips were unscratched. It looked like it was boxed out of the factory yesterday. It seemed like there was one of everything. SKS carbines were piled on top of M-1 Garands, which leaned against Mannlicher-Carcanos (the gun that killed JFK), flanked by Czech LMGs and rusting Mausers.

Later, back in Mogadishu, I had the opportunity to examine a Breda Model 30 Italian Light Machine Gun. The Breda, although one of the first machine guns made with a quick-change barrel, and while exhibiting excellent workmanship, was a badly flawed design. A delayed blow-back operating weapon with a recoiling barrel, it has a large bolt with multiple locking lugs, and the magazine is permanently attached and is loaded with a twenty-round charger. On top of the receiver are an oil pan and pump. Because of faulty loading and ejecting inherent in its design, weapons oil is injected onto the rounds as they're fed through the side-loading fixed-box magazine. It obviously didn't fair too well in the sandy wastes of Ethiopia and Libya, leading to the old joke about Italians making better shoes than machine guns.

Dan and I meticulously disassembled it. All parts were serial numbered and matching. Ski petitioned to have it sent back to the US to a museum to no avail. Large quantities of captured and confiscated weapons were shipped to the embassy compound, where they were later destroyed. I heard stories about mint-condition nineteenth century Wilkinson dress swords and antique flintlocks being destroyed alongside stacks of battered Kalashnikovs. Unfortunately the well-deserving soldiers and Marines of Operation Restore Hope were restricted from bringing home a war trophy. The ATF strikes again.

Some of the people who justly deserved a war trophy were the US Marines of India Battery, 3/11 Marines who manned several outposts of camouflage-net-covered sand bags sited along the embassy's outer wall, topped with shards of broken glass, and the main outer gate to the US Embassy compound. I spent a little time wandering around the perimeter and getting to know the leathernecks responsible for the security of my work site and the area where I slept (quite comfortably) in an open, GP medium tent with a sand floor. The positions were all two-man positions that included night vision devices and an automatic weapon, either an M249 SAW or an M60. While some automatic weapons positions had range cards, others did not; it seemed to be a gunner prerogative rather than a result of SOP or orders from their tactical small unit leaders. Then again, some had non-existent fields of fire.

Most of the Marines I spoke to eschewed the M249 SAW, citing its inaccuracy. They preferred their M-16A2s—every Marine a rifleman. This included the M249 in the sandbag position just outside my office. One day I sprinted up there after some shots rang out. There was a wooden ladder up to the machine gun position, since the post was on a platform built into a corner of the wall. As I cleared the ladder into the position, I noticed no one manning the M249. I got on the gun, charged it, and began searching for targets. When I asked one of the riflemen why he was using his M-16 and not the SAW (thinking maybe they'd had problems with it), his reply was, "I can't hit shit with that, sir!" After the shooting died down they told me I was welcome to man the gun whenever there was trouble. Fine with me. Now I always knew where to find a squad automatic, and I much prefer a SAW or an M60 to a '16 any day.

Their disdain for the belt-fed light machine gun was because they were artillerymen re-designated as infantry. They weren't as well-trained or experienced with the SAW as infantrymen would be. I'd trained on it at Aberdeen as a National Guard infantry second lieutenant while escorting a group of cadets in 1984, and then again as a young infantry captain at Benning in 1990. With my experience with full-auto crew-served weapons, I had no doubt I could employ it against any targets that popped up. As I was a former M60 machine gunner, the M249 on our wall quickly became my assigned weapon as far as the Marines were concerned. Fuck the major in charge of the MI guys. I was a soldier, damn it, and I sure wasn't going to stand around with my dick in my hand or cower behind the wall if the shit hit the fan.

I often went up to that observation post to shoot the shit with the Marines. On the southwest corner they had a good view of a Somali prison, where nighttime executions were a common event with the Marines holding front row seats from this outpost, no tickets required. When I heard this I couldn't help but hum the opening bars of Elvis

Costello's "Watching the Detectives," changing the lyrics to "watching the executions." I was up there one afternoon when they dragged three men out, hands bound behind their backs, threw them to their knees and shot them in the back of the head with a pistol. The executioner actually took his cigarette from his mouth, turned in our direction, and waved. It was times like that that made you wonder what the fuck we were doing over there.

One morning Lance Corporal Jessie Nunez engaged a Somali armed with an RPG spotted crawling over the embassy wall just across the street from the prison. Despite the occasional sniper rounds thudding into their sandbags, and the nightly harassment of nearby Somali versus Somali firefights, they spent most of their day shifts bored by routine and harassed by Somalis begging for food. Since they were Moslems, we tossed them our pork entrees. Fuck 'em if they couldn't take a joke.

These Marines and personnel from the Force Service Support Group guard force handled perimeter security and reaction teams. Additionally there were sniper posts located on top of various buildings in the compound, as well as on K-7, a building outside the embassy. K-7 was considered key terrain because of its commanding height and fields of fire. Marine artillerymen from Echo Battery 2/12 Marines attached to the 3/11 Marines also performed mounted and dismounted patrols outside the embassy and the airfield.

On January 10 at about 1:30 in the morning, two of the Marines providing security for my detachment, Corporal Jerimie Bartley and Lance Corporal Shawn Henderson, were part of a fifteen-man patrol traveling in Humvees. They told me they spotted armed Somalis and their patrol dismounted near K-7. Moving stealthily down the alleyway while hugging the walls, the Marines were fired upon by an unknown number of Somalis. Going to ground, most of the patrol quickly burned off some rounds, but the whole firefight was over very quickly; their lieutenant was screaming ceasefire before some of the Marines were even able to fire their weapons.

The Marine scout-snipers from on top of K-7 engaged multiple targets, using either a .50 Barrett or a Remington 700 (no one I talked to would confirm which), and claimed two kills that were later confirmed. The patrol accounted for another confirmed kill and a probable. Luckily there were no friendly casualties. Luckily, because after the unit consolidated, the Marines found that a round had hit the feed tray cover of an M60 machine gun. The Marines weren't going to be lucky forever, though. It was on a patrol like this just two days later that the Marines lost one of their own.

Tuesday night, January 12, 1993, Lance Corporal Domingo Arroyo of the 3/11 Field Artillery, USMC, a veteran of the Persian Gulf War, became the first Marine combat fatality of Operation Restore Hope when he was fatally wounded in the head during a nighttime patrol. Arroyo was part of an eleven-man squad/patrol conducting a night security sweep outside the Mogadishu International Airport in an area of abandoned warehouses when it encountered light automatic weapons fire and exploding grenades. A fierce firefight took place, and after about five minutes the patrol leader ordered the Marines to break contact. The unit fell back from the hasty ambush, exited the kill zone, and moved to its rally point. After consolidating and making a headcount the unit determined it was missing one man. The patrol received reinforcements from a Quick Reaction Force mounted in three armored vehicles, and then returned to the ambush site, engaged the Somalis in a second firefight, and recovered Arroyo's body, roughly thirty minutes after the initial contact with enemy forces.

I heard about this the next day and was commiserating with some of the Marines on our perimeter when one of the Marines said, "Hell, sir, you talked to Oscar just the other day." I was flummoxed and asked him what he was talking about. He told me Oscar was the Marine I'd given a can of snuff to. I was too stunned to speak. Now there was a face to the name, and I knew the guy. He was dead, and this war had just got very personal for me.

Lance Corporal Richard Duarte, a close friend of Arroyo's, was grieving for his buddy when I spoke to him the next day while he was manning Post Three Alpha in the embassy compound. He and Arroyo had gone through boot camp together before being assigned to the same platoon. All Duarte could talk about was getting the Somalis responsible in the sights of his '16. Another Marine who knew Arroyo, Corporal Blackburn, squinted piercing blue eyes at me, and in a slow Kentucky hillbilly twang said, "Wish I had my deer rifle over here—my 8 em-em magnum; I'd make some sonofabitch pay." Lance Corporal "Thumper" Perry agreed with his friend. For Arroyo's friends, payback was just a short time in coming, but not before another American would be shot.

The Marines at the old soccer stadium considered the area hot. And hot it was, with sniper fire a part of daily life. I was sniped at every time I went over there. Sometimes more than once. Either the Sammies couldn't shoot for shit, or they weren't trying very hard. A few hours after Arroyo was killed, a sniper fired three rounds at a patrol just south of the stadium, wounding the patrol medic, a US Navy corpsman, in the left shoulder. This really pissed off the USMC. Nobody, but nobody, shoots one of their corpsmen. Hours later, the Marines gunned down a Somali stupid enough to threaten them with a weapon.

Our rules of engagement were limiting the amount of payback that US forces could dish out. More Americans would die before anybody put a serious hurting on the Somalis. On January 25, a night with no moon, Lance Corporal Anthony Botello, twenty-one, volunteered to take the point on a night patrol outside the Stadium's perimeter. The patrol was making a security sweep in an attempt to locate some of the troublesome snipers who plagued the stadium compound. Before the patrol moved out, Botello told his squad leader, Corporal Scott Richards, "Let's get it done tonight. Let's come back." The patrol moved down a trail between a group of squatter huts. Botello's team leader, Corporal Bill Lamb, walking behind Botello, heard the steely rasp of a door latch being lifted. Botello stopped and told Lamb that he heard voices up ahead; not an uncommon occurrence for patrols in that area of operations.

Lamb was wearing night vision goggles (NVGs). Through the fuzzy green haze of the NVGs, Lamb spotted a man waving and speaking as though issuing instructions to others. Somalis, prompted by the sounds of armed men moving through their neighborhood at night, often stepped out of their houses when Marine patrols passed by, only to duck back inside after recognizing the Marines. This time two Somalis cocked weapons. Lamb and other Marines in the patrol heard the weapons' actions being worked. Hampered by the rules of engagement, the Marines didn't immediately react, until Lamb saw a Somali only five meters away drop to one knee and raise his rifle at Botello.

Lamb fired four rounds. After that everyone opened up, including a Somali on a rooftop, who sent two green tracers streaking towards point man Anthony Botello. Botello went down with a round in his chest. It had punched through his arm and penetrated his chest cavity at an oblique angle by entering through his unprotected armpit. The patrol heard Botello yell as he was hit. Despite orders to fall back on line so an M60 machine gun team could lay down suppressive fires, Lance Corporal Michael Soman, twenty-one, and PFC James Allison, twenty-one, rushed forward to rescue Botello. Soman threw the wounded

Marine onto his back and carried him to safety while Allison provided covering fire. Botello was Medevacked to the Swedish hospital. He died an hour later.

We were all getting some payback though. Our soldiers and Marines were killing Somali gunmen in little skirmishes, ambushes, and sniping actions on a daily basis. I was accompanying a Civil Affairs unit on one of its routine meet-and-greets. We pulled up two Humvees in front of a house, and as some of the CA types went inside with our interpreter, the rest loitered outside. I was hanging around the trail Humvee, enjoying a cigar. I had my pistol with me but also had an M-16, courtesy of one of the CA NCOs. All of a sudden, the shit really hit the fan with everybody screaming and shooting. I dropped down on a knee behind the Humvee and looked up the street to see a Somali in a blue shirt stand up behind a junk car and start banging away with an AK.

I snap-shot him. Taking a quick sight picture on his upper body, I gave him a quick double-tap and he went down. The rest of the guys outside had been banging away as well. As we secured the area, I mentioned I thought I'd accounted for the guy behind the car, but I knew the other guys were shooting too. Guy behind the car? Everyone had been returning fire at two Somalis shooting from the building across the street. We ran over to the junk car and there was one dead Somali with an AK. My rounds had hit him high in the chest and in the neck. Everybody sees things differently in a firefight, I was just lucky I was looking in that direction, as that guy was starting to put fire on us and no one else saw him.

After one of my contact trips to check on the linguists and give them their pay, I returned to Mogadishu and the office in the embassy compound to find a note waiting for me. I was to sign for and pick up some classified documents at the SCIF, pronounced "skiff." A SCIF, or Sensitive Compartmented Intelligence Facility, is usually a vault, but in this case, it was just a doorless room in the embassy with a shelter-half tarpaulin across the entrance and a bored-looking warrant officer sitting behind a folding wooden field desk. A Beretta 9mm was on the table within easy reach.

I identified myself, and he looked over his shoulder and called, "Hey, Lieutenant, we got us a visitor." The lieutenant came out. He was a freckle-faced kid a few inches shorter than me in a brown army t-shirt.

I identified myself. The el-tee told me to come with him, as the documents were being held in a field safe with another MI unit. We walked over there; I signed for the documents, and was thanking the el-tee when he asked, "Sir, where did you go to school?" Recognition suddenly dawned. I knew he wasn't asking about college or the military, but high school. I looked at him and said, "Hell, Mike, how many Rob Krotts do you think there are in the world?"

Mike Morrisroe grew up just down the road from me in rural McKean County, Pennsylvania. My parents were godparents to his kid brother. Mike and I went to the same little high school—about eighty kids per graduating class—and to the same weekly catechism center for our Catholic parish. A few years behind me, he had received an appointment to West Point. I was wearing my uniform with a nametape, whereas he was just in a t-shirt. Plus I'd identified myself. I sure wasn't expecting to meet anybody from home. We caught up on things and I told him I'd see him around. A few days later he showed up over at the office and asked if he could talk to me. When we were alone he said, "Did you call my mom?" I laughed. I'd called my parents and had my mother call his mother to say I'd seen Mike, he was doing a good job, and was fine.

Mike suddenly realized what was up: "You've got sat phone access!" The MI unit I was with had a sat phone link. This was back in the day when calling home from the field overseas was practically impossible, before hand-held Iridium and Thuraya sat phones were available. We had kept it quiet, or we'd be deluged with troops lining up to call home. The first time I called Judy, she was in shock. The sat link got us to any military phone or switchboard in the world, so I would call the Pentagon switchboard. They had no idea where or how the call was originating. I'd just say, "I'd like an outside line please," and they'd connect me to AT&T. As Reston, Virginia was just down the road from the Pentagon, it was a local call, and no charges to talk to Judy. When I called home I just called the unit at Fort Monmouth and the CQ (charge of quarters sergeant) would give me an outside line, and I'd call home on my AT&T calling card. Long distance from Monmouth, NJ—not Mogadishu!

Besides Mike, I bumped into a few army acquaintances as well. When we were told that the Operation Restore Hope mess hall had been completed by the friendly Brown and Root contractors and was open for business we were ecstatic. No more MREs! The mess hall would open every day at 1400 and serve one meal until, I think, 1900. The first day it was chicken cacciatore, buttered green beans, escalloped pota-toes, mixed fruit cup, and Kool-aid. The second day it was chicken cac-ciatore, buttered green beans. . . . Yeah, you got it, the same meal for a week or more. They'd unloaded one pallet or shipment of each and we had to eat it up before they brought in anything else.

One day while eating this fare, standing up at a four-foot high ply-wood table, I glanced up from my cardboard tray to see Major Tim McNulty. Grinning at him I said, "Hey, sir, how are you?" He was very perplexed until he glanced down at my nametag. It wasn't that he could-n't recognize me, it's that he couldn't recognize me out of context, just as I had not immediately recognized Mike Morrisoe. McNulty was very surprised to see me. He was a transportation officer for whom I'd briefly worked in a staff job at Fort Devens. As soon as he read the name tag, he took on that look that regular-army REMFs (Rear-Echelon Mother Fuckers) gave me whenever I popped up in a war zone some-place: "What the hell are you doing here, and I don't think I want to know/by the way, shouldn't you be in jail somewhere?"

When I was sent over to the Special Forces office in the embassy compound, I expected I might bump into some one I knew. There was a soldier at the front door. I didn't know his rank right off because he wasn't wearing his BDU jacket. It turned out he was a captain. Although I had an appointment, he wanted to play keeper of the gate. Lots of testosterone and even more attitude for no good reason. There were too many of those guys swaggering around. They spent all their time in the compounds, lifted a lot of weights, and didn't see any action. I really didn't have time for any of them. Given the fact that I was outside their chain of command and could operate more freely, they liked me even less, I'm sure. Not to mention my salary.

The commander of Special Operations Forces Somalia was Colonel Bill Faistenhammer. His father had been Colonel Ludwig "Blue Max" Faistenhammer— a well-known Special Forces officer in Viet Nam and later commander of 10th Special Forces Group. Ludwig had gone to St. Bonaventure and while there met his future wife, an Olean girl. Bill had gone to school in Olean and later, West Point. He saw my nametag on my jacket and immediately said, "That's a good Olean name." I got along well with Bill and did everything I could to support the SF mis-sion in Somalia.

At one point a Special Forces A-Team had a need for Rehanwayen dialect speakers. This wasn't the first such specific request. SF and other units were encountering problems when their interpreters, because of their accents or lack of local clan knowledge, were recognized by the locals to be from a rival clan. It wasn't good for business. Despite Mosely's contention that we didn't need to know what clan an interpreter was from, I'd made it my business to track that information on my own. Fortunately for us, I'd kept a cheat sheet of sorts in my notebook. Whereas Carl and Neil only knew a few of the Somalis personally, I was keeping by name notes on all hundred of them, just like I'd been taught to keep notes on my men as a platoon leader, forming my own sketch personnel files with notes on family, background, personality, and characteristics and abilities. Next to every name in my book was the interpreter's clan affiliation and region of origin or, for interpreters born outside of Somalia, the area from which their family originated.

It was rapidly becoming old home week for me in Mogadishu. A few days later I was standing in line at the Mogadishu Airport waiting to manifest for one of my various hops around Somalia when somebody tapped me on the shoulder. It was Jack Wheeler, an old friend from Fort Benning. Captain Wheeler, Team 3, C Co., 96th Civil Affairs, had the dubious distinction of being the only military police branch captain in my Infantry Officer's Advanced Course. He said, "What the hell are you doing here?" He wasn't surprised when I told him. He'd seen my first feature article in *Soldier of Fortune* with a photo of me, a two-page spread, where I was bare-chested, holding a spear, and dressed as a Samburu warrior right down to the goat fat and ochre in my hair, on a lion hunt with local warriors. He had told his friends, "I know this crazy sonofabitch!" Jack was working as a civil affairs officer. I told him I was on my way to visit a civil affairs unit near Bardera in a few days' time. We shook hands and then had to go our respective ways. I didn't know what a surprise Wheeler had in store for me.

The USMC helicopter crew chief didn't have time to fuck around with me. And it was obvious he had no inclination to do so. I couldn't really hear what he said, but the screaming face looked like it was yelling, "Get the fuck off my helicopter!" Fuck. I jumped out and hit the sand in a tumble before he could boot me out. I picked myself up and dusted off my knees as I forlornly watched the helicopter fly away. I looked around and saw nothing but African savannah—thorn trees, scrub, and sand—for as far as I could see. Shit. All I had with me was my LBE with two canteens, Kabar knife, and poncho; my Israeli paratrooper knapsack full of US greenbacks (nearly one hundred thousand dollars); and my 9mm pistol.

I adjusted my gear and trudged off in the direction the crew chief had pointed. After a few hundred meters I saw an MRE cardboard case cut open and placed on the ground as a sleeping pad, with a poncho strung overhead for shade. Oh, yeah, the Bardera Hilton. Okay, somebody was here. A bit further and I found the airfield. Sitting on the dirt strip was a Southern Air Transport C-130 with a busted landing gear. Off the airstrip was a beat up GP small tent with the ubiquitous wooden field table in front of it. There were two dirty and unhappy-looking soldiers sitting there with a radio and sign that said, "Welcome to Bardera International Airport." Great.

Why the hell the Marine pilot had dropped me off so far away I have no idea. He could have landed near the C-130. I walked over to the two soldiers. They just looked at me disinterestedly. They looked bored to tears but were beyond the point of caring who the hell I was or where I came from. Strange, especially given my less than clean-cut and decidedly un-GI appearance. I said hello and then jacked a thumb at the broke dick C-130 and said, "What's with the C-130?"

"What C-130?"

"That C-130 right over ... ah, yeah, gotcha. Can you guys tell me where to find the Civil Affairs people?" They pointed me in the right direction, and I was off trudging through the scrub again. I found what can only be described as a gypsy camp of ponchos, shelter halves, and tarpaulins thrown together to build an ops tent. I was introducing myself to an NCO standing outside when I heard a voice from inside the tent say, "Well, Krott, it's about fucking time. We've only been waiting for you for two weeks." I walked inside, surprised to see Captain Dennis Kennedy, Civil Affairs branch, formerly lieutenant, infantry of the 1/17th Infantry Battalion, 2d Infantry Division, Camp Casey, Republic of Korea.

I had introduced Dennis to his wife. I was sitting in the Club 54 in Tongduchon outside the Camp Casey gate with my girlfriend Kyong. Kyong was a Korean-American and US government employee who worked at Camp Casey as a GS-12, the civilian equivalent of a colonel. She knew anybody who was anybody, and on this particular night some Korean girlfriend of hers was sitting with us. This third wheel, albeit extremely attractive, was cramping my style. Dennis walked by and I introduced them, problem solved. Kennedy married her. When I asked after her, I was worried that it hadn't worked out, but Dennis assured me he was happily married with three kids. While we were chatting we both had a butt burning. As I never remembered Dennis smoking and I only smoke cigarettes in the field, I asked him, "You smoke at home?" He laughed and said, "You ever see a ninety-pound Korean woman mad?"

I finished my business there, paid off our interpreters, and caught a ride out on the non-existent C-130. I still have a SAT t-shirt emblazoned with the Southern Air Transport logo and the holy trinity of spook work: Admit Nothing, Deny Everything, Make Counter-Accusations.

After returning from that trip I quickly made another visit to Balidogle to pay our interpreters there. Balidogle Air Base had been renamed Camp Arroyo. Damn right. I don't know if there was any official USMC involvement and didn't really care. I was happy to see the sign out front. That night I froze my ass and was whipped near to death by wind and sand while sleeping in the open on the roof of the Balidogle airport terminal. The most exciting moment of the trip was watching a latrine burn merrily. Troops were trying to burn the shit and it got out of hand.

On another contact visit I got stuck. It was one of those can't-get-there-from-here situations. In order to get back to Mogadishu, I had to catch a ride on a C-130 supply flight returning to Mombasa, Kenya. When I deplaned in Mombasa I was forced to stay in a US Army compound with no chance of getting out into the city (which I'd visited before in 1988). That sucked. No seafood dinner at the Castle Hotel restaurant, no night clubbing, no dusky Kenyan maidens, and worst of all: no cold Tusker beer.

To keep the troops occupied, there was a movie tent with a VCR and large-screen TV. As I walked into the movie tent, a movie was just ending and the troops were debating what to watch next. Looking over the pile of dusty videotapes I suggested *Blue Velvet*. It was quickly seconded by the two or three GIs who had seen it before—yeah, a David Lynch film. The other thirty or so recent high-school graduates were in for a surprise. Right at the point where Dennis Hopper slaps Isabella Rosellini and yells, "Shut up. It's Daddy, Shithead. Get me my bourbon!" and after he gets on his knees, stares at her crotch, and sniffs from an inhaler murmuring, "Mommy, Mommy," one of the wide-eyed soldiers looked over at me, grinned appreciatively, and said, "Man, this is messed up," and went back to watching the movie. Dean Stockwell as a mincing homosexual singing Roy Orbison's "In Dreams" cinched it. They didn't know what to think.

When I returned to the Embassy I walked back to the office and briefed some Aussies in front of their headquarters in the embassy compound. The 513th MI BDE shared the building with them, so I got to know some good troops like corporals Raynor, Cripps, and Leppens. These were the first of the Australian contingent to arrive in Somalia. Later, there were over nine hundred Australians wearing those funny-looking hats deployed in support of Operation Restore Hope. They had just taken over US responsibilities in Baidoa. It was the largest deployment of Aussie troops since their participation in the Vietnam War. Although their officers were equipped with well-worn Browning Hi-Power 9mm pistols, the Diggers were carrying brand-spankin' new Steyr AUGs. Sweet. Also sweet was one of the MPs—as in female, blonde, Aussie, one each. She turned a few heads, and her sunny smile was a welcome sight on many days after the stress of downtown Mogadishu. I swapped a half-pint of Jack Daniels from my stash for some gear from down under. Because of this and some subsequent wheeling-dealing, I was known to a few of the Australians.

A few days after the Australian contingent was reinforced, I went up to Baidoa to take care of business and bumped into some of them as they were taking over the mission there. I was in Baidoa to check on an interpreter assigned to a USMC civil affairs team. Business done, I had some time to wander around until my flight out of there arrived. I watched some Aussies prep for a patrol. I tagged along with some inquisitive Diggers and inspected some "technical" vehicles captured by the 15th MEU USMC at Baidoa. Besides the usual shot-up Toyota trucks (one of which mounted a 106mm recoilless rifle) there were a Fiat 6614 APC (which mounts a 12.7mm machine gun) and a US-made truck mounting an anti-aircraft gun. The Fiat with the recoilless rifle, according to a placard attached to it, had been used to kill twenty-five civilians. Painted on the side was a slogan in Somali, which one of my interpreters translated as, "We must Kill and Loot. Nobody will survive when we attack." One of the other slogans on a technical said, "Ruthlessness and Gold is my Religion." The Aussies, newly arrived in country, just shook their heads at that one. Yeah, welcome to Somalia, mate.

The Aussies offered me some Vegemite, a yeasty paste they spread on perfectly good toast during breakfast in order to ruin it, but since my

Aussie "mate" Corporal Jeff Henley had introduced me to it in El Salvador four years previously, I decided to pass and wait another four years before I tried it again. They wanted to know if I was going out on patrol with them; I told them I'd have to pass, as I had to pay some of our guys up there and check on their performance. I watched as the Aussies unloaded and formed up prior to moving out to a feeding center. A few hours after they left in a convoy of trucks, word came back that one of the Diggers accidentally discharged his Steyr in the back of a vehicle. The round struck the barrel of his mate's Steyr, splintering the round and wounding two with the fragments. It was one of the first of several incidents involving the AUS-Steyr that would plague the new weapon in Somalia.

I left Baidoa later that day in a USMC helicopter. I was running for it before it left and piled into the back out of breath. They'd held it for me, and as I was getting myself sorted, I noticed three passengers, all US Army infantry colonels. Oh, shit, I thought, I really don't want to catch any shit from them or get the usual third degree: who was I, why was I here, etc. etc. I needn't have bothered. They all looked at me, put their heads together for a brief discussion, and then one leaned over to me and asked, "Are you Rob Krott?"

When I nodded yes, one moved closer and said, "We've been looking for you!" (Oh, shit! What have I done now? I was thinking maybe somebody had blown me in for shooting some Somalis with a US Army weapon.) They wanted to talk to me about Operation Restore Hope. Their generals had sent them over as fact finders. Full colonels in the Pentagon will often be sent for coffee. These guys were all young colonels, fast-burners on the career track. My name had obviously come up in some briefing and probably cropped up several times during their visit in Somalia.

One of their questions was, "How do we get out of here? How do we get rid of this Tar Baby?" I was dumbfounded. I replied succinctly and honestly: "Sir, the food has made it to the feeding centers, we've done the job. Declare this a success and pull everybody out." They looked at each other and nodded heads. The whole experience was extremely surreal to me.

I was only two years out of the Infantry Officer's Advanced Course at Fort Benning, and I had three full-bird blue-flame specials with lots of merit badges on their uniforms, guys soon destined for stars, asking me how to get us out of Somalia? Fuck me. I couldn't believe this was happening. If I hadn't recorded it in my journal later that day, I would-n't believe it now. I got off the chopper and waved goodbye, thinking, "We're in deep shit when the Pentagon is asking Rob Krott what to do."

After visiting the Aussies in Baidoa, it only seemed logical to check out the Belgians in Kismayo, a port city south of Mogadishu where Somali workers were unloading grain shipments. I had some people down there who needed paid and one who needed an ass chewing. I flew in on the Kiwi Bird, the New Zealand Air Force shuttle, and wandered around the shot-up terminal building trying to bum a ride to the port. On top of the terminal building, 10th Mountain Division troops watched the access road to Kismayo airport and the troop barracks in the terminal building. The security detachment was well armed with M-16s, M203s, a Mark 19 grenade launcher, as well as an M24 sniper rifle. The exit road had traffic control barriers made out of 55-gallon drums filled with sand. They were prepared to stop any vehicle-mounted attack or truck bomber. No Beirut barracks type bombings were going to hap-pen here.

Things were tense in Kismayo. The Belgians at the port had taken casualties in a flurry of grenade attacks in the past twenty-four hours. On the ride through town, the driver of the Humvee tossed me his M-16, gunned the engine, and told me to be ready. I slapped up on the magazine, pulled the charging handle to the rear just far enough to see brass, released it, and tapped the forward assist. I am happy to say the trip to the port was uneventful. Dodging sniper rounds in Mogadishu was bad enough: I wasn't looking to add, "survived grenade attack in Kismayo" to my resume. In Kismayo I took care of business and said hello to Jack Wheeler. I told him what a great time I'd had visiting Dennis Kennedy.

The Belgies at Kismayo were paratroopers wearing maroon berets with SAS *Who Dares Wins* cap badges. The Belgians believe berets are a good Pysops weapon, and ever since their combat jump on Stanleyville in the Congo in the 1960s, it's been their custom not to wear helmets in combat. Armed with FNC Para folding stock carbines and little else, they'd encountered an ambush just a few hours before. Damn if I'm always a little late to the party.

One Belgian paratrooper showed me the shrapnel wounds marked with mercurochrome dotting his leg that he had received a few hours earlier. The Belgians' doc had simply dug out the frags, given him some aspirin and sent him back to duty to monitor patrol reports. His sergeant walked over to me and proudly displayed the shaved spot on the top of his head where a frag had been dug out. He was obviously already in the prone when that particular grenade exploded. Hell of a way to ruin a beret.

Wandering around the port I encountered a bizarre sight: a fat, rotund Merchant Marine captain in his ice cream suit, complete with Bermuda shorts, knee socks, and captain's hat, had come ashore from a Scandinavian freighter loaded with food aid. He was acting like some asshole tourist with his Nikon around his neck. What got everyone's attention was the ninety-pound spinner, a Thai girl of about nineteen, on his arm. Miniskirt, halter top, lots of hooker makeup, and heels. She sailed the globe with him, taking care of his needs and no doubt driving the entire crew crazy with lust. One of his perqs. He was definitely doing better than he ever could in Copenhagen or Stockholm or wherever he was from.

What a life.

Leaving Kismayo, I almost drove into a large firefight between General Morgan's fighters and one of the other Somali militia factions. Kismayo was definitely hot. If one side didn't get you, the other would. The only time the Somalis agreed on anything was when they were trying to kill Americans.

On the road to the airport we got sniped at. *Pop, pop, pop.* A round hit the hood (later inspection found a bullet hole in the rear fender as well) and I returned fire hastily. Riding shotgun, I dumped about half a magazine from the driver's M-16 out the window into the brush. A lot of combat is like that: put down fire even though you might not have a definite target. You may never know if you hit anything or killed anybody. Though it does provide more than a small amount of personal satisfaction!

But even in places like Kismayo, where ambushes were common and inter-clan fighting was a daily affair, the troops all said the same thing: "I'd rather be here than in Mogadishu." Life in Mogadishu at that time (January through March 1993) was fairly routine. Marines leaving the compound for a patrol locked and loaded their weapons and prepared themselves for the daily dangers of traveling the mean streets of the "Dish." Contested and hot areas like the port, as well as areas congested with Somalis and street side vendors, were avoided whenever possible. Sightseeing was discouraged; some troops never even left their com-

April 1992. An old man on a
bicycle–life goes on in Sisak.

Although many buildings
received small arms and artillery
damage (a common sight in
southern Croatia) the owner of
this building is lucky as it is still
standing.

Rob Krott

The author as a 22-year-old infantry platoon
leader, Camp Casey, South Korea, 1985.

US Army

The author issuing orders to a Croat Commando unit while on patrol
in the Serb-held Krajina Border region.

Author's collection

The face of a Free Democratic Croatia. "Blondie" left a good job and a comfortable life in Zurich to return home and fight. Croatia, April 1992.
Rob Krott

Commando company commander Predrag Matanovic, Richard Vialpando (ex US Army) and John Rajkovic, a 19 year old Croatian-Canadian, ham it up after a mission. Sisak, Croatia, 1992.
Weapons are a Singapore SAR-80, Rumanian AK 47, Smith and Wesson 6" in .357.
Rob Krott

The author inspects a Croatian Commando unit prior to moving out on a recon patrol near Zazina, Croatia. The unit is a provisional LRRP team, Commando Company, 2d Infantry Battalion (light).

Author's collection

Boat drills on the Kupa River. John Rajkovic standing. "Hey, it beats swimming, guys."

The snakelike course of the Kupa River formed a border/no man's land between Croatia (10 km "downriver") and the Krajina Serb Republic (10 km "upriver").

Rob Krott

Opposite above: Looking for a match for that last smoke before patrol. The author is third from the right. At 5'10" many of the Croats towered over him. Sisak, Croatia, April 1992.

Author's collection

Opposite below: Pando with Blackie's girlfriend; "Italiano" with girlfriend; the author "sleeping."

Author's collection

Above: Predrag Matanovic, 22, a company commander in the 2d Battalion and a veteran of the fierce fighting south of Sisak.

He is shown here with his weapons of choice: 100-round drum-fed silenced Czech MGV 176.22 Rimfire submachine gun and a SAR-80. He usually carried both in combat while walking point for his company.

Predrag was grievously wounded in August 1992 near Dubrovknik.

Author's collection

Right: "Jeff," A British merc in a ghillie suit with a sniping rifle.

Rob Krott

Above: Police inspect bomb damage to the Restaurant Karablja. It was bombed after its owner returned to Serbia.   Rob Krott

Below: The author with a Croat-made Zagi 9mm submachine gun.   Author's collection

Above: The author in front of the Balidogle Airfield control tower in Somalia. The airfield was later renamed Camp Arroyo.

Below: Somalia, north of Merka. The author laughs at the antics of a German woman he administered first aid to after the Landrover crash.

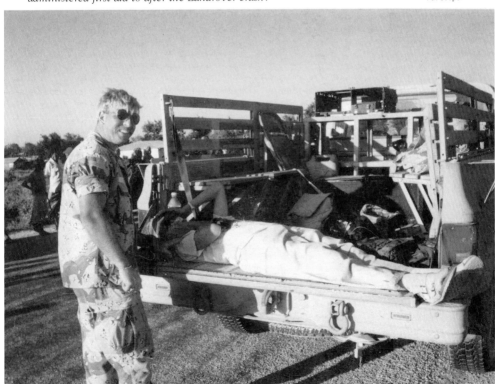

Above: Col. Zjelko "Nick" Glasnovic, commander of the King Tomislav Brigade, Tomislavgrad, Bosnia, 1993.   Photo courtesy "Mike Cooper"

Below: Col. Zjelko Glasnovic briefs a platoon before a patrol in Bosnian mountain country. The patrol's purpose was also to "show the flag" in what was, until recently, bandit country.

When is the last time you saw a brigade commander set the pace for a bunch of 18- and 19-year olds and almost kill them?   Rob Krott

Above: The author cleans his new Romanian AK-47 in the barracks at Zazina.
Author's collection

Below: French mercenaries, Bosnia, 1993. From left to right: Bruno, François, Christophe.
Author's collection

German soldiers of fortune, Heiko (left) and Homes (right). Homes is carrying a PKM general purpose 7.62 mm machine gun.

Author's collection

Uwe "Honecker" Herker of the King Tomislav Brigade rests whilst on patrol in the western Herzegovina mountains near Crvenice, Bosnia, 1993.

Author's collection

A gun position on the front line in Bosnia, 1993.

Rob Krott

Left: On the frontline outside Tomislavgrad, Bosnia, 1993.

Carlo, the Italian mercenary from Viking Platoon, is wearing a sleeve patch with the HOS insignia.

Rob Krott

Below: Members of Viking Platoon in front of one of their Russian jeeps.

From left to right: Jim, Mike, Kane, Roger.

Front, kneeling: Ike.

Rob Krott

Above: Observing targets in a Chetnik (Serb) held village from a newly dug-in 20mm AA gun which had been brought up to a forward position under cover of darkness.

This was a "surprise" for the Chetniks who were in positions only 400 meters away.

The photo was taken on the author's 30th birthday.

Rob Krott

Right: Andy Kolb, a German volunteer.

He ran recon missions with "the Cobras," an ethnic Croat recon platoon near Mostar before unit attrition caused him to transfer to the King Tomislav Infantry Brigade.

He was KIA at Gornji Vakuf, Bosnia in November 1993.

Author's collection

Another photo of Andy Kolb together with one French and three more German mercenaries near Crvenice, Bosnia, 1993.
Rob Krott

Above: A King Tomislav Brigade mortar crew setting up. The soldier on the far right was only 15 years old.　　　Rob Krott

Below: Aisha, a King Tomislav Brigade medic, on a rest break during a combat patrol in the mountains.　　　Rob Krott

Above: Foreign mercenaries with a Viking patrol jeep. From left to right; British, German, Italian, British, Scandinavian. The two Brits are "Jeff" and "Pat."

Below left: Mike "Ranger" McDonald.
Photo: Courtesy of Mike McDonald

Below right: The author in full US Army officer's mess dress blue uniform, two weeks after leaving Bosnia.
Author's collection

pounds, while others were outside the wire, patrolling or conducting missions daily.

But there wasn't much to see. And what there was to look at all looked the same. Typical scenery in the Dish: rubble, rubble, and more rubble in the streets, with more bombed-out buildings, some trashed vehicles, and crowds of miserable-looking Somalis here and there. Dotting the city in little shantytowns, hootches made of curved poles covered with hides, tarps, or grain bags were preferred to bombed-out buildings by nomads who had left the countryside. The overall destruction of the city was an overwhelming sight. What wasn't outright destroyed in the civil war amongst Somali factions had been looted and sold to Arab merchants and shipped out of the country. In the words of a 10th Mountain Division officer, 1st Lt. Bill Shomento, "They sold their country to the Stone Age."

One day one of the MI soldiers saw some Somalis working in the street with shovels and pointed them out to me, "Hey, Mr. Krott, they're fixing the road." I just laughed. I'd seen the same thing in other parts of Mogadishu. They weren't working on the streets. They were digging up telephone cable to sell.

It's surprising that in the light of the deaths of two Marines and the constant violence directed against US forces that the MARFOR commander, Major General Charles E. Wilhelm, obviously in the winning hearts and minds mode and not the war-fighting mode, published a letter to his troops calling for an "attitude check." Major General Wilhelm instructed the Marines to ask themselves some of the following questions: "Am I still waving to Somali children? If the answer is "no," we aren't accomplishing our mission. Am I swearing at Somalis or blowing the horn of my vehicle when I get caught in a traffic jam or crowd? If the answer is "yes".... When I'm on patrol and a crowd forms, am I pushing Somalis or pointing my weapon at them? If the answer...." Get the picture? Wilhelm's closing line was, "The people of Somalia need a friend—not just another oppressor in desert camouflage utilities." It's a lesson we're still trying to learn and apply successfully in Iraq.

Unfortunately it was the privates first class, lance corporals, and corporals who had to deal with these quandaries. And these oppressors in desert camouflage utilities were just a little bit tired of having glasses stolen, being hit by rocks, getting sniped at, walking on dangerous night patrols whose purpose and wisdom was widely debated in our press, and losing friends in nighttime ambushes. The NCOs and line officers had to deal with the pronouncements from the politically motivated "echelons above reality," carry out combat-type missions in what was touted as a humanitarian effort and not a police action or a war, and put-up with the usual paint-the-rocks-white BS. They did their best.

At one daily briefing a sergeant major stated, "Trash and sanitation is your priority, right after killing people" and the rules regarding vehicle speeds through downtown Mogadishu were again emphasized, though the conversation went something like this: "Speed limit in the compound is five mph, and through Mogadishu it is thirty mph." "But Sergeant Major, what about getting shot at?" asked a Senior NCO. "You can't outrun a bullet, so you might as well slow down and see where it's coming from," replied the Sergeant Major.

That pretty much summed up duty in Mogadishu.

When the US went into Somalia, we had only five native Somali speakers in the entire US military. One was a navy female who had applied for a discharge under conscientious objector status. She was told, we've got some good news and some bad news for you. The good news is your conscientious objector status is approved. The bad news is it won't take effect until we're done with the mission in Somalia! Another Somali speaker was a USMC reservist. Ordered to active duty, he was sent over and assigned as Wilhelm's personal interpreter and advisor on Somali culture.

One day one of our interpreters pointed at this Marine and Major General Wilhelm, the commander of MARFOR-Somalia. They were talking to two Somalis, one in white shirt and one in a blue shirt. Our interpreter went into a panic—Wilhelm was speaking with Aideed's son. Our interpreter knew him from school in Mogadishu as a child. When asked whether it was the Somali in the white or blue shirt, he panicked and shouted, "No, no, it's the Marine!" Hussein Aideed, USMCR, was the son of Mohamed Farah Aideed. He was serving under his mother's name. While supposedly assisting Major General Wilhelm, he was reporting all kinds of confidential information through contacts to his father. Hussein was shipped home and then later brought back in a deal worked out with his father to serve as a liaison for US forces. Later he left California (supposedly AWOL from his reserve unit) and returned to Somalia for an arranged marriage. He assumed leadership of the *Habr Gedir* clan and the Somali National Alliance after his father died in 1996.

Nearing the end of my first three months on contract (and qualifying for a hefty ten thousand dollar bonus), I got a call from the Australians at Balidogle. There was a problem there with one of our interpreters. He'd previously been caught in possession of *khat* and a large sum of Somali pounds while AWOL and riding around in a Somali vehicle with some locals. Now he'd been found escorting a militiaman inside the perimeter while he made a sector sketch showing the defenses, weapons emplacements, and troop positions. He was shipped back to Mogadishu under escort and I received high-priority travel orders to take him back to DC. They were endorsed by Lieutenant General R. B. Johnson, commander JTF-Somalia (and later commander of UNITAF). A personal note was written at the top of the interpreter's travel orders I was handed: "Mr. Krott, get him out of here immediately!" followed by his signature.

We took the interpreter, whom I'll call "Egal," to the airfield. The next plane leaving was a medical flight. No weapons were allowed on the airplane by international law. I was told we couldn't fly, as we weren't wounded. I presented my travel orders and the one for Egal with the general's note and asked the USAF clerk, "How many times do I have to bash his head against the wall before I run in the bathroom and put my finger down my throat? He's wounded and I'm sick. Put us on the plane."

It was a tedious flight to Germany. At Frankfurt we had to buy civilian clothes at the PX because our connecting flight was commercial, not military. Egal was seated about ten rows behind me in the plane. Of course, good Muslim that he was, he kept ordering up beer and whiskey. About half way across the Atlantic he started getting a little obnoxious. I'd informed the flight attendants of the situation, and when they expressed their concern about his continued demands for more alcohol, I urged them to keep him well supplied. If he caused a problem I'd smack him upside the head. Happily. The booze eventually put him under.

Upon arrival I dragged his ass to the terminal. Once there, we were met by Mosely and some other pogues from the office, and Egal immediately started ranting and raving. I was polite towards him, so that Mosely and company wouldn't start in on the whole situation right there in the airport. Egal thought I was being two-faced, as I'd had little to do with him on the way home, and didn't want to sit near him on the plane. It didn't really matter, they couldn't pay him off and fire him fast enough. What was funny was that even though he had been caught red-handed, he still thought he could lie his way out of the situation!

While I was back in Virginia, BDM offered me a plum job as a Special Warfare coordinator at the Joint Readiness Training Center (JRTC) then still at Fort Chaffee, Arkansas. Out in Arkansas interviewing for the job, I contacted an old friend from some Central American adventures. David "Rocky" Eales, a former Marine lieutenant, was a highway patrolman and a tactical officer on the Oklahoma Highway Patrol's Tactical Team. We'd last seen each other at a Guatemalan paratrooper base four years previously on my second trip to Guatemala. On a previous trip to Guatemala, I'd hooked up with Lance Motley from *Soldier of Fortune*, Barry Sadler, and Gerald Leguire, a seasoned paratrooper, weapons expert, adventurer, and my best friend for the past twenty years.

Rocky and I had a good time in Guatemala where we'd jumped with their airborne unit and later went over to El Salvador where we made an O'dark-thirty jump into an unsecured drop zone with a unit of El Salvadoran SF. Later that year, me, Rocky, and Leguire jumped in the Dominican Republic with their paratroopers. So we were former partners in crime, and while we had stayed in touch it'd been almost four years since we'd seen each other. I drove across the border to Oklahoma and Rocky met me halfway. We spent the night drinking and catching up. The next morning I showed up at the BDM office at Fort Chaffee a little hung over, slightly, but not noticeably, the worse for wear.

The deal BDM offered me was to hang out for a few months and then move to Fort Polk, Louisiana, where JRTC was being relocated. It was suggested that if I wanted to go back to the Balkans on my own, that would be a good thing. I went back to Virginia, packed my gear, bought a plane ticket, and got dumped by my girlfriend when I told her my plans. Judy had not been happy with the separation and my general demeanor after returning from Somalia, and she was even less pleased with the idea that I was now happily running off to another war zone.

President George H.W. Bush sent US troops to Somalia in December 1992, just weeks before his term ended, in a UN humanitarian mission to bring food to starving Somalis. He said the mission would last about a month. After twenty-four Pakistani soldiers were killed, the mission expanded under President Bill Clinton into a quest to restore law and order amid widespread anarchy, and to track down Somali warlord Mohammed Farah Aideed.

Searching for Aideed, US Rangers and Delta Force raided a hotel in Mogadishu on Oct. 3, 1993. After a helicopter crashed, they were sucked into a seventeen-hour gun battle in which eighteen Americans were killed.

I was in Nairobi when some of my interpreters there on leave informed me that two BDM interpreters were also killed. You won't find them mentioned in any of the books, or in the movie *Black Hawk Down*, or included in the list of KIA, but they were riding in trucks with the 10th Mountain Division troops who were trying to break through to the beleaguered Rangers. Mobs dragged the bodies of dead Americans through the streets. Clinton later withdrew US forces. Somalia is still awash in civil war and anarchy. People are still suffering.

It was all for nothing.

CHAPTER 5
SOLDIERS OF FORTUNE

"There is no hunting like the hunting of man, and those who have hunted armed men long enough and liked it, never care for anything else thereafter."
—Ernest Hemingway

While in sunny Somalia I sent a Christmas card to an acquaintance of mine, Robin Anthony (a nom de guerre), a Croat-American with good contacts in Croatia. I stated my intention to go back to the Balkans and do something meaningful. I called my friends at *Soldier of Fortune* magazine in Boulder, Colorado, as soon as I got back from my vacation in hell at Somalia's Mogadishu embassy resort complex. That's when I heard about *Soldier of Fortune*'s training team mission to Bosnia. Unbeknownst to me at the time, Robin Anthony's distant cousin, Colonel Zeljko Glasnovic, was commanding the King Tomislav Brigade, a Croat infantry unit in Bosnia. Lieutenant Colonel Robert K. "Bob" Brown, the publisher of *Soldier of Fortune*, suggested that I assist the King Tomislav Brigade, since several of their training cadre along with the Brigade Executive Officer, Juri Schmidt, had recently been killed in action.

In its hayday of the late 1970s to early 1990s, *Soldier of Fortune* provided extensive coverage of the war with reports from various freelancers as well as with trips to the war zone by its regular contributors. During that same period, the magazine sponsored training teams of experienced combat veterans (mostly Vietnam veterans) to various combat zones and hot spots around the world to assist democratic governments and freedom fighters in their struggles against the spread of Communism and good old-fashioned tyranny. Teams of as many as ten men or as few as one assisted and advised the anti-Soviet Afghan *mujahideen*, the Nicaraguan Contras, the Burmese Karen guerrillas, the

119

El Salvadoran Army, Laotian Hmong resistance fighters, and even the Lebanese Christian militia.

In December 1992, an eight-man training team spent two weeks training Croatian troops in western Bosnia. The *Soldier of Fortune* team that offered their skills to the Bosnian-Croats of the fledgling Croat Defense Force of Croat Herceg-Bosna was a group of former regular military personnel in their forties and fifties with combat experience in various war zones around the world. The team of middle-aged military adventurers consisted of team leader Lieutenant Colonel Robert K. "Bob" Brown, USAR (ret.) who had just turned 60; Colonel Millard "Mike" Peck, USA (ret.); Colonel Alex McColl, USAR (ret.); Major John Donovan, USAR (ret.); Major Bob MacKenzie (traveling as Bob Jordan), late of the Rhodesian SAS and South African Defense Force; Paul Fanshaw (a *nom de guerre*), formerly of the French Foreign Legion, the USMC, and the 82d Airborne; and Peter Kokalis, a civilian firearms technical expert.

Peck, McColl, Brown, and Donovan were all retired US Army Special Forces field grade officers. No strangers to the sharp end, these guys were adventurers with the financial security and wherewithal to hit the world's hot spots as they pleased. Their idea of a fun vacation was going to a new war zone or observing coups and revolutions in some shitty little third-world country. They enjoyed "going to see the elephant." Or, like John Donovan and Alex McColl, the group's most avid parachutists, they received a healthy adrenaline rush by going someplace exotic, jumping out of a perfectly good airplane, and earning a set of foreign jump wings.

It was not the mercenary magazine's first involvement in the widening Balkans conflict. *Soldier of Fortune* had covered the war in the Balkans extensively starting with contributing editor Major Mike Williams' trip to check out the fighting in Slovenia and the early skirmishes between the Zengees and the Chetniks near Osijiek. Williams is the subject of the book *Major Mike*, co-written by the late Robin Moore, who also authored *The Green Berets* and *The Hunt for Bin Laden*. Besides being a World War II and Korean War veteran, Williams is one of the twenty "Originals" as they're known: the first twenty Special Forces officers who served under Colonel Aaron Bank and formed the US Army Special Forces. Mike's good friend, the late Jack Hemingway (son of Ernest Hemingway), was also an "Original." Mike went on to serve in the Rhodesian Army's Grey's Scouts (mounted infantry) as a major and had been involved in other soldier of fortune-type activities over the years. We had jumped together on several occasions and I've been proud to be considered his protégé. I think of him as my "godfather."

The feedback from MacKenzie, Williams, and the other *Soldier of Fortune* correspondents who'd already been on the ground in the Balkans proved invaluable to the team. The *Soldier of Fortune* training team's mission preparation was based on an estimate of the situation formed from their reports. Concerning the team's decision to pick sides and make preparations to aid the Croats, Bob Brown reported in his magazine that with the "continuing analysis and evaluation over the ensuing months, it didn't require a degree in nuclear physics to conclude that the Serbs were the aggressors and that the Serbian policy of expansionism and 'ethnic cleansing' was creating a nightmare of civilian massacres and mass rape unseen in Europe since World War II."

Brown decided to organize a major training effort and what was essentially a two-week vacation in war-torn western Bosnia for Bob's cronies and ski buddies. The whole operation was coordinated through contacts in Bosnia established through Robin Anthony and his family connections to Colonel Zeljko Glasnovic. Glasnovic was commanding a brigade of the *Hrvatski Vijece Obrane*, or Croatian Council Defense Force (HVO), which consisted of locally raised troops in the heavily contested mountain region of western Bosnia. This light infantry brigade was responsible for the defense of an area between Split, Croatia and Sarajevo, Bosnia-Hercegovina. At that time most of the King Tomislav Brigade troops were young men in their late teens and early twenties, locally recruited militia without any former military experience. The ranks were leavened with foreign military volunteers, many of them expatriate Croats or foreigners of Croatian descent.

Brown knew that Glasnovic had lots of bodies in his light infantry brigade, but was desperately short of experienced personnel. The unit lacked training, and was made up essentially of militia recruits and a few JNA veterans in their forties and fifties, and even some old salts in their sixties and seventies with nothing better to do. It was in need of professional military training in operations, tactics, and weapons. The ethnic Croats from Tomislavgrad and its environs were sprinkled with a handful of foreign volunteers from Canada, Australia, New Zealand, Germany, England, and the US.

Between the foreign volunteers with prior military service and a few former regular soldiers and trained conscripts from the old JNA, Colonel Glasnovic had himself a cadre. Of sorts. At the time he was only too happy to accept additional foreign volunteers with professional military credentials to help beef up his brigade—if, of course, you could afford to be a volunteer. You had to get yourself to Zagreb and then arrange your own transportation to Tomislavgrad, usually a grueling twelve-hour bus ride down the coastal road from Zagreb. Just because you showed up to volunteer didn't mean you'd be accepted. Even if Colonel Glasnovic assigned you a weapon and found you a place to sleep, that was about all you were going to get from the HVO. In December 1992, pay for a sergeant was only about thirty US dollars a month, paid in Deutschmarks. As Brown said, "It would take several years at that wage just to pay the cost of your airfare to Zagreb." Then again, money wasn't the prime motivator for most of the volunteers making the long journey to the Balkans war zone.

After mulling things over, Brown decided that helping the King Tomislav Brigade was not only a worthy cause, but also a good opportunity. The team members could get a good firsthand look at the current situation in Bosnia, and there'd also be a story or two in it for the magazine. The offer of direct military assistance from the retired colonels at *Soldier of Fortune* was a godsend.

According to Brown, "All the Croatians we spoke with emphatically noted that they did not need or want troops from the West—or even offensive air strikes." The Croats of the King Tomislav Brigade merely wanted the opportunity to defend themselves against what they considered to be Serbian territorial aggression. Speaking to the *Soldier of Fortune* team, Colonel Glasnovic echoed the sentiments of his men: "How can we successfully fight the Serbs and their T-84s with our few captured T-54/55s? We're even forced to reload rounds for our tank main guns. For God's sake, give us a fighting chance by removing the arms embargo." General Russo, the former French Foreign Legionnaire who was the commander of Croatian special operations forces, told Brown that they needed anti-tank weapons like French MILANs (*Missle d'Infanterie Léger Antichar*) and American TOWs (Tube-launched, Optically-tracked, Wire-guided heavy anti-tank assault weapon). Anything to battle the JNA's T-72 tanks.

Brown sent an advance party of contact man Robin Anthony as interpreter and Special Projects Director Alex McColl to Bosnia. Colonel McColl would advise Brown to green-light or abort the planned operation. Their job was to finalize the subjects to be taught, arrange for training aids (blackboards and chalk were about it), insure trainees were selected and schedules laid on, provide for an adequate supply of ammunition and explosives for training, check on classrooms and weapons firing range areas, arrange for interpreters, organize living quarters for the team, and a dozen other niggling tasks. After this and all the myriad details assigned to the advance party were accomplished, they contacted Brown and provided an update on the situation and communicated their needs. Once McColl gave Brown the green light, the team left for Tomislavgrad.

Brown's training plan was that *Soldier of Fortune* magazine's contributing editor for demolitions, Major John Donovan, would teach the Croat HVO troops how to blow things up in a creative manner with much panache and élan while Peter Kokalis, the magazine's technical editor and "Full Auto" columnist would instruct a course on the employment of squad automatic weapons (light machine guns). Colonel Mike Peck and Major Bob MacKenzie would provide classes on sniping, tactical reconnaissance, and combat patrolling operations. Colonel Alex McColl meanwhile would train the brigade staff in the more cerebral areas of staff management and organization, field artillery fire control, and crater and fragment analysis.

The *Soldier of Fortune* training team didn't see any active combat while they were with the King Tomislav Brigade. There was an occasional air raid alarm and a few unexplained bursts of automatic weapons fire in the middle of the night, but all in all the trip was uneventful. As Brown wrote later, "We also made many new friends, ate too much red meat, drank respectable amounts of good, cheap red wine and, of course, ogled the young lovelies."

Although the lack of action and danger was sometimes disappointing, the team understood their primary mission was to function as a training team, was not to run around in the woods like a bunch of eighteen-year-old trigger pullers fresh out of basic training. For the two weeks they were in Bosnia, they had their hands full just training HVO troops in the rudiments of modern land warfare. The consensus was that the team could have stayed busy for a good six months. Hence Brown's encouragement on his return for me to go over and volunteer.

In addition to combat time garnered in most of the late twentieth century's brush-fire wars, all of the magazine's training team members had literally had years of on-the-ground experience in training indigenous troops in foreign countries. Alex McColl, Harvard Law School graduate and retired US Army Special Forces colonel, was the director of special projects for *Soldier of Fortune* and a director of Refugee Relief International Incorporated. Alex belied the myth that America's best and brightest avoided service in Vietnam. His first tour in Vietnam saw him assigned to the Military Assistance Command-Vietnam's (MACV) legendary Studies and Observation Group, formerly known as the Special Operations Group. After duty with MACVSOG he did a stateside tour and then returned to Vietnam for a second tour (April 1967 to November 1968), where he was a District Senior Advisor to the ARVN before going back to MACVSOG. There he worked with OP-35, the clandestine reconnaissance teams which conducted missions "over the fence." Alex was quite probably the only person to ever be a graduate of Harvard College, Harvard Law School ('60), the Special Forces "Q" Course, the US Army War College, and the MACVSOG parachute school at Long Thanh, Vietnam. Alex trained the Croats in staff management and organization.

Besides his six years in the US Army and US Marine Corps, Paul Fanshaw is a twelve-year veteran of the French Foreign Legion, where he was a SCUBA trainer with the 2d Foreign Parachute Regiment (2d REP). Fanshaw was decorated for the combat jump on Kolwezi, Zaire, and was at one time the platoon sergeant of General Russo, OIC (officer in charge) of Croatian Special Operations, while the two were Legionnaires in Djibouti. Fanshaw trained Contras in Nicaragua in 1987 and accompanied Brown on trips to El Salvador and Afghanistan, and into Burma following the death of my friend and fellow *Soldier of Fortune* correspondent, Lance Motley. Lance was KIA while operating with the Karen National Liberation Army, and Brown and Fanshaw went over to confirm the details of Lance's death. He later tagged along with Brown to the Gulf War. Fanshaw has appeared on the cover of *Soldier of Fortune* at least twice. It's rumored he was once a CIA asset.

John Donovan, the magazine's contributing editor for demolitions, owns Donovan Demolition Inc., of Danvers, Illinois, and is a former Special Forces major. Donovan had trained troops in demolitions before as a member of SOF training teams in such exotic locations as El Salvador and Afghanistan. "Big John," as he's known, is also an accomplished master parachutist, having earned parachutist badges from several foreign countries.

Bob MacKenzie, or "Bobby Mac" as many of us called him, was a standout in the small world of professional soldiers for hire. Robert Callen MacKenzie was the genuine article when it came to real life, real world mercenaries—a soldier's soldier. Bob served as an airborne infantryman with the 101st Airborne Division "Screaming Eagles" in Vietnam, and was medically discharged for wounds. In 1970 he enlisted in the Rhodesian Army's Rhodesian Light Infantry (RLI) under the *nom de guerre* of Bob MacKenna. He volunteered for the elite Rhodesian SAS and quickly rose to the rank of captain, serving as the Squadron Commander of C Squadron, SAS. Receiving several awards for bravery, including the Bronze Cross of Rhodesia and the Silver Cross of Rhodesia for "conspicuous gallantry and leadership in action,"

Bob MacKenzie was the most decorated American to serve in the Rhodesian conflict. He participated in such famous cross-border missions as "Operation Dingo," the 1977 airborne assault on the ZANLA base at Chimoio, Mozambique. At Chimoio MacKenzie's SAS A Troop parachuted into the middle of approximately eight thousand guerrillas from five hundred feet in one of the most daring airborne assaults in military history. A total of ninety-seven SAS and forty-eight RLI paratroopers supported by helicopter gunships jumped into Chimoio and routed eight thousand armed insurgents and killed over a thousand in close combat. MacKenzie made a total of nineteen combat jumps, including HALOs (High Altitude Low Opening), while serving throughout southern Africa. He also participated in the clandestine raid on the Munhava oil storage depot at Beira, Mozambique in 1979.

He left service in Rhodesia as a major when the political sell-out occurred. Like many other Rhodesian vets who refused to soldier for a regime run by their old enemies, he offered his services to the South African Defense Forces. In South Africa Bob MacKenzie continued to soldier as a Special Forces officer in the rank of major for eighteen months. In 1981 he joined the Transkei Defence Force, where he served with distinction as second-in-command of the Transkei Special Forces Regiment. In the Transkei SF Regiment, Bob ran special operations in the bush of the South African homeland nation against SWAPO terrorists for the next three and a half years until 1985. That's when he made the mistake of attempting to have his passport renewed at the American consulate.

According to Bob, the consular official looked at his passport and said, "My God, what have you been doing over here all this time?" When he found out that MacKenzie had spent the last fifteen years serving in three foreign armies (as a field grade Special Forces officer, no less), and killing Communist terrorists he threw a hissy fit, refused to renew the expired passport, and arranged to have Bob returned to the United States. Well, that was Bob's story, anyway.

I chatted with General Ron Reid-Daly, founder of the Rhodesian Selous Scouts, at the SAS reunion dinner in Durban in 1999. He mentioned what I'd heard from others—that Mac was a CIA asset. Coincidentally, MacKenzie's wife, Sibyl Cline, is the daughter of Ray S. Cline, a former Deputy Director for Intelligence of the CIA.

Robert K. Brown, the final member and leader of the team, first served in the US Army as a lieutenant in the Counter-Intelligence Corps (1954–57), following graduation from the University of Colorado. An avowed anti-Batista activist, Brown flirted with Castro revolutionaries, actually traveling to Cuba before switching sides after it became obvious that Castro was a Communist. He became involved in various guerrilla operations run by anti-Castro exiles as well as an attempt to overthrow Haitian dictator François "Papa Doc" Duvalier. He returned to active duty as an Army captain in 1967, and after the Special Forces "Q" course, a brief assignment to the 5th Special Forces Group G-2 staff, and duty with the XVIII Airborne Corps Advanced Marksmanship Training Unit at Fort Bragg, he eventually found himself in Vietnam.

In Vietnam, Brown was assigned as the battalion Intelligence officer (S-2), 2d Battalion, 18th Infantry, 1st Infantry Division, despite problems with his security clearance because of all of his Cuban adventures. After taking on some extracurricular tasks following the Tet Offensive, he was cited by the local coordinator of the Phoenix Program for "planning and executing many successful operations against the Viet Cong in Thu Duc." With the help of John Paul Vann, the highest ranking civilian advisor in the Vietnam War, Brown returned to the 5th Special Forces Group and was given command of an A-Team, Team A-334 at Tong Le Chon. After Vietnam Brown finished out his hitch on active duty as a company commander at Fort Leonard Wood and was discharged in 1970. He remained active in the US Army Reserves, eventually retiring as a Lieutenant Colonel. Brown started *Soldier of Fortune* on a shoestring in 1975, and was soon able to finance adventures to any hotspot in the world including Rhodesia, El Salvador, Afghanistan, Laos, Suriname, and, now, Bosnia.

When the *Soldier of Fortune* team arrived in Bosnia, foreign volunteers, mostly of Croatian descent, made up the cadre of the King

Tomislav Brigade's Basic Training Center. Many of them were veterans of the disbanded HV International Brigade. Other foreign volunteers came from Germany, Australia, the US, Canada, the UK, France, and New Zealand. Money definitely wasn't their prime motivator. Tony Vucic, a Croat–Australian, was assigned as Kokalis' interpreter for the machine gun course. Another volunteer from Down Under, Major Dennis Radovich, an Australian with more than eighteen months service in the HVO, was the OIC for the King Tomislav Brigade's basic training center. Radovich was later featured on the cover of the May 1993 *Soldier of Fortune*.

The *Soldier of Fortune* team was surprised to find an American serving with the King Tomislav Brigade. Tom Kundid, twenty-one, was a Croat-American from Westchester County, New York. His mother and father were both born in Croatia. Tom left for Croatia in February 1992 with six or seven other volunteers. The Croatian community in Queens coordinated their journey to Zagreb, where Tom's uncle worked for the Defense Ministry. Tom was only nineteen at the time and had no previous military experience. With Tom was a US Army Airborne veteran, Pesa Nastazio Marin. Marin was later captured by Serb forces along with another American, Colton Glenn Perry. They were held as POWs for three months before Senator Alphonse D'Amato (R-NY) could effect their release to the *Chargé d'Affaires* of the US Embassy in Belgrade.

When *Soldier of Fortune* met up with the American volunteer, he'd been fighting in the Balkans for over a year. Tom first enlisted in the *Frankopan Zinski*, the Croat Army unit named after two famous Croat kings, who had employed a large number of foreign volunteers. In the *Frankopan Zinski* with Tom and the rest of the New York contingent was the former Canadian light infantryman and French Foreign Legionnaire, Zjelko Glasnovic, who later was promoted to full colonel (and eventually brigadier general) in the Croat Army and commanded the King Tomislav Brigade.

Tom left the *Frankopan Zinski* after five or six months because the unit was experiencing a period of relative inactivity. His father was from Imojski in the Croatian-Bosnian border region, to which he was headed. He arrived in Imojski, visited his father's relatives, and joined a military police unit of the *Imojski Bojna*. I'd heard of the *Imojski Bojna* when I was in Bosnia. They were a very professional regular Croat Army battalion actually fighting in Bosnia, a fact that President

Tudjman wanted kept quiet. Kundid spent about a week in Tomislavgrad with the small group of foreigners coalescing there, including their commander, Juri Schmidt. Kundid was surprised to see Glasnovic, his old comrade from *Frankopan Zinski*, commanding the local HVO troops. Tom met Bob Brown and some of the members of the training team during their stay with the King Tomislav Brigade, but was less than enthralled by some of the foreign volunteers he met there, so he left Tomislavgrad for Mostar where he joined the HOS.

Kundid had some interesting experiences in the King Tomislav Brigade. "When I was in Mostar we talked to the Chetniks on the radio all the time. They had the high ground and we fed them map coordinates for Muslim positions and adjusted fire for them. My cousin used to eat lunch with friends in a Chetnik unit." At the time of our conversation in 1994, Tom told me that, "Serbs and Croats have agreed not to fight each other any more in Bosnia, because they know what land belongs to whom. The Muslims are trying to grab territory and the idea is for the Serbs and Croats in Bosnia to clean up the Muslims, and then sort things out in the Krajina and Sarajevo later. In Sarajevo the Croats have joined with the Serbs against the Muslims." While this certainly held true for some time in various parts of Bosnia, like every other agreement it was subject to change at short notice.

Shortly after the *Soldier of Fortune* team's mission to Bosnia occurred, the headline in the Zagreb newspaper, *Globus*, screamed, "I Taught Croatian Soldiers How to Shoot Serbs at 1,000 Meters." The quote, which was attributed to Bob Brown, wasn't completely accurate, but it was based on fact. Bob MacKenzie and Mike Peck had conducted a sniper training program for a group of selected personnel temporarily held in reserve at the King Tomislav Brigade's headquarters in Tomislavgrad, some seven miles behind the frontline trenches. Peck's last assignment in the US Army had been as the chief of the DIA's Special Office for POW/MIA Affairs, a job from which he resigned in protest after eight months.

Peck is a highly decorated (multiple Bronze Stars, Purple Hearts, Silver Stars, and a Distinguished Service Cross) officer with extensive experience in Special Forces including Delta Force. He is a former instructor at both West Point and the US Army Ranger School, and a veteran of Operation Urgent Fury, the invasion of Grenada. In 1964 Peck was the sometime commander and sometime executive officer of ODA-224 (a Green Beret A-Team) at Phu Tuc. After his first tour in

Vietnam as a Special Forces lieutenant he returned to serve a total of four tours in Vietnam. In Vietnam Peck earned one of his Purple Hearts the hard way, when he was shot in the head. Peck had been forced to play dead, waiting for the NVA to loot his body; when two of the enemy approached him to loot his handgun from his body, he shot them both point blank.

As in the case of MacKenzie's previous visit to Croatia, he found the Croat-Bosnian troops of the King Tomislav Brigade to be "everything an instructor could want: intelligent, physically fit and enthusiastic." According to MacKenzie, the King Tomislav Brigade militiamen enthusiastically participated in his courses because "they were motivated by a strong desire to defend their homes, or to recapture houses now occupied by the Serbian army. Some of them had fought from their bedroom windows before being driven out by enemy tanks." MacKenzie knew what he was talking about; he'd seen it in Petrinja. The troops were eager to learn and soaked up the training like a sponge. MacKenzie was pleased with their motivation and with their performance. The Croat recruits were quick learners and got everything right the first time around.

Bob MacKenzie was a firm believer in the dividends paid by military sniping operations. Writing in *Soldier of Fortune*, Mac said, "Sniping, when used against unarmed civilians or conducted from the bell tower of a university campus, is nothing less than murder. Properly used in the military context, however, sniping is a very efficient method of killing one's most dangerous opponents before they get a chance to kill you, or disrupting enemy operations and morale for only the cost of a few well-placed bullets."

MacKenzie and Peck met Glasnovic at his brigade headquarters. MacKenzie was impressed with Glasnovic, whom he later described to me as "a good guy who knew he needed assistance." Glasnovic told MacKenzie and Peck that they would have only three days to turn a group of King Tomislav Brigade soldiers into accomplished military snipers. Military sniping courses in professional western armies usually run from two weeks to a month or more in length. Glasnovic, a veteran of both the Canadian Army's Princess Patricia's Light Infantry and the French Foreign Legion, knew this, but just couldn't spare his troops from the line for a longer period of time. MacKenzie and Peck also had serious demands placed on their time with all the other courses they were slated to give during their brief two-week stay in Tomislavgrad.

Glasnovic had rounded up twenty of his brigade's best shots and equipped them with a motley collection of scoped rifles for the three-day sniping course. MacKenzie and Peck spent the day organizing resources for the course and preparing lesson plans. At 0800 the next day, the instructors were introduced to their class of twenty sniper-trainees, mostly eighteen- to twenty-year-olds with a few older thirty-something year-old NCO-types in the brigade headquarters classroom. When MacKenzie and Peck asked the twenty students if any of them had killed an enemy soldier, no one raised his hand. But they all claimed to be pretty good shots who had done a lot of deer and small game hunting in the mountains during peacetime. They now had their Chetnik hunting permits. No bag limits.

MacKenzie found that the sniper-trainees were equipped with a wide variety of "sniping rifles." Fortunately many of the rifles were brand new and all were in good condition, including several examples of Bob's personal choice for military sniping, the Austrian-made Steyr SSG. There were also a dozen Yugoslav M-76 Dragunov-style sniping rifles. The issue sniping weapon of the JNA, the M-76, was found in significant quantities amongst all the Balkan combatants. MacKenzie and Peck would soon find that this modern production-made sniping rifle was actually a good deal less accurate than the other rifles. Indeed the M-76/Dragunov is all but worthless in the accuracy department at ranges beyond four hundred meters. A good shooter can do equally as well with a well-maintained assault rifle with open sights and can easily exceed the M-76/Dragunov's capabilities with one of the World War II generation bolt-action military rifles with standard open sights.

Civilian hunting rifles with telescopic sights were also being used for sniping by troops of the King Tomislav Brigade. Prior to the war, Yugoslavia had a large military weapons and sporting rifle industry, manufacturing large quantities of small arms for export. Hunting rifles, mostly copies of the Winchester Model 70 bolt-action sporter, were manufactured for export in such popular calibers as .270 Winchester and .308 NATO by Zastava (Star). Many people in the Balkans owned hunting rifles, and in 1991, during the initial hostilities in Slovenia and the opening days of the Croat-Serb conflict in the Krajina (aka the Serbo-Croat War), and throughout the war in Bosnia and in the Kosova conflict, these sporting rifles played a major role in arming the hastily formed local militias and equipping ad hoc sniping teams. In the hands of a skilled marksman they are effective sniping weapons.

Besides the ubiquitous Yugoslav hunting rifles, MacKenzie had one sniper equipped with a scoped FN FAL and another sporting a Winchester .30-30 lever action with scope. But the prize of the bunch was a Barrett Light Fifty rifle. The Barrett Light Fifty is a Browning machine gun .50-caliber sniping weapon developed as a long-range sniping and interdiction weapon and as a possible defensive weapon for light vessels. Designated the M82A1, it was field tested in the Gulf War by US Special Operations snipers. The Barrett Light Fifty was also used with good effect in Somalia by US Marine snipers I witnessed shooting from the embassy compound in Mogadishu while I was there. I've already mentioned that on one occasion the shots were made at night and left some very surprised Somalis sprawled in the dust of a nearby alley.

All of the weapons were equipped with telescopic sights of varying manufacture, including civilian models by Tasco, Bushnell, and (on the SSGs) Swarovski. Some of the scopes required maintenance and repair, and some of the mounts needed adjustment. With the differing reticules and adjustment drums, MacKenzie knew that the zeroing exercises were going to be interesting and time consuming. There would be little opportunity for by the numbers group instruction in this area.

After their initial assessment of the sniping class's experience, abilities, and equipment, the two Americans presented a special bloc of lecture material on the moral and ethical aspects of military sniping. This was a real problem in the Balkans, where any idiot with a scoped rifle, including foreign volunteers, could call himself a sniper and usually spent a majority of his time pot-shotting civilians. Sarajevo became known for its sniper alleys where civilians had to run for their lives, ducking for cover to avoid a sniper's bullet.

The last time I talked to Bob MacKenzie was at the 1993 *Soldier of Fortune* convention in Las Vegas. MacKenzie told me about a Serb sniper in Sarajevo, a former instructor for the Sarajevo Police department's SWAT team. The former policeman would select different categories of targets on any given day. Bob was shocked and disgusted that such a former professional had degenerated to shooting civilians. MacKenzie couldn't understand it. "Some days he would just shoot, say, journalists, and another day he might shoot only grandmothers or people driving cars. Something must have made him snap, to make him do this. The man used to be a cop, now he's a terrorist."

In training, MacKenzie and Peck especially tried to impress the professional ethics of the military sniper upon the young militiamen. Many of them had no doubt been traumatized by the war, and putting them on the ground as well-trained snipers with the right equipment could prove disastrous if they weren't indoctrinated against committing atrocities. The two American instructors explained the importance of the sniper and his impact on the battlefield as a combat multiplier: a soldier worth many times his number in combat because of his skills.

The two combat veterans also touched upon the personal characteristics required of an effective sniper: patience, determination, maturity, and the ability to work alone. After the ethics lecture the class moved on to fieldcraft instruction. Camouflage, concealment, stalking, tactical movement, and the selection of hides (usually a dug-in, covered position) and alternative positions are equally important, if not more so, than marksmanship to the combat sniper. An excellent long distance shooter is worthless as a sniper if he doesn't have the requisite fieldcraft skills to successfully stalk his quarry and provide for his own survival, whereas a so-so shooter who can move like a cat in the woods is going to rack up a respectable bodycount and at the same time come home to tell the tale. Snipers must have greater than average intelligence. Sniping is more than just being able to shoot; many of their ancillary tasks, such as scouting, reconnaissance, and acting as forward observers for artillery, require as much practice and effort as their marksmanship, as well as a certain level of cerebral acumen.

Your average civilian off the street can't even begin to read a military map; it takes a certain modicum of intelligence and more than a little training, yet it's a very necessary skill for a professional military sniper. Snipers have to be able to work independent of orders, exercising initiative and discipline. As one sniper instructor says, "We have the capability to watch people die; their heads explode, or whatever. It's the mark of a true professional to carry out the mission."

MacKenzie and Peck taught security techniques for the sniper, how to safely enter and leave friendly lines, coordination procedures when operating with patrols, use of artillery support, ballistics, ammunition selection, and picking a team partner (an observer). All this was touched on as quickly, but as thoroughly as possible, during the first morning. That afternoon the two sniping instructors took their charges to the rifle range. Even though the twenty sniping students were supposed to be fairly good shots, they still needed remedial marksmanship instruction.

MacKenzie and Peck went over the basics of rifle marksmanship, with the sniper-trainees spending the rest of day one and most of day two firing shot groups at one hundred-meter targets. The instructors adjusted the scopes as necessary after the shooter fired a "tight" shot group to determine required corrections of elevation and windage. By the end of day two, they had the class shooting accurately out to five hundred meters, where most of the trainees were able to consistently score torso hits on man-sized silhouette targets. MacKenzie told me he felt that given the time available this was a reasonable standard, so the class spent the third and final day conducting field sniping exercises and going through a review of sniping methods.

MacKenzie and Peck's next training class was on troop-leading procedures for officers. The classroom was filled with thirty-seven platoon leaders and company commanders, a large portion of the brigade's company-grade leadership. The officers were eager and ready to learn from the American trainers. It was only a one-day course of instruction; the young officers were needed at their units. MacKenzie and Peck, the two field grade officers with years of combat troop leading experience at the company level, spent a long day in the classroom using terrain models (sand tables) to instruct on the planning and execution of combat operations, estimates of the situation, backward planning time management, conducting rehearsals, preparing and issuing orders, and use of supporting artillery, armor, and troops. Officer courses in other armies spend months on these subjects; the officers of the King Tomislav Brigade were forced to soak up whatever they could in one day. They were luckier than most.

Like all combat veterans and military professionals in a war zone, both Major MacKenzie and Colonel Peck were itching to get in on the action, so Glasnovic gave the two a break from their instructor duties and took them on the all expenses paid grand tour of the frontlines. Meals and hotel surcharges extra. They put on their web gear and picked up an FN FAL rifle and an old Russian PPsH-41 submachine gun for personal protection. These submachine guns were more common than you would think: Croatia produced a copy of the PPsH-41, the Sokac M-91, in 1991-1992. The receiver was identical to the original, except it was chambered for 9x19mm caliber, and had a plastic pistol grip and a folding stock like the CZ-24 Czech submachine gun. There was a standard model, a silenced or suppressed model, and an early version with wood furniture instead of plastic. But it was strange to see soldiers running around in the 1990s with a weapon from World War II.

Glasnovic picked up MacKenzie and Peck in his jeep at the Hotel Tomislav and the three, who'd become good friends, drove up to the frontline trenches where the King Tomislav Brigade's troops were dug in amongst the snow and ice-covered slopes of the Bosnian mountains. MacKenzie later wrote in *Soldier of Fortune*: "We visited his men's snow-covered bunkers in Ardennes-like forests, on a rocky hilltop anti-tank strongpoint overlooking the bare windswept plains, and in mud-filled trenches facing similar Serbian ones, reminiscent of WWI." MacKenzie reported that the troops were well supplied and their morale was high. He attributed their successful halting of the Serb offensive there in western Bosnia to the King Tomislav Brigade's efficient use of the terrain for defensive operations and to the unit's high *esprit de corps*. After their frontline tour MacKenzie and Peck returned to their roles as visiting instructors one more time, teaching a class on combat patrolling techniques to some of the brigade's NCOs. Like the other courses it was critical material that really needed more time to be taught completely and thoroughly, but any training was better than none.

Peter Kokalis was slated to run training courses on squad automatic weapons and light machine guns. Kokalis conducted an intensive three-day course of instruction, emphasizing such aspects of machine gun employment as the cone of fire, the beaten zone, firing from enfilade, and fire discipline. Kokalis oversaw three days of range firing. As a former eighteen-year-old US Army PFC assigned as an M-60 machine gunner and the graduate of two machine gunner's courses (this was before I saw the light and motivated by greed and the desire to work less, got myself a commission), I was interested to hear about Peter's experience with the Bosnian-Croat machine gunners, and spoke with him about it at length.

Like the rest of the training team, Kokalis was staying in the King Tomislav Hotel, which was formerly the government-run tourist hotel, the Duvno Hotel. He jokingly referred to it as a half-star facility. Even with the stained carpets and the paint peeling from the walls, by East-European standards it was average, but in comparison to your basic stateside Holiday Inn it was certainly decrepit and seedy. Given some of the places I've holed up in around the globe, especially in East Africa, it was as good as the Hilton to me.

Kokalis shared his room with his interpreter, Tony Vucic, the Croat-Australian assigned to him for the duration of the three-day machine gunner's course. The Tomislavgrad air raid siren woke Kokalis up one evening (a common event when I was staying in the Tomislav a few months later) and jolted him from his slumber. It was probably the adrenaline highpoint of his stay. When he asked his interpreter if they should get dressed and go downstairs, Vucic said, no, don't worry about it unless they heard incoming artillery. Kokalis figured since he was on the top floor of the hotel, it might be too late to do anything if that happened, but he rolled over and went back to sleep anyway. The Serbs didn't shell Tomislavgrad that night and allowed Kokalis to get his rest. He needed it because in the morning the machine gun expert was back at work instructing a group of machine gunners from the King Tomislav Brigade.

Arriving at the firing range, a farmer's unplowed field with a nearby mountainside as a backstop, Kokalis found a grab bag of automatic weapons. There were three World War II German machine guns, an MG34 and two MG42s, as well as three MG 53s, three PRC Type 80s, two HK 21s, and one Czech ZBvz30J, the only light machine gun amongst an eclectic collection of heavier GPMGs. Because of the arms embargo and the severe logistics and ordnance problem, the Bosnian Croats were armed with a hodgepodge of weaponry. But according to Kokalis, "What they lacked in logistics, the Tomislav gunners made up for in enthusiasm, dedication and performance."

Like MacKenzie and Peck, he found he had an eager group of students. The wide array of fully automatic ordnance made Kokalis' task both challenging and interesting. The cold weather proved to be a bit of a distraction for the weapons technician accustomed to the warmer climes of Arizona, but Kokalis got down to work. He conducted blindfolded disassembly-assembly drills, ensuring that the gunners would be able to perform basic operator maintenance in the dark if necessary, and cross-training on all the guns so that the machine gunners could function as fully trained professional gunners on all available guns, and not just on the particular model that they currently carried. By the time a Bosnian soldier learned the ins and outs of every weapon in his unit's inventory, he was nearly as good a small weapons expert as a US Army Special Forces 18B weapons sergeant.

In addition to this quartermaster's nightmare of weaponry, Kokalis noted that there was also a wide assortment of ammunition for the Kalashnikovs, with the rifle rounds bearing head stamps denoting their origins from Yugoslavia, China, Bulgaria, Romania, and Poland. All the ammunition for the Type 80 machine guns was, as denoted by its Arabic markings, from either Egypt or Iran. I never paid too much attention to the ammunition origins of my issue, as long as it was clean and reliable. But I always inspected my rounds and then put several magazines, or at least a few rounds if ammunition was limited, through my weapon to insure that not only was the weapon functioning and reliable, but that it would continue to function reliably with that particular ammunition. The Kalashnikov series of rifles is very forgiving if operator maintenance is neglected, but the cartridge has to fire, and getting a particular lot of corroded ammo that causes cases to rupture and jam the weapon, or rounds with bad primers that don't fire, will certainly ruin your whole day. I've heard horror stories of units being issued crates of faulty ammo all from the same factory lot without any other replacements available. On a subsequent trip to Bosnia, Kokalis found a Croat machine gunner going into combat loaded down with old, defective ammunition.

When I saw Bob MacKenzie for the last time at the 1993 *Soldier of Fortune* convention in Las Vegas, he told me he was going back to Bosnia. As promised, he returned a few months later in early 1994, and worked for Glasnovic's new unit, the First Guards Brigade "Ante Bruno Busic." Headquartered at Capljina, it was one of the new professional brigades, equipped with its own organic armor and artillery support— a vast improvement over the largely light infantry units of poorly-equipped militiamen like Glasnovic's previous command, the King Tomislav Brigade.

After leaving Bosnia in January of 1995 Bob MacKenzie hired on with GSG Ltd. GSG (Ghurka Security Guards) was a privately owned British company with its head office in St. Helier, Jersey, the Channel Islands, and branch offices in Katmandu, Durban, and Nairobi. GSG was co-owned by Anthony Husher, a former officer in the British Green Jackets and Rhodesian African Rifles; Jon Titley, an ex-British Ghurka officer with service in the Oman; and Mike Borlace, a pilot who flew fighters in the Royal Navy and helicopters for the Rhodesian Air Force before becoming a captain in the elite Rhodesian Selous Scouts. If Borlace and MacKenzie didn't know each other from Rhodesia, then Borlace probably knew of MacKenzie, the only American commander of an SAS squadron.

The company employed retired Ghurkas in security and paramilitary jobs. While working for GSG, a few employees were wounded in firefights in Mozambique, others cleared minefields in Kuwait, drove UN trucks in the Balkans, guarded foreign embassies, and conducted anti-piracy patrols off the coast of Africa. MacKenzie and Andrew Meyers, a former Coldstream Guards soldier and also a veteran of Glasnovic's brigade, were hired by GSG for a contract in the West African nation of Sierra Leone. They arrived there at the end of January 1995. Fortunately, as it turned out, I was on another contract at the time, or Mac would have got me in on the job.

Sierra Leone's leader was then Chairman Valentine Strasser, a former Sierra Leone Army captain. Strasser, head of the National Provisional Ruling Council, and his right hand man, Major Abu "ABT" Tarawali (a Fort Benning-trained officer) contracted GSG for sixty Ghurkas to provide basic military training to the Republic of Sierra Leone Military Force (RSLMF) and train a crack Commando unit, the Sierra Leone Commando Unit, to battle bandits of the Revolutionary United Front (RUF). MacKenzie, commissioned as a lieutenant colonel in the Sierra Leone Army, was the first commander of the SLCU and was assisted by Lieutenant Meyers and Lieutenant James Maynard. They handpicked 160 men from the Sierra Leone Army, issued them new Kalashnikovs, French Foreign Legion pattern uniforms in Portuguese camouflage, and dark green berets. In the field MacKenzie habitually wore his tan SAS beret or a camouflage boonie hat with US airborne wings attached and US battledress uniform with his 101st Screaming Eagles Airborne Division combat patch on the right shoulder.

Shortly after assuming the contract in Sierra Leone, Mike Borlace, MacKenzie, and Tarawali were checking out possible sites for their training camp (Camp Charlie) when they made their first contact with the rebels. Leading a group of SLCU recruits near Mile 91 (91 miles from Freetown), they encountered a burning village as well as the rebels who'd torched it. They quickly routed the rebels.

On February 17, MacKenzie and Meyers had just left Camp Charlie, their training site at Mile 91 deep inside RUF territory, with six Ghurkas and a truckload of Sierra Leone soldiers on the only road to Freetown when they were ambushed. MacKenzie's vehicles sped through the killzone and stopped for the troops to dismount. Seizing the initiative, Bob led his small group of Ghurkas and indigs in a flanking maneuver. Confronted with an aggressive response and automatic weapons fire, the rebels melted back into the thick bush. After a quick search of the area, MacKenzie found three blood spoors—his small force had drawn blood without sustaining any casualties themselves.

MacKenzie's troops couldn't even walk through the bush quietly, set OPs or ambushes, or for that matter even maintain anything resembling small unit discipline. Part of the problem might have been the *ganja* (marijuana) that was issued with their rations. They fired their weapons on automatic from the hip and many had cut the stocks off their rifles so the weapons would look cool. MacKenzie wanted six months to train his troops before going into the bush after the RUF. But his two victories, small as they were, against the RUF had so impressed the high command that they wanted immediate action. Safely ensconced in Freetown and removed from the realities on the ground, they believed the RUF could be routed and defeated by any organized offensive action directed against the rebels. They wanted MacKenzie to take his Ghurkas on a direct action mission against the RUF and win the war now: forget about the training program.

With only three training days in Camp Charlie, MacKenzie realized how hopeless this task was for his 160-man unit. Some of them wore civilian clothes under their uniforms so they could drop their weapons, discard their uniforms, and run off into the bush if they made contact with the RUF. No one could read a map; compasses were worn as decorative necklaces; and the troops were regularly lit up on booze and ganja. Despite all this, Mac decided to go for it in the best SAS tradition—"Who Dares Wins."

The SLCU had no leaders save for MacKenzie and his two British lieutenants, so he couldn't break the unit down further than two maneuver units. These he designated A Group and B Group. Leading A Group, MacKenzie along with Meyers, Major Tarawali, and six "non-combatant" Ghurkas for communications and medical support, would assault the left flank of the hill occupied by the RUF camp. B Group and Lieutenant Maynard would move north on the right flank to secure a second, smaller hill situated southeast of the RUF camp. Maynard's unit would set up "stop-groups" on the trails winding through the bush to ambush any fleeing bandits.

At 0900 on February 23, 1995, MacKenzie's force loaded into two trucks and two Land Rovers to begin movement. At 1500 hours a Mi-24 helicopter flown by a Russian contract pilot hovered over Camp Charlie. On board was a Nigerian officer sent to Camp Charlie as an air liaison officer (ALO) to coordinate the two Nigerian bombers on loan to Sierra Leone for an air strike against the RUF camp. The pilot dropped to the ground, hovered, and almost landed, but quickly pulled cyclic and flew off. The helicopter and the Nigerian ALO left without any communication. Attempts to make radio contact with headquarters for an explanation were futile. At 0800 the next day, February 24, the Nigerian air support hit the wrong hill, alerting the RUF to an impending attack.

The bush was fairly dense, with visibility anywhere from two to twenty meters. MacKenzie, Tarawali, and Meyers were leading their troops, A Group. Approaching the crest of one of the hills in a fairly loose formation, they came to a piece of open ground. In the middle of it was a chalkboard on an easel and a flattened area where it appeared people had been sitting. As they were examining it, they suddenly came under fire from not more than fifteen or twenty meters away.

Tarawali was hit and went down, killed in the initial burst of fire, and four SLCU troops were wounded. Mac always led from the front. Although he was wearing the dark green beret of the SLCU when they were ambushed, sometimes Mac had worn a Kevlar helmet in Bosnia. On the back of it was sewn a Follow Me patch, the motto and insignia of the Fort Benning Infantry School. Mac rallied his force and returned fire to the front. Attempting to carry out the wounded and Major Tarawali's body, the SLCU troops came under heavy fire and a Ghurka went down, wounded. MacKenzie, still up front and shouting orders, laid down suppressive fire while directing the withdrawal.

As the RUF fire intensified, the SLCU troops panicked, abandoning the dead and wounded, and fled to the rear, trampling the Ghurkas tending their wounded comrade. MacKenzie ordered the Ghurkas to fall back, and they grabbed the wounded Ghurka to carry him out. The senior Ghurka medic then saw Mac take rounds through both legs and one in the back. Dropping his rifle, Mac fell to the ground as Meyers ran over to help him. The last anyone saw of the two, Meyers was bending over MacKenzie to render first aid. It was later learned that the RUF carried MacKenzie's and Tarawali's bodies off into the bush. Both were presumed to be KIA. Meyers did not make it out. Initially it was rumored that the RUF dismembered and ate the bodies.

War correspondent Jim Hooper later interviewed a RUF prisoner in Freetown who saw Andrew Meyers two or three days after the incident. According to the prisoner, Meyers was in great pain from a stomach wound. Seven Italian nuns held hostage by the RUF stated upon their release from captivity that McKenzie's head was mounted on a pole outside the hut in which they were held. Nearby lay his emasculated body, identified by his distinctive military tattoos. It's possible that parts of him were ritually cannibalized by the West African rebels.

Bob MacKenzie had soldiered through Africa's most violent bush wars in the 1970s and 1980s, survived numerous mercenary contracts around the world and close combat operations during a major offensive in the bloody Balkans, only to die in an unimportant skirmish on an unnamed hillside in an unknown African backwater.

CHAPTER 6

VACATIONS IN HELL, PART II

"It's a town full of losers and I'm pulling out of here . . ."
—Bruce Springsteen lyric from "Thunder Road" used as the funeral
memorial card epitaph for Andreas Kolb, age 19, German volunteer in
the King Tomislav Brigade

It was mid-March 1993, and though I hadn't remembered it yet, it was
also my thirtieth birthday. I was momentarily ignoring an omelet *sa
sirom* swimming in grease and asking myself what the hell was I doing
in a dumpy Bosnian hotel eating Nicaraguan peanut butter for breakfast. While the air raid sirens drove me nuts, no less. Well, sports fans,
it's really a simple answer: I was bored.

Prior to leaving for Bosnia I had received my marching orders from
Brown and a good Intel brief from my friend, Major Bob MacKenzie,
and from Colonel Alex McColl. MacKenzie's assessment of the King
Tomislav Brigade was that the unit had some keen, smart individuals,
but its small unit tactical capability was zero. According to Mac, the
troops didn't even know how to battlesight zero their Kalashnikovs and
were reluctant to train because they thought they knew it all. "Training
wasn't that great. It was run by some flaky ex-corporals," he reported,
and warned me to "watch out for some wise-ass officers wearing pistols
who think they know it all." As it was, I didn't have much luck in avoiding either flaky ex-corporals or wise-ass officers wearing pistols . . . or
was it flaky officers and wise-ass ex-corporals? Same difference.

MacKenzie also told me about a run-in he had with a British merc.
Gus (a *nom de guerre*) started off on the wrong foot by telling Bob that
he was a professional mercenary with years of experience in Africa
(which was actually a good description for MacKenzie), and that he had
guarded a particular railroad bridge in Mozambique. Bob just shook his
head, turned, and prepared to walk away. He knew for a fact that the
bridge the Englishman had just mentioned was actually in Angola. But

before he could remove himself from earshot, Gus next went on to tell him that he had worked for the South African Army, the SADF (South African Defense Force), at the time. It was all Bob, the former SADF Special Forces major, could do to keep from falling over with laughter. The SADF spent the majority of its time trying to blow up the bloody bridge, not guard it. Gus got smart and shut up when someone clued him in that MacKenzie was not only an ex-major, SADF-type, one each, but had previously commanded a squadron of the Rhodesian SAS.

I was pretty well briefed, but not very well equipped, so I bummed some web gear and uniforms from Mike Smith. Smitty used to be my supply sergeant when I was a nineteen-year-old Pennsylvania National Guard platoon leader. Now a prominent local businessman who owned an army surplus store across the street from the armory, he opened up his backroom for me. I needed some gear because much of my own stuff was still sitting in a tent in Somalia. Plane tickets came cheap, courtesy of some super-saver vouchers from my favorite (and only) sister. In a week's time I was en route.

Three other Americans, two of whom were Croatian War veterans, were planning on accompanying me. Carl Graf was leading the charge. I'd met him at the *Soldier of Fortune* convention, along with Heath Peterson and Eugene Lee, a Croatian 3rd Brigade veteran. Carl Graf served with the 25th Infantry in Vietnam, 1965-1966, and was honorably discharged in 1967. He lived in Rhodesia from 1975 to 1980 and traveled around southern Africa. Graf served briefly as a volunteer in Nicaragua. He was an international volunteer with the Croatian Third Brigade from December 1991 to March 1992, when he was billeted near Krumelvic, Tito's hometown, and attended a sniper school there.

Eugene Lee, like many other foreign veterans of the war, had no prior military service before traveling to Croatia to join up in January of 1992. On his flight from Frankfurt to Graz, he bumped into a group of twenty-three mercenaries from Russia, Poland, and Czechoslovakia. Lee found himself sitting next to a Russian captain on his way to Belgrade. Only three of the mercs were traveling on to Zagreb with Lee; the rest were headed to Belgrade to fight for the Serbs.

Lee served with the 1st platoon, 3rd Battalion (*Brinje* Wolves) of the 133 Brigade headquartered at Otocac in the Krajina, about fifty miles from the coast and Rab Island. The only non-Croatian in the unit, he was discharged as an HV lieutenant on May 21, 1991. On June 17, 1994, the Republic of Croatia awarded him the *Spomenicom Domo-*

vinskog Rata—the combat service medal of the war for the Croatian homeland.

Peterson, Lee, and Graf, all good guys, had to change their plans, dropping out at the last minute. Along with Graf at the convention was another American, an acquaintance of Graf's. James (a *nom de guerre*) claimed he was a former Marine and a four-year veteran of the 82d Airborne Division. I didn't remember having ever met him; he was originally going to accompany Graf from California, but ended up meeting me in Boston. I still give Carl a hard time for foisting him on me. We met the third member of our scratched-together team in Europe. Mike Cooper (a *nom de guerre*), thirty-six, formerly a British Army combat engineer corporal, was at that time earning a living teaching people (i.e., police forces and military units) how to blow things up. I knew Mike from *Soldier of Fortune* conventions and through mutual friends.

We first met when Cooper staggered up to me at the 1992 SOF convention, brilliant, charming, and definitely three sheets to the wind. We hit it right off. In order to protect his anonymity, I can't say too much about his background. While serving with British Army engineer units he saw service in Northern Ireland, where his duties included work with radio-controlled EOD (Explosive Ordnance Disposal) robots. He had an interesting tour in the Philippines in the immediate post-Marcos transition period, where he got involved because a friend of a friend had been blown away in his own garage by a Marxist New People's Army Sparrow team (assassination team). The NPA were the same people who killed Colonel James "Nick" Rowe, my old boss at Fort Bragg, where I was briefly his acting battalion S-3. Mike trained CHDF (Civilian Home Defense Force) units in counter-guerrilla COIN tactics and advised friends in the Philippine Police Force on technical matters.

Before I left I also got a call from some people in Dallas, Texas, who were all excited about going over, but they were typical time wasters. All gung-ho and swearing they're committed, they bug the hell out of you for information and then never show up. One International had told me how all his old friends and several acquaintances were talking about going to Croatia to fight in the war—a common story I've heard from nearly every foreign Balkans veteran I've met. After reading *Soldier of Fortune* or *Combat and Survival* or *Raids*, it's good beer talk on a Friday night, especially for impressing eaves-dropping bimbos and other macho-posturing wannabes: "Yeah, let's, like, go to Bosnia and be mercenaries." These poseurs are more interested in talking than doing, and no one actually packs a bag. It's all just verbal masturbation from guys on bar stools getting their jollies by talking about being a "merc." If you make plans to go with others and actually get to the point of buying plane tickets, they suddenly discover problems or responsibilities they never knew they had. "I really want to go, man, but I just got this really great job at Burger King and if I miss a payment on my '83 Celica . . ." It's like the scene in *The Dogs of War*, where the mechanic says that he can't go on the mission because of his wife.

As late as 1995 I got phone calls asking "do they still need mercenaries in Bosnia" from the same Neo-Nazis in Germany who had previously told me in April 1993 that they were going to Bosnia next week. This they said to me in front of Uwe Honecker, a German merc, who had just returned from Bosnia with me. Uwe just looked at me, smirked, and whispered, "These guys said the same shit a year ago when I went. It's all bullshit. If they really wanted to go they'd be there already, or they'd go back with me next week." He was right. Despite all the bravado there were no takers four days later to leave with Uwe for the easy eight-hour train ride to Zagreb.

As for the guys from Texas? I expended valuable time coordinating their travel and procuring information for these Walter Mitty armchair heroes and they didn't show. They still owe me an apology, an explanation, and fifty bucks for phone bills.

James and I met Mike in Frankfurt, which I'd left a few days previously on my way back to DC from Somalia. We arrived in Zagreb via train from Germany and encountered no serious problems along the way, though a German *Grenzschutze* policeman did ask me why I was going to Zagreb. I told him in my very best *Hoch Deutsche*, "*Ich besuche meine Oma.*" I'm visiting my grandma. Yeah, right. He took one look at our gear—which included two US Army duffel bags and a British Army rucksack—nodded his head, smirked, handed me back my passport, and with a "*Danke schoen, mein Herr,*" wished me well. Must be my blond hair and blue eyes.

In Zagreb I linked up with my contact in Parliament, Mr. Branko Barbic, a chemist who had left Australia and returned to his native Croatia to help clean up the mess the Tito regime had made of Croatia's environment. Branko treated me to an espresso in the Parliament's dining room. He passed us on to some Croatian-Americans who were helping him funnel foreign volunteers into Bosnia. At this time there was a loose network of Croats and Croat émigrés helping the war effort in Bosnia. Some of our arrangements were actually made through the Ford dealership in Zagreb! With the assistance of two stunningly attractive young Croatian-American businesswomen, including a good-looking redhead from Cleveland named Bozana, we got on a bus bound for Tomislavgrad.

Twelve hours and a really rough bus ride later, we arrived in Tomislavgrad and met Colonel Zeljko "Nick" Glasnovic, the King Tomislav Brigade commander, and sat down for an interview in the seedy Hotel Tomislav. I delivered a package from Zeljko's mother, Neda Glasnovic, whom I had met in Zagreb. Mrs. Glasnovic was a kindly woman whose other son, Zeljko's twin brother Davor, was enduring a typically brutal captivity as a POW held by the Serbs. Davor "Joe" Glasnovic had been captured after his leg was shattered by an armor-piercing bullet during a firefight with Serb forces. Glasnovic had to deal with the certain knowledge that his brother was receiving harsh treatment, and played the back and forth game of negotiating his exchange. The family received a photo taken of Joe in captivity. He was missing his left ear.

We sat and talked about my background. Glasnovic readily accepted me as an officer in his brigade because I had recommendations from his cousin as well as Glasnovic's recent acquaintance, Lieutenant Colonel Robert K. Brown. According to the Colonel, I wasn't the first American outside of the *Soldier of Fortune* crew to visit his brigade. He told me an American artilleryman had journeyed to Bosnia. Assuming he'd find fully equipped modern batteries with high-tech frills like laser range finders, he was highly disappointed when he encountered the brigade's antique field pieces such as World War II Russian PAK guns. They had spot-welded a cheap, made-in-Japan .22 rifle scope onto one of the guns to help in sighting. The former artilleryman didn't last long. Laser range finders. Yeah, right. So much for what they teach at Fort Sill. I imagine the King Tomislav Brigade gun-bunnies are still laughing.

Glasnovic (who was about forty) had been sent from Zagreb to Tomislavgrad to organize and lead the local militia units there. Before his arrival things were in really bad shape. When we first met, he was a colonel in the *Hrvatski Vojnik*—in effect, a Croatian regular army officer. A Croatian-Canadian, he had spent five years in the Canadian Army gaining valuable experience as a soldier in Princess Patricia's Light Infantry headquartered in Edmonton, Alberta (where I would later live for four years). Colonel Glasnovic and I, after completing our military service, had both worked as federal correctional officers for our respective countries. This gave us a wealth of strange and humorous stories and a shared, but rather twisted view of the human condition, as you can well imagine. He had grown tired of working as a correctional officer and joined the French Foreign Legion, where he served for a couple of years, including a deployment to the Middle East during Desert Storm. Like many other former Legionnaires serving in the Balkans, he left the Legion before completing his service in order to fight in a real war.

But for him it was more than the allure of adventure: invaded by the might of the Yugoslav Army and Chetnik militias, Croatia, the land of his fathers, was fighting for its very survival. So in the early days of the fighting, Glasnovic journeyed to Croatia to offer his services. He served for a time in the Frankopan-Zinski, an elite unit named after two famous Croatian kings, heavily staffed by former Legionnaires. After fighting the Serb Army and the Chetniks of the so-called Serbian Krajina Republic, he was transferred to Bosnia when fighting broke out there.

Badly wounded in 1992, he was hit three times and would have died except for the determination of four of his soldiers, who carried him out to medical attention. One of the stretcher-bearers who refused to leave him was a sixty-eight-year old World War II veteran, who had fought the Chetniks in the same hills fifty years ago. Another was Glasnovic's personal driver, a quiet, steady man who practically worshiped his brigade commander. Glasnovic inspired unswerving loyalty and intense confidence in his men. A lot of this was due to the man's overwhelming personal charisma. Anybody I know who ever served with him respects him immensely.

A significant number of French Foreign Legion vets were serving in the Balkans conflict. *Vive la Morte! Vive la Guerre!* By my count, at least twenty-seven Legionnaires, including Eric Di Tomasso, twenty-three, one of Glasnovic's fellow Canadian veterans of the French Foreign Legion, died fighting in the Balkans. Di Tomasso, a Brossard, Quebec native, served eight months in Bosnia before being killed in action on August 24, 1993, while attempting to save the life of a fellow soldier. At nineteen, he had joined the Canadian Reserves and completed basic training at the Canadian Army base at Petawawa, Ontario, before joining the French Foreign Legion in 1992. Di Tomasso served in Africa and in Spain before joining Croat forces with three other

Legionnaires. He was quickly promoted to captain and put in charge of a platoon-sized unit. He was leading a ten-man "Commando squad" against Bosnian Muslims in Rastani, Bosnia, when he was killed by a burst of machine gun fire. *Vive la Legion Etrangère!*

General Russo, commander of the HV special operations at that time, was a former Legionnaire. Besides Colonel Glasnovic, three other Legion vets were serving in Tomislavgrad when I was there. A fourth Legionnaire, the only American and a stay-behind from the *Soldier of Fortune* training team, had just left. Paul Fanshaw, a well-known *Soldier of Fortune* and good friend of Bob Brown's, had once been General Russo's *sergeant chef* (platoon commander) in Djibouti. A veteran of both the US Marines and the US Army, he jumped with the Legion into Kolwezi during the Shaba Rebellion in Zaire. From what I was told, Fanshaw had a falling out with another ex-Legionnaire (actually "Pat Wells"), and left for Germany. I had an extra two hundred bucks with me that Brown had asked me to loan Fanshaw, but I never met him there. He left the brigade before I arrived and without informing Glasnovic, who still thought he was living down the hall from me in the hotel when I arrived.

In the late winter of 1992–1993, fighting broke out in western Bosnia between the ethnic Croat forces of the HVO and their nominal allies (against the Serbs), the B-H *Armija* and the Muslims serving within the HVO. The Muslims had refused to relinquish control of the towns and villages in the Bogojno region as directed by the United Nations peace plan. Fighting with their former allies, the Muslims, broke out twice. Combat was vicious and close. They were fighting over neighborhoods. Nearby Mostar, a Muslim stronghold, was in a Croatian "province."

The Bosnian civilians suffered the most, especially during the artillery and mortar bombardments. Up to that time, the HVO was pretty evenly matched, tactics-wise, against the Muslims, as well as the Serbs. Regarding tactics, it was more like 1914 than 1993. In some sectors opposite trench lines were only two hundred meters apart, though at one time there were bunkers separated by only forty meters of no-man's-land. Tanks were used as mobile artillery and following massed artillery barrages, troops were literally sent "over the top" to attack enemy fortifications. It was the Somme with a rock n' roll soundtrack.

The fiercest fighting was around the small city of Gornji Vakuf, now known to the veterans of the fight as "Vakuf," where half a dozen

Muslim snipers armed with small-caliber hunting rifles racked up an impressive bodycount. The Muslim snipers consistently hit their targets in the head and chest. There were Bosnian mountain boys with hunting and shooting experience in the Muslim ranks.

During the sniping in Vakuf, one Croat trooper was shifting around in his hole when he heard a voice drift across no-man's-land: "Go ahead . . . move a little more to the right, and I'll get ya." There were several Muslim snipers, supposedly trained by mujahideen Special Forces-types from various Islamic states, assisting the Bosnian-Muslims. Equipment was anything with a scope. I personally inspected an American hunting rifle, a .22 long-rifle caliber Marlin lever action, equipped with a Weaver scope. It was a rifle like I'd seen in many gun racks at home in Pennsylvania. This one had accounted for over a dozen Croat troopers before someone bagged the Muslim sniper using it. Say what you want about squirrel guns.

A Brit serving with the King Tomislav Brigade told me, "Vakuf was a bloody meat-grinder. They [the Croats] lost nearly fifty killed and around 140 wounded up there. More than they lost on the whole line." When Glasnovic called up an additional 180 men from his unit's reserve rolls, only about sixty showed up. No one wanted to go to Vakuf.

"Major" Jurgen "Juri" Schmidt, a former *Bundeswehr* officer from Cologne, was the executive officer of the King Tomislav Brigade at the time of the fighting in Vakuf. He had served six years in the West German Army, rising to the rank of lieutenant in a *Jaeger* (mechanized cavalry) unit, as well as serving in the French Foreign Legion. He is sometimes referred to as a *Fallschirmjaeger*, so it is assumed he was also parachute qualified. He had served with the anti-tank unit of 134 (Zadar) Brigade of the HV during the initial phase of the war in Croatia 1991–1992. In 1992 he moved on to Bosnia and enlisted in the Eugen Kvaternik Brigade of the HVO at Bugojno. Later he found his way to the King Tomislav Brigade.

Schmidt, by all accounts a fine officer and a considerate planner, grabbed twenty new recruits, mostly seventeen- and eighteen-year-old kids, and headed east to the fighting. Schmidt was there with his twenty-man detachment of newbies ostensibly to season the troops a little. Major Schmidt moved north to Vakuf with another group of Croat soldiers to the little hamlet of Duratbegov Dolac, and became decisively engaged with a much larger Muslim force. A British volunteer, Steve Green, when first hearing of Schmidt's death, said, "Good, serves him right, going off like that. A German paratroop officer should know better." Green later told me somewhat derisively, "He lost it when his best mate got it. He got them (the recruits) all killed and himself slaughtered as well."

The more accurate version of Schmidt's death, as told to me by Croats who were there, was that the Muslims had managed to outflank the Croats on both their left and right and were beginning to direct accurate sniper fire on the smaller force. Schmidt realized this and led the withdrawal as his force managed to break contact and attempted to exfiltrate south at night, only to be ambushed by a group of Muslim HOS (aka HOS-MOS). Some of the dead were found with coup de grace shots to the head, evidence that the Muslims achieved fire superiority in their ambush and later swept through the kill zone, methodically putting security rounds into dead and wounded alike. One wounded survivor, a young Spanish merc, Bruno Ruso (a *nom de guerre*), refused to talk about the ambush. An Austrian merc, who was Juri's close friend, said he was pinned down by snipers before he could escape, an account which some of the other mercs later questioned. The experience shook the Austrian volunteer up so much that he left the Balkans for good. Schmidt's body was later recovered lying in the middle of the road, stripped of his weapon, equipment, and uniform.

After I was in the King Tomislav Brigade for a couple of weeks I asked around about Juri, because Bob Brown and all the folks from the *Soldier of Fortune* magazine training team had liked and admired Schmidt and wanted to know some details about his death. Every time I brought up the subject of Juri's death with some of the survivors of the Vakuf fight, people got nervous. I later heard rumors to the effect that Schmidt was possibly shot in the back. The only motive for such a heinous act that I heard was that some people may have believed he was either linked with German Intelligence or rumored to be so, and had discovered too much about the black market in stolen German cars and illegal arms shipments in Tomislavgrad. Many people believe that the death of the German officer has never been explained satisfactorily. When I was in Germany some months later, a friend of Juri's on active duty with German Military Intelligence interviewed me. There wasn't much I could tell him about Schmidt.

I would later learn how easy it was to become a subject of unfounded rumor and suspicion by fellow "mercenaries" and how quickly they would condemn a fellow soldier to death.

Tomislavgrad was a strategic objective for the Serbs. Their aim in 1992 and 1993 was to cut off southern Croatia by driving through central and southwestern Bosnia, severing the Tomislavgrad-Split corridor. Tomislavgrad's geographical links to the Croatian homeland were tenuous at best: all traffic to western B-H near Tomislavgrad from the Croatian coastline had to be transported by ferry, because the bridge was blown. If the Serbs could take Tomislavgrad, they could cut off the southern peninsula of Croatia and isolate Dubrovnik.

Tomislavgrad had a bit of the old Wild West lawlessness to it. But there was little if any crime, because uniformed cops were everywhere (especially after the pretty new blue uniforms arrived), and everyone carried a gun (sometimes two) and occasionally, a grenade—hey, you never knew when it might well come in handy. Early on in the war, gangs held up cars just outside of town and there were several cases of kidnap for ransom until HVO troops under Glasnovic's command got the situation under control. The mountains of western Herzegovina had, moreover, always been known for banditry: the *hajduk*, or "mountain bandit," was part of its historical and cultural tradition, and "brigandry," a term considered archaic in the modern world, was still a punishable and fairly common crime during Tito's regime.

Although Tomislavgrad is Croatian in language, culture, and heritage, the town is actually located in Bosnia-Hercegovina, nearly thirty kilometers east of the Croatian border. On maps, Tomislavgrad was still marked as its former name, "Duvno". This small city is the birthplace of Tomislav of the Trpimirovij dynasty, the first Croatian ruler (910–928 AD) to be crowned a *kralj* (king). An important figure in Croat history, King Tomislav was crowned at Duvanjsko Polje in 925 AD, defeated the Hungarians, established the Drava and the Danube rivers as the northern border of Croatia, fought the Bulgarian empire, and united the Pannonian and Dalmatian duchies, creating a sizeable state. The canton of Bosnia-Hercegovina, *Hrvatski Zajednice Herceg-Bosna* (the Croatian Community of Herceg-Bosna), was unmistakably Croatian. The Croatian flag flew everywhere. I never saw a Bosnian flag, the six gold *fleur de lis* on a field of blue, known to many of the HVO troops as the Muslim flag. Most cars bore Croatian license plates; Croatian crests and badges adorned HVO uniforms (many troops were still wearing their Croatian Army HV insignia and various Croatian Army unit badges); and people drank Croatian beer, smoked Croatia Filters cigarettes, and spent Croatian dinars.

The day after I met Colonel Glasnovic, we rode out to the King Tomislav Brigade training facility together. Glasnovic had a great sense of humor: most mornings, he'd pick me up after breakfast for the ride to the training school and entertain me with funny stories and jokes from his vast repertoire. You should hear the one about the leprechaun and the meat-puppet sometime. When we arrived at the training school I was surprised to find that upstairs, right next to one of the troops' barracks rooms, was a schoolhouse that housed a classroom for ten-year-old girls. I looked in on the troops being trained downstairs on landmines and basic demolitions by a very knowledgeable old soldier, a former JNA engineer sergeant. Glasnovic believed in tactical and technical training conducted by former active service professionals.

At the schoolhouse I met Roger Risberg, twenty-five, a Swedish veteran of the French Foreign Legion and at the time the de facto commander of the *Viking Vod* or Viking Platoon. The Viking Platoon was a seventeen-man unit of Swedish and Norwegian mercs, which, according to their beret badges, included graduates of the Swedish Coastal *Jaeger* School and veterans of Sweden's Lapland *Jaeger* Regiment and Life Hussar Regiment. Roger's boys had their own transport—three surplus Russian Gaz jeeps purchased in Stockholm and convoyed all the way to Bosnia. That was a selection course in itself. Their second-in-command was Simon, a Croat-Swede. Shortly after I arrived, Simon was recalled to active duty with the Swedish Army to be a peacekeeper in Beirut. After Mogadishu, I thought *I* was on Vacations In Hell, Part II, but trading Bosnia for Beirut, damn. Talk about jumping out of the frying pan.

Proving that the Balkan merc business is a small world indeed, Roger and I soon discovered that we knew each other by reputation when we had served in the same HV infantry battalion in Sisak, Croatia, in 1992. We were both in that lovely town on the Kupa River at different times, missing each other by days as we passed in and out of the unit's *kaserne*. We immediately struck up a friendship on first meeting. We had several Croatian friends in common, including one of my unrequited infatuations, Mirijana Zugaj. It seems we'd both pursued her with unrestrained ardor despite her slight boyfriend problem, Butch the MP—the idiot with the .16 gauge shotgun-pistol. Roger and I complimented each other's taste in women and had a good laugh over Butch and how Mirijana had strung both of us along.

Roger is the quintessential soldier. If the UN would just recruit guys like this into a peacekeeping army, pay them a fair wage, ship them from hot spot to hot spot, and let them do their job, there wouldn't be any Sarajevos, Beiruts, or Mogadishus. Well, not for long anyways.

There's a war story about one of the men in the Viking Platoon that I call "Kane and the Kalashnikov." The night after Roger and I bumped into one another, we all got together in the hotel bar and later moved on down the street for a night of boozing and skirt chasing. Kane, a former *Jaeger* (Ranger) sergeant in the Swedish Army and one of the Viking Platoon sergeants, carried a folding stock Kalashnikov. Some so-called experts denigrate the folding stock Kalashnikovs, but they serve their purpose for mechanized troops, and are nearly as accurate as fixed stock Kalashnikovs at ranges under two hundred meters. Most combat engagements, especially those in urban warfare, take place under one hundred meters anyways, so what the hell. Kane also carried a Serb fragmentation hand grenade, its shiny, stainless steel spoon protruding conspicuously from his breast pocket. More than just a fashion accessory for an otherwise drab-looking camouflage field jacket.

Kane was the designated driver/bodyguard for the Viking Platoon. Roger was no dummy. In light of the recent murder of two British mercs by the Muslims they were training, and the ever-present specter of the occasional act of random violence, traveling with a good bodyguard was a wise precaution. Tomislavgrad was something like Dodge City with teenagers carrying Kalashnikovs, and most men wearing a pistol on their hip. Have I mentioned that most of these guys spent all day sitting in bars drinking? Anyways, it was nice to have Kane around during our lets-get-acquainted-and-engender-camaraderie-amongst-foreign-mercs party. After a pivo or two, some half-drunk Croat civilian walked up and said something to Kane. Roger, who had picked up considerably more Croatian in the last year than I had, translated.

"He says, 'That Kalashnikov makes me nervous.' "

Kane smiled and said, "Well, I suggest you go somewhere else then."

We all laughed, Roger translated and, well, you get the idea.

Kane and I became good friends and he was interested to hear that I had grown up near a town in Pennsylvania named Kane, after Thomas Kane, its founder. Kane, Pennsylvania, always had a large Swedish population, and the next county over even boasts a town called Sweden Valley. After Simon, the Croat-Swede who was the Viking Platoon's designated interpreter, unfortunately had to return to Sweden, the Swedes became dependent on Tony, a young Croat who spoke fluent English, for interpreter support. Tony really liked to style American fashions and usually sported the latest nightclubbing gear as recently seen on MTV. He also had an eye for the ladies and was usually off chasing one, if not actually in the young lady's boudoir, when you needed him. Two other Swedes, Bjorn "Doc" Qvarnstrom (the platoon medic) and Mike (a *nom de guerre*) both wanted to join the US Marines. I told them I'd check into it for them.

Two more Swedes I got to know fairly well were Jim and Ike (*noms de guerre*). A Norwegian, Thore Hansen, a lieutenant in his own army, claimed to have a background in special operations, including being trained by 10th Special Forces Group personnel. Most of the other men didn't care a whole lot for the guy, especially after he bullshitted them about training Contras in Nicaragua or something like that, but he seemed like he had a good heart. I told him I'd find something for him to do. He ended up returning to Norway. There was also one American with the Viking Platoon. His story is important because it shows what kind of trouble you can get into as a foreign volunteer, and how close you can come to getting locked up, thrown out of the country, or just plain whacked without even seeing it coming.

Looking very forlorn, Howard (*nom de guerre*), twenty-two, showed up one day at the school fresh off the Zagreb to Tomislavgrad bus, and in the custody of the local military gendarmerie. The MPs had him because he was walking around town in black BDUs wearing a full beard (and therefore looking a little too much like Muslim HOS), all the while taking pictures of the King Tomislav Brigade headquarters building. Not smart.

I showed the Tomislavgrad brigade MPs my HVO ID card and got Howard released into my custody. A former PFC mortarman with the 8th Infantry Division, he had either a Chapter 9 discharge (alcohol/drug rehabilitation failure) or a separation for unfitness and unsuitability for military life, which would be a Chapter 13. I forget exactly what he told me. But it wasn't encouraging. We really didn't have much for a PFC artilleryman to do in our program of light infantry skills and tactics, except help teach basic soldier skills, but there was a chance he could work with the brigade's mortars as a crewman if he had any motivation. Howard freaked everybody out by fumbling with a loaded Kalashnikov without asking someone to show him how to operate it. After I got him squared away with a weapon and a room in the Tomislav Hotel, he bugged out after about two days.

Without telling us or making any coordination, Howard just up and moved to Suica with the Viking Platoon. This really pissed Glasnovic off, because the Viking Platoon was attached to a different brigade, the Jajce Brigade, and Howard had one of Glasnovic's weapons. Glasnovic, quick to anger, wanted to ship his ass out of the country, but I interceded. Howard has no idea how close he came to being arrested for weapons theft and desertion and thrown in an HVO military stockade. But he managed to integrate himself well with the Viking Platoon and spent a lot of time behind the wheel of one of their Russian jeeps. Howard kept his beard and his chubby frame's spare tire increased with the meat, cheese, and beer diet of the HVO. He later accounted himself well as a mortarman with the brigade's mortar platoon.

I kept my distance from Howard so he'd do the same. I didn't want him to keep his distance from me so much as I wanted to keep him away from James. Unbeknownst to Howard, and for a reason unknown to me, James wanted to kill him. I'd had to sternly order James to cease and desist in his homicidal plans for Howard's demise. James by this time was a borderline psychopath and sometimes very difficult to handle. Of only moderate intelligence, and somewhat emotionally disturbed, he fell into the "I can do anything I want here" mode—a common denominator among some would-be mercs who think they can be a law unto themselves, and gravitate to places like Bosnia just for that purpose.

Guys like James are more trouble than they are worth. Mike Hoare, the famous mercenary leader of the 1960s and 1970s, had a simple method of dealing with them when he commanded 5 Commando in the Congo. He either shipped them back out on the same plane they came in on or he summarily executed them when they screwed up. But options like this weren't open to me. Because I regretted having anything to do with James' arrival in Tomislavgrad, I felt honor bound to mitigate his actions. I was afraid that if Howard hung out in Tomislavgrad, James would "do" him sometime when I wasn't around to intervene. More than one military adventurer has got it in the back from someone who developed a casual dislike for him. It's easy to get yourself fragged when you're surrounded by criminals and amateurs.

The day after Howard showed up, we went out to the schoolhouse again, helped the class zero their Kalashnikovs, and taught them some basic patrolling techniques. Amongst the group were five young Germans and a Frenchman. The Germans were Michael "Homes"

Homeister; Marco; Uwe "Honecker" Herker; Heiko; and Andreas "Andy" Kolb. The Frenchman, Christophe (a *nom de guerre*), was a two-year French Army veteran and former Paratrooper. A sixth German, Mark (a skinhead), was in the rear, nursing a bullet-shattered leg held together by sixteen screws, and milking it for all the feminine sympathy he could get. It wasn't much. For some reason, he reminded me of the ex-Nazi playwright character in Mel Brooks' movie "The Producers." He was an avowed National Socialist with a very skewed view of the history of western civilization.

Homes, twenty-six, was the leader of the German mercs in the brigade. A skinhead and card-carrying member of the FAP (*Freiheitliche Deutsche Arbeiter Partei*, or Free German Worker's Party), Homes learned to soldier in the West German *Bundeswehr*, where he was a combat engineer specializing in explosives, demolitions, and mine warfare with the *2d Kompanie, Pioneerbatalion 1*, for three years until his discharge in 1989. Homeister's military experience would come in handy in Bosnia. He signed on as a volunteer in February 1993, just two weeks before my own second tour in the Balkans began. With only two weeks more time in country than me, he was already considered an old hand.

I was impressed with him from the start. He would prove himself to be a steady, dependable professional soldier. A good friend of mine from Fort Benning, Tom Kelly (a *nom de guerre*) would later serve in the KTB with Homes, and his opinion of the German soldier of fortune was the same. Kelly and I were infantry lieutenants living in adjoining rooms at Fort Benning for six months during our Infantry Officer Basic Course. He later went on to serve for five years as a paratrooper in the French Foreign Legion and later, after Bosnia, re-enlisted in the US Army, where he is a Special Forces senior NCO. If my evaluation of Homes' soldiering ability doesn't carry any weight, then Tom Kelly's should!

Homes told me he was motivated by an idealistic impulse to help the Croats, whom he felt were the victims of Serbian aggression. At the same time, he figured he'd get some real combat experience and get a chance to kill some "commies," as he referred to the Serbs. Homes was a skinhead who formerly advocated some rather racist ideas and had spent a little time in a German jail for a minor misunderstanding with some Turkish gentlemen. Surviving incarceration in the German penal system as a Nazi amongst the Turkish gangs was a character-building experience. He was a very tough guy. Homes had some serious tattoos, including *ACAB* tattooed on his neck, which stands for: "All Coppers Are Bastards." But don't get the wrong idea. Homes was a very intelligent young man with a good understanding of the military-political situation in the Balkans. Joining the fight in Bosnia was a simple matter for Homes: he took a train from Germany to Zagreb and from Zagreb he rode a bus to Tomislavgrad.

Because of his prior military experience with the *Bundeswehr*, Homes was enlisted as a volunteer in the King Tomislav Brigade without any problems. He was another good example of the universal soldier type. His constant companion was "Susie," his PRC Type 80 machine gun (a Chinese copy of the PKM), though he preferred a Jugo Model 53 "Sarac," which is a copy of the World War II German MG-42 machine gun. He liked to wear *flectarn*, the new German Army camouflage uniform that very much resembled the old World War II SS fall-summer camouflage. Put an American Kevlar "Fritz" helmet on his head and look out. He could have been on the cover of *The Forgotten Soldier*, Guy Sajer's classic memoir of duty with the Charlemagne SS Division on the Russian front.

Homes had some amusing stories to tell about plundering East German Army munitions depots after the Berlin Wall came down. It seems that the German far right wing acquired a sizable supply of plastique explosives as well as other goodies. They also had lots of disgruntled, unemployed military veterans from both sides of the wall that know how to use the stuff. Scary, huh?

Marco, on the other hand, was just the opposite. A strange looking-character who had lost an ear in a car accident, he acted even stranger. Glasnovic finally threw him out of the Brigade after seeing him drunk as a skunk and causing trouble on main street in Tomislavgrad at 0730 one morning. Uwe Herker, twenty-one, aka "Honecker" because of his East German roots, was another skinhead and avowed National Socialist. Uwe was a slightly built youth with the face of an angel. He was wanted by the German police for various crimes, mostly political, including a bombing. Heiko, another East German, was the stereotypical blond, blue-eyed Nordic German with some experience in the East German Army. Heiko didn't speak any English and didn't say much anyways. His East German-accented slang was so guttural I had problems understanding him. According to Uwe, Heiko had raped and killed a woman (not necessarily in that order) during the recent fighting versus the Muslims. I'm not sure if I want to believe that. He was on the scary side, but never caused any trouble and soldiered on.

But in my opinion the best of the bunch was Andreas "Andy" Kolb, nineteen, from Muhlhausen, Germany. When Kolb arrived in Bosnia in early 1993, it was his intention to make it as a freelance photographer and journalist, but before long he was drawn into taking a more active part in the war. Andy was a very intelligent young man determined to be a professional mercenary. I repeatedly told him there wasn't much money in it. Andy spoke excellent English so I gave him a US Army Ranger handbook. He appreciated that because he'd recently visited his cousin, who was in the US Army at Fort Benning. Andy had a penchant for World War II history, specifically the US Marine Corps campaigns and battles in the Pacific. I found this interesting because when I was his age, I was caught up in reading about Otto Skorzeny, the Brandenburgers, *Kampfgruppe Peiper*, and other German special operations in World War II, rather than studying Iwo Jima or Guadalcanal. Go figure.

The last day of class in our infantry skills and tactics training course for the HVO troops was anti-tank weapons. While the troops received hands-on instruction, Colonel Glasnovic showed us a South African Defense Force promotional video on the ARMSCOR 40mm grenade launcher. The launcher, with its six-round cylinder, looks a lot like an oversized revolver pistol. Then we got to play with one. It has an optical sight with a dot reticule aim sight that requires the firer to keep both eyes open. It took me some getting used to, as my dominant eye wanted to focus on the scope itself rather than looking through it to the target. Maybe it has something to do with me being a hillbilly.

Glasnovic gave me some pointers and I soon got the hang of it. The funny thing is, the ARMSCOR MGL was obviously sterile (it had no markings), but the boys in South Africa had screwed up when they packed the official SADF demonstration and promotional VHS video with the weapons. Oops. I'm sure somebody in Pretoria got the sack for that OPSEC goof.

The previous evening we'd drawn four Romanian Kalashnikovs and also picked up three Degtyarev light machine guns with their unique top-mounted pan magazines. The Degtyarev machine guns we rescued from the armory were factory ordnance marked 1944. For a machine gun nut like me they were a great find. I had a GI Joe as a kid that came with a Soviet uniform and a Degtyarev, complete with removal pan magazine. I always thought the Degtyarev was interesting. It just looked so radically different from other machine guns. The Russians first made the Degtyarev (DP) 7.62mm machine gun in 1926. It is unique because it was the first use of the Kjellman-Frijberg locking system in Soviet machine guns. Yes, I'm sure this just excites everyone reading this beyond all belief.

These old Russian machine guns were just sitting in the armory, supposedly unserviceable, so we took them back to the hotel and stayed up until about 0300 cleaning and repairing them. Later on in the morning we zeroed our Kalashnikovs and test fired the venerable, old Russian bullet hoses. It was a hoot. We got some good familiarization on the gun and sent some rounds down range. It also pleased Glasnovic that we had repaired and put into service three machine guns.

Weeks later when we wanted to use them in a class to train some of the brigade's infantrymen, we couldn't find them, and no one had any answers. Since we'd secured them in the school's arms room, I believe that some of the training school support staff, who were Muslims, appropriated them. They then no doubt ended up on the Tomislavgrad arms black market as part of an arms shipment, either to the nearby Muslim forces, to Kosovo, or to Macedonia. I heard that weapons were being bought up piecemeal in the bars around town until a sizable shipment accumulated for shipment. Glasnovic raised a little hell about the disappearance of the guns, but I never heard what the final outcome was. I was pissed off about it, but questions got me nowhere, and mindful of what might have happened to Juri Schmidt, I shut up about them.

Black-marketeering of weapons in the Balkans was big business, both on a large and small scale. When I was in Bosnia, Kalashnikovs were for sale on the black market from two hundred Deutschmarks on up, depending on type. G-3s and Argie FN-FALs were much tougher to get, and if you did get one, the problem was that .308 ammo was in short supply. Pistols were in great demand. Tokarev pistols cost between three hundred and five hundred Deutschmarks, while CZ pistols commanded prices around a thousand five hundred Deutschmarks. On the Balkans arms market anything was available for a price: Skorpion machine pistols, ARMSCOR MGLs, RPGs, you name it. But again, after I heard rumors of possible foul play being involved in Juri Schmidt's demise and his supposed investigation of black market activities, I tried not to express any interest in the local illicit arms trade.

After we had finished zeroing the now perfectly functioning Russian machine guns, we walked back to the schoolhouse in time to join the troops, who were falling out into a road march formation. We humped back up the valley out of the village and up into the hills, with the troops carrying the anti-tank weapons that they were going to fire as a live fire demonstration. The target was an old stone house and not all the rounds were on target. Some duds plowed into the soft mud for Mike to EOD while I accompanied the troops, led by Colonel Glasnovic, on a near-vertical death march up and down the Bosnian countryside. James stayed behind to help Mike with the duds. I'm not sure exactly what he thought he could contribute, but he did avoid a tough, day-long combat patrol through the mountains. He made noises about me being a chicken. That's right. Mike and I have a long-standing agreement. I don't ask Mike Cooper to lead infantry assaults up hillsides and he doesn't ask me to dispose of unexploded ordnance. If you don't know what you're doing, my advice is not to mess with it, especially if it has a propensity for going boom and splattering your body all over the countryside.

While Mike was taking care of the duds I was off on a reconnaissance and security patrol, a show-the-flag operation to any bandits or Chetniks that might be skulking in the area, and familiarizing myself with mountainous terrain. Mountainous is an understatement when describing western Bosnia. It was the first real physical exertion I had after nearly two weeks of travel, gear unpacking/packing, and getting organized in Tomislavgrad. All the walking and PT I'd done in Somalia had been done on the flat. As I am a Pennsylvania mountain boy, my legs were still in fairly decent shape, but the steep grade of the Bosnian mountains and the insufficient tread of my jungle boots conspired to give me a hearty workout. I was only a day away from thirty, and I kept thinking about the training "death marches" I'd made as a seventeen-year-old basic trainee.

The training school's medic, Aisha, a really good-looking brunette, was fetchingly dressed all in black—black fatigue pants and tight black turtleneck sweater—with a knife stuck in the top of her right jackboot. My kind of woman. I have to confess that I did enjoy watching her shapely ass climb up and down those mountain passes. Not that I was going to say anything about it, not while she had that bayonet stuck in her boot.

Aisha had been a nurse before the war and was an asset to the unit. There were women serving in various capacities in the Balkans. Some were even in frontline units, which is something I didn't agree with.

They did okay in static positions but could be a liability if the battle-front became fluid. Several King Tomislav Brigade troops were killed and captured because they had to slow their retreat, ahem, *withdrawal*, to carry a female soldier who couldn't hang with the pace of their movement. I wish the Senate Armed Forces Committee, and all assorted non-veteran liberals and draft dodgers who want to put women in the combat arms of the US Armed Forces would take note of some real world experiences rather than listening to feminist propaganda. Now we've spent five years at war in Iraq and hundreds of women have been killed and grievously wounded. Okay, I'll get off my soapbox about women in the military now.

Aisha had no problems keeping up with the demanding pace as we scrambled up and down the mountain ridges. Glasnovic barely broke a sweat, while many of his troops half his age were hard pressed to keep up. He was almost always in good humor, but had a ready temper when confronted with a discipline problem or a personal affront. When it came to combat, nothing much seemed to faze him though. Walking down a dirt road through a mountain village on the patrol, he showed relative unconcern when a grenade went rolling past us. I just about shit myself and I went down on one knee. I stopped at taking a knee actually, as I nearly dived into a pigsty for cover before I noticed there was no fuse assembly–the brain can process a lot in about half a second. One of his troops had dropped it. He was obviously carrying it John Wayne style by clipping the spoon (safety lever) through his gear, lending credence to the oft-repeated Bosnian mercenary's quip, "The average age of a combat soldier in Vietnam was nineteen. In Bosnia that's their IQ."

I've always maintained that this is how I'll buy the farm someday, by accident because some newbie or amateur does something really stupid. Just like when I was with the 513th Military Intelligence Brigade in Somalia and that real idiot for a company clerk named Davis who wanted to play John Wayne all the time tried to toss a Willy Peter grenade to my friend Ski. I probably have more close friends messed up as a result of dumb actions like that than from actual hostile fire. I don't like messing with grenades or sims unless I absolutely have to. I had a flashbang go off prematurely at Camp Dublin in Iraq. Someone I was working with was removing spoons and straightening pins to use them with a pull cord in training. I picked one up without inspecting it first, and barely got it out of my hand when I heard the fuse initiate. I turned my head and body away, but it still burnt the back of my jacket, scorched my shirt at the waist, and blew my cell phone (a total loss) off my belt. My ears rung all day long and the blast injury to my right ear probably contributed to me being Medevacked to the Baghdad CASH shortly after Christmas 2005 for convulsions linked to an inner ear problem.

It was an enjoyable and educational hump over the mountains and back down the valley and around to Tomislavgrad. This was definitely different country than the low, rolling hills of the Kupa River valley where I had run operations with the Croatian Commandos a year previously. The patrol was a good introduction to the sights and sounds of western Herzegovina. With nary a rest break our patrol meandered along the mountain ridge and then down along the valley slope through a few alpine villages. I took in the rugged mountain terrain, the rock-strewn hillsides dotted with sheep, the small villages of quaint cottages, nearly unchanged for generations, populated with local peasantry. The people, especially the bent-backed *babushkas* and the old shepherds, made me think I was stepping back in time.

The day after our death march from hell was the morning of my thirtieth birthday where I found myself trying to swallow a mouthful of Nicaraguan peanut butter. The Communist peanut butter, which was stale and no doubt part of a mis-directed relief shipment, stuck in my throat for several reasons. The label said, "Sold for the Nicaraguan Sandinista government in a show of solidarity by the British Socialist Party." The left-wing pukes. After ignoring the air raid siren for a while and finally eating the greasy cheese omelet, I left for my first visit to the line.

I went up to my room for my equipment and weapon. I loaded up my gear, did a quick pre-operations check as I always do, checking each and every Kalashnikov magazine. Any time I'm issued magazines, I disassemble them and clean them, just like my rifle. I check every round as I load it. Loading an old, previously misfired round into the middle of a magazine can definitely cause a significant emotional event. I had two canteens full of water, some MRE rations in the cargo pockets of my old US woodland BDU pants, my E&E (Escape and Evasion) kit and first aid kit in my buttpack, and my Cold Steel Trailmaster Bowie on my LBE belt. Lastly, I had my Kalashnikov, tuned up and sighted in. I wore an old patrol cap but my Kevlar helmet was slung over one of the canteens.

I sat in the dining room with a cup of coffee and waited for the Colonel. His driver came in to fetch me and we walked out to the jeep. Glasnovic was carrying his .308 German G-3 and his driver had a Steyr

Mannlicher .308 sniping rifle with optical sights. I was the odd guy out with my battered Romanian Kalashnikov. I would happily have carried a G-3 if there was one available, but the 7.62 Kalashnikov cartridge is no slouch either, and I had plenty of extra magazines and ammo for the AK.

We drove out of town along the snow-covered dirt roads to the frontline. Things were relatively quiet with another ceasefire in effect although there had been some pot-shotting going on. We stopped first in Suica. A Serb MIG pilot had been shot down in Suica by a SAM-7, a Soviet hand-held anti-aircraft heat-seeking missile. The pilot ejected and his aircraft exploded, showering the farmer's fields with debris. The local HOS troops pulled the hapless pilot from his harness before his canopy could collapse: he never even touched the ground. His Skorpion machine pistol, a real prize, was quickly appropriated.

The Yugo Skorpion is a nice little toy. The 7.65mm (.32 ACP) Model 84 machine pistol is identical to the Czech Skorpion and was manufactured under license in Yugoslavia by Zavodi Crvena Zastava. It is a blowback-operated, fully automatic "machine pistol" measuring only 10.63 inches with the stock folded and weighing just 2.89 pounds empty. It's basically a phone booth gun—the guy you shoot needs to be in the same phone booth with you—but it is a great weapon for using against a room full of surprised colonels or taking some one out at close range. There was at least one rear echelon Commando in Tomislavgrad who would drunkenly swagger into the Tomislav Hotel bar and wave his Skorpion around. Loaded? Unloaded? Of course everyone in the place (also drunk, naturally) had to handle it and admire it. I usually picked that moment to finish my coffee and go elsewhere.

After inspecting some of the HOS artillery positions in Suica, we drove closer to the actual fighting in another sector and checked out a mortar platoon. Debussing at the base of a small hill, we walked up a well-trod path through the woods to the bunker line. Equipment was a mix of captured Serb tubes and the new Croat 82mm mortars. One of the old salts in the platoon was wearing a World War II field cap with the old World War II *Ustasha* badge of Ante Pavelic's fascist Croatian State attached to the front. Outlawed by Tito, it was no doubt passed on down through the generations, father to son, as a family heirloom.

I saw a very young looking mortarman and asked him his age. Fifteen. Hell, I thought, I'm nearly twice his age. Then I glanced at my beat-up old Seiko's calendar and realized I was twice his age. Today. It was my birthday. Out loud, I blurted, "Today's my birthday!" The mortarmen all laughed and offered their congratulations. Glasnovic laughed, rubbed his own graying hair, and called me a youngster. I continued trooping the line with Zeljko.

This sector was defended by some of the nearly two hundred HOS troops loyal to his brigade. The troops were well dug-in, for a Chetnik tank and infantry advance was stopped there earlier at terrible cost. The previous night, more troops and weapons had come up under the cover of darkness. They spent the early morning hours digging in on the edge of the woodline and preparing for the attack at first light. As we hunkered down in the position with the troops we cut loose with a single barreled M55 20mm anti-aircraft gun in the ground support role. We cranked off several rounds into the fortified Chetnik village nearby. Zeljko gave me an expended round. "Happy Birthday," he said.

Beat the hell out of a cake.

CHAPTER 7

MANY SOLDIERS

"I see many soldiers; could I but see as many warriors!"
—Nietzsche, *Thus Spake Zarathustra*

After we cranked some cannon rounds off at the Chetniks, I used a pair of binoculars to survey the Chetnik positions. Colonel Glasnovic's driver used the optics on his Steyr-Mannlicher SSG to scope out the Chetnik positions. I remember him as a taciturn, steady individual. He had a reputation as a beady-eyed killer and as an exceptional marksman. I was told that he had confirmed kills out to seven hundred meters. I've fired the SSG before and found it to be a good sniping rifle with a smooth trigger pull and a light recoil. MacKenzie considered it to be the best off-the-shelf military-tactical sniper rifle of the day.

I didn't need the binoculars to see that the Chetniks in the village were beginning to return fire. While we were in the woodline, we weren't in fighting positions. I was starting to feel a bit exposed, as incoming fire was chipping the bark off the trees a ways down the hillside. I was re-evaluating my previous exuberance in opening the dance. If we started to take heavy automatic weapons fire or even worse, return cannon fire, we were going to be in a world of hurt. I was looking through the binoculars and trying to pinpoint the sources of enemy fire. I noticed some smoking fires where our rounds and those of the others on the line firing had obviously hit.

I wasn't the only one concerned about our lack of cover in an escalating firefight. Glasnovic suggested we get moving. The King Tomislav Brigade troops manning the gun were already putting another clip of rounds into the village. We went from there to some 203mm gun positions where the troops were ensconced in some well-fortified, cozy bunkers. The artillery observation post (OP) we humped up to on a nearby ridgeline had a well-built bunker for a living area but the OP positions themselves, skylined on the ridge, had no overhead cover or camouflage.

The King Tomislav Brigade gunners put another clip of 20mm into the Chetnick lines and then the shit really started to fly. As our lines continued to fire on the enemy positions, the Chetniks got their act together and the return fire began increasing. We were crouched down next to the bunker and not really protected, trying to use a few pine tree trunks as cover. With enemy small arms fire clipping through the trees around us, it soon got too hot to be out there in the open. Glasnovic led us back down the hillside, ducking and running along a line of thin scraggly pines as the rounds snapped through the trees.

Later in the afternoon we took a welcome respite in one of the bunkers. We ate lunch and waited for the coffee to brew while it started to drizzle and then finally piss down rain outside. It was a long, cold, wet day at the front. The mountains of western Herzegovina can be a very inhospitable place in the springtime, but it was a very good way to spend my thirtieth birthday.

That night we returned to Tomislavgrad, and with us some of the troops came back off the line to their families. "Tough day at the office, honey?" It was a welcome pleasure to see the well-worn dirty carpet of the Hotel Tomislav lobby. I trudged in wearing my muddy mountain boots to get a hot shower, a change of clothes, a plate of hot veal medallions, and a cold Karlovaco. This would then be followed by a cappuccino and a cigar as I relaxed in the hotel bar. I could always count on some good conversation, some interesting war stories, and perhaps a chance to ogle some of the local lovelies. What a way to fight a war. It was almost civilized.

Too bad I wasn't getting paid.

The next day we were back to work training troops. We worked with a group of about twenty soldiers, teaching patrolling techniques, establishment of a linear ambush, and various immediate action drills. Tuesday, March 16, we received a new bunch of trainees. They went through the usual administrative garbage in the morning and after lunch went to the range for some basic rifle marksmanship. This group had received a day's worth of rifle firing several months before when they were drafted into the military police reserve; therefore, they all considered themselves expert shots requiring no further training or practice.

This was a prevalent attitude amongst the "veterans." Whereas professional soldiers take every opportunity to confirm their rifle's battlesight-zero and enjoy practicing marksmanship, the mark of the rank amateur is his disdain for firearms drills and marksmanship training. All this platoon of civilians in camouflage had done so far was go door-to-door looking for deserters.

I was out bright and early to the training school to set up a rifle range. We had built some targets earlier and I simply paced off a zero range and then longer ranges, placing targets at one hundred and one hundred fifty meters. As far as the marksmanship ability of some of the troops was concerned. I was actually being quite optimistic. The range was just part of a farmer's pasture. The backstop was the bare hillside. We kept an eye out for wandering sheep.

Later in the morning we were joined by Pat and Mejor, two supposed former French Legionnaires. Pat Wells was an Englishman from Bristol with an accent that was, at times, completely incomprehensible, and John Mejor, his sidekick, was Belgian-Hungarian. Pat claimed he had served as a rifleman in the British Army, joining the Gloucestershire Regiment for three years when he was seventeen. He also claimed he completed his five-year hitch in the Legion, serving with the 13 DBLE in Djibouti and the 6 REG in L'Ardoise, with deployments to Chad and the Central African Republic. Talk about some good stories. He said he left the Legion as a corporal and joined the HV in Osijek in 1991 and then went over to the HVO. It all sounded good, but his background has since been called into question by other British volunteers and other French Foreign Legion veterans.

Pat had introduced himself to me the previous evening at the hotel. He wanted to get in on our training gig and on the Brigade's tit, so to speak, as well. According to Pat, Mejor had left the Legion before his five-year enlistment was up to serve in the Balkans. Without a passport, he was pretty much a stateless person. Since he spoke no English, Pat had to translate for him. In the morning, with Pat and Mejor assisting, the five of us taught squad tactics starting with basic movement formations and techniques (the "wedge"). I know I can be pedantic at times when it comes to training. But constant repetition and reinforcement is the only way to indoctrinate green troops–if they carry out their drills as if they're second nature, it will eventually save lives. This led to some long-running jokes and a sign above the others' quarters reading "Welcome to Wedge World."

Our interpreter was Miro, a young Croat military policeman. Miro was a big-time fan of the rock group, U-2. Their new album *Achtung, Baby,* was the thing to have in Tomislavgrad. I made a friend for life when I gave him my cassette tapes of *The Unforgettable Fire* and *Under A Blood Red Sky*. Miro's school English was only slightly better at times than my military Croatian, but fortunately we both had copies of the same *Englesko-Hrvatski* dictionary. I'd forgotten much of my military Croatian in the past months since leaving the Sisak Commandos, and didn't have time for an adequate review after getting back from Somalia. Miro helped me with a few key phrases I jotted down in my notebook.

In order to teach tactics without an interpreter you really only need the basic words and phrases pertaining to the subject matter, e.g., *zasjeda*—ambush, *sigurnost*—security, *mitrajet*—machine gun, etc. The rest is simply demonstration and do as I do, the "follow me" method of small unit tactical instruction. Troops, especially if they're motivated, usually pick it up fairly quickly. Just as in Sisak, on some days I could instruct in German since there was a German-speaking Croat or two in the group who could interpret for me. On other days I used a mishmash of Croat, German, English, and sign language interspersed with hasty sand tables. Most of the time though, we depended on an interpreter to rove around between the training groups and solve any serious communications problems. The classes were split into eight- to eleven-man squad-sized groups to train on tactics within sight of each other. When I had time, I would draft everything out into English and give it to Miro to translate the night before. That way he was familiar with the subject, and I had it all in simple Croat to refer to. My vocabulary expanded as I learned new words and phrases.

One group of eager trainees included the five or six Germans and two French volunteers. It was easy for me to instruct them. Most had two years of national service. They soaked up everything I threw at them. Later Glasnovic mentioned that some of the Germans we'd trained (the team led by Michael Homeister) begged him to go out on patrol. He consented and they'd returned successful, having killed at least two Chetniks.

Chris, another military policeman, also acted as our interpreter. He was an Aussie of Croat parentage and supposedly a veteran of the Australian Army. He boasted (just a little too loudly) that he was an Aussie SAS trooper. I doubted that he was even ex-military, let alone

SAS, just because of his youth and his disinterest in infantry tactics. Besides that, he took no real interest in training his fellow Croats in anything resembling military skills, and he was so immature I couldn't see him passing selection on "the Golden Roads" for Australian SAS. The Australian SAS is an elite unit closely patterned after the famous British special operations unit. SAS troopers are experienced, mature troopers who have volunteered from other units and passed a rigorous selection course. Chris had neither the intelligence and character, nor the experience required to be SAS. Also, any SAS veteran would have been proficient with a variety of weapons. This guy was clueless. Another imposter.

These Croat MPs were not organized military law enforcement professionals like those you'd encounter in other national armies. The case in Croatia, or even the Balkans as a whole, was that military policeman were usually just draftees like any other trooper, except in addition to a uniform and a Kalashnikov, they also got a pistol, an armband, and sometimes a white holster for their sidearm and some white webbing. Habitually a lot of them were kids who swaggered around safely away from the frontlines, thinking they were hot shit and were going to be hot shit after the war when they talked their way into the regular police force. Guys like my old buddy Butch in Sisak. Chris also swanned around in a BMW, courtesy of some well-to-do relative or perhaps a dirty deal on the black market.

Chris told me that he led the patrol that the Germans had participated in. According to Chris, they picked their way through two minefields while negotiating no-man's-land. Even though it was a reconnaissance patrol, Chris abruptly changed it into a combat patrol when a golden opportunity presented itself: three Chetniks had impatiently left their positions to go meet their reliefs. Placing the Germans in an overwatch position, Chris and one soldier crept forward, slithered into the abandoned positions, and waited. The three Chetniks, late for their changeover, walked right into it. The ambushers opened up with their Kalashnikovs on full automatic at nearly point blank range. The Serbs never had a chance. Two went down, dead, and the third fell wounded, but regained his feet and hobbled to cover, screaming for help. Chris and his buddy legged it back to the rest of the patrol and exfiltrated back to friendly lines as Serb artillery fire rained down on their old position. The King Tomislavgrad Brigade's foreign volunteers were steadily whittling down the enemy ranks.

The day's training started off with a blackboard review of the squad tactics our trainees had already learned. Following that Mike taught a class on early warning devices. He used field expedients and a set of surplus US Army PEWS (Platoon Early Warning System)—a ground surveillance radar system that he'd rebuilt himself from surplus scrap. Next they had the five steps of building a good two-man defensive fighting position drilled into their heads. Croat soldiers usually favored a circular foxhole-type position with the uncamouflaged dirt and rock piled in front. The occupant of the hole then looked over this parapet (there being no overhead cover) to observe and fire. Consequently, a lot of the boys got it in the head and face. We wanted to rectify that situation.

While I translated two other classes into Croatian with Chris' help, the other trainers took the troops up into the treeline for some practical application. Later, when the troops took a break for lunch, we adjourned to the nearby mom and pop corner store for a much-needed instructor break so I could brief everyone on the afternoon's training plan regards change number sixteen. We had no sooner walked inside than two more foreign volunteers entered. Pat knew them and made the introductions.

Steve Green, a Brit who claimed to have seven years as a tanker in her Majesty's service before the downsizing of the British Army, was now serving as an infantryman in the King Tomislav Brigade. It seems a few of the mercs in the Balkans would have remained on active duty at home if it weren't for the Cold War's demise. He'd been wounded months previously. The other Brits referred to him as a wind-up merchant, since he liked to spread rumors and generally run-off at the mouth. Physically he wasn't much to look at. About 140 pounds dripping wet, he was a real pencil-neck. Glasnovic didn't think much of him. He was the same guy who made all the negative comments about Juri Schmidt: nothing like stomping on a guy's reputation after he's dead.

With the wind-up merchant was a former Danish Army TOW anti-tank rocket gunner and self-admitted ex-con. His real name was Anders, but everyone called him Andy, Andrew or "Pingo." Anders' plan, which he was very vocal about, was to serve in the Croat Army until after the war, receive citizenship, and then stay in Croatia. My immediate thought when I heard this was, "Why would anyone want to leave the social welfare paradise of Denmark to be a pig farmer in a small mountain village in western Bosnia?" I suspected he was a wanted man in Denmark or just another loser who couldn't cut it anywhere else. He claimed to be ex-Spanish Foreign Legion, and all his war stories revolved around getting drunk and being thrown in the stockade. Anders was surprised to see an American and told me that in his year in the Balkans I was only the second Balkans merc he knew of who was formerly a serving officer in another army. I assume that Juri Schmidt was the first.

A few moments later Johanna, a tall, shapely, green-eyed, brunette, Swedish journalist-type and the best looking thing in fatigue pants any of us had seen in quite awhile, came in looking for Roger. She'd obviously homed in on news that a fellow countryman was serving as a "mercenary" in Bosnia, and was after Roger and the boys for a sensational story. Her arrival prompted another round of introductions. We chatted awhile about Mogadishu, which she'd just left. The members of the fourth estate are the true "whores of war," and this was especially true in the Balkans, where they made a hell of a lot more money than any of the mercs did. Several journalists made their reputations on their coverage of the war in Bosnia (Maggie Kane and Christiane Amanpour, for example), yet the press hypocritically called the foreign volunteers opportunists. Well, I'm here to tell ya sports fans, there weren't too many rifle-toting opportunists there at two dollars a day.

Hildebrandt, one of Johanna's colleagues, walked in, looked at the American flag patch on my BDU jacket, and said, "My God, are you really an American?" Yes, I replied, and introduced him to James, who remained sitting on the floor in a corner nursing a beer, looking as much like Jack Nicholson as possible, and acting twice as demented as he usually did. He said hello, and Hildebrandt did a double take because, even though James was white, he spoke a stereotypical LA homeboy black English, what they now call Ebonics. Before the preponderance of hip-hop music videos and movies, most English-speaking Europeans found it absolutely incomprehensible. By now the store-cum-watering hole was becoming decidedly crowded. Johanna finished her drink, we exchanged goodbyes, and as she left I said, "See you in Angola." I laughed afterwards, because it reminded me of a scene in the movie *Under Fire*, where the Hawaiian shirt-wearing mercenary character played by Ed Harris sidles up to Nick Nolte's photojournalist during a Managua street celebration after Somoza's fall and says, "See you in Thailand."

The whole time I was in Bosnia, the mercs there were all fantasizing about leaving the Balkans for the big bucks in Angola. It was laughable because most didn't have enough money for bus fare to Zagreb, let alone a round trip ticket to Pretoria or Luanda. Angola was heating up again because Jonas Savimbi was upset with the outcome of the free elections. Savimbi didn't get elected, so he took his UNITA freedom fighters back into the bush to wage more guerrilla war against the formerly Communist MPLA government forces. Word had it that the oil companies were paying big bucks for mercenaries to take back refineries from rebel control.

I found out later that the rumors were true. Both the MPLA and UNITA were hiring South African mercs. Nearly the entire complement of 32 Battalion, an elite counter-insurgency unit formed for duty in Angola, went over to Angola to fight. On both sides. The South Africans had disbanded the unit after the Cubans left Angola and free elections were held. Pay was between one hundred and two hundred dollars a day––good money for merc work at that time—depending on experience and qualifications. I circulated what hard information I had at the time, most of which was from Carl Graf. Carl had lived in Angola for many years and kept tabs on the military and political situation there.

It was probably a good thing that I missed the job in Angola. In early 1993, London-based Heritage Oil in conjunction with Ranger Oil of Canada approached Eeben Barlow (founder of the South African mercenary corporation Executive Outcomes) to recapture the Angolan's Soyo oil production facility from UNITA guerrillas. A force of sixty mercenaries accomplished the mission. EO began conducting additional operations in Angola that captured the attention of every soldier of fortune, would-be mercenary and armchair Commando. I eventually made it to Angola in 1996 as a "ground security consultant" for Chevron Oil, but that's a tale for another book. Another job that passed me by because I was in Bosnia was a gig in Azerbaijan. It was supposedly set up by some oil interests in the US, but it turned out to be a scam perpetrated by a phony oil-man. Several guys spent weeks training Azeris in shitty conditions and not getting paid.

During the time I spent in the Balkan war, no one ruled the night in Bosnia. As was the case in many other conflicts involving irregular forces and untrained conscript armies, nobody fought or moved tactically at night. Colonel Glasnovic wanted to change this: we thus incorporated night training exercises into the schedule. In the early evening, the classes were on occupying a patrol base; after dark, the troops learned noise, light, and litter discipline and the use of night observation devices (NODs), using examples from the brigade inventory that we serviced and repaired.

Seeing his foreign help fixing unserviceable equipment such as NODs and World War II machine guns made the Colonel happy. Equipment in the under-equipped HVO was at a premium. Much of their equipment was *Hrvatski Vojnik* castoffs. Most of the night vision equipment was Russian, including many of the same models now imported for sale in the US. We cleaned the stuff up, tinkered with it, checked connections, and installed batteries until we got it all working. It just takes a little know-how and some effort.

The night patrolling FTX (field training exercise) consisted of three patrols each with a two-man team of trainer/advisors. Patrols were to link up on a known terrain feature, a prominent wooded hilltop, after conducting route recons and navigating by compass azimuth and terrain recognition. They would engage in force-on-force hasty ambushes. Glasnovic gave me some trip flares and hand-held flares to use as training aids. After the prerequisite stumbling and cursing, and some "bang, bang, bang" as well as the opportunity to react to flares, the patrols linked up. Getting them into a perimeter in the pine forest at night was another story. It was an absolute total goat screw with everyone using flashlights, yelling, and generally bitching because we were making everyone train past dark.

Unfortunately Green and another Brit began playing "silly buggers" and sending patrols to the wrong locations. They were purposefully attempting to screw up the entire training exercise. They thought it was funny. No wonder the Croats didn't respect them. One squad actually refused to continue training and said they were going to go home. Lots of luck I told them; the bus wasn't due until midnight.

Right there on the hilltop, by flashlight, we conducted a hasty after-action report on the training exercise. What the exercise demonstrated was that even in small fire team units, the King Tomislav Brigade was woefully unprepared to conduct nighttime operations. More training and experience would be required, but at least we were off to a good start. Unfortunately the bulk of the brigade was too busy trying to hold the line and couldn't conduct regular training exercises. Another problem was lack of experience. No one knew how to plan or conduct a training exercise.

From there, each patrol moved to the firing range about four klicks away for a squad night live fire. This was the first opportunity many of them had to fire as an organized fire team or a squad on their leader's order. The unit leader used tracers to direct their fire. It was also the first time many of them had fired at night. In my opinion, any opportunity for a soldier to put rounds down range is good training. Much modern day infantry do not shoot enough in peace time, and in war time it's too late to practice.

Training was complete sometime around 0100. We all loaded onto a bus for the ride back to Tomislavgrad, and the instructors jumped off at a house used to billet some of the Brigade's foreign volunteers. After a mug of hot tea and a plate of bangers (sausages), everybody began to talk shop. The guys passed around some grenades—always an attention-getter/conversation starter in a small room.

The small, black-plastic fragmentation grenades were considered practically worthless, but they were actually offensive grenades well suited to room and bunker clearing. Rated higher on the mercenary's grenade appreciation scale were the apple-green-colored Serb grenades, but they were in short supply. Thirdly, there were the Croat-made striker mechanism type grenades requiring removal of a safety cap to expose a plunger/striker which had to be smashed against a helmet, rifle buttstock, etc. to arm. In many people's opinion, this is a less than ideal method of ignition. Consequently they were considered unsafe and were very unpopular amongst we mercs. All this was explained to Mike while Pat and Mejor chatted away in French. This was all stuff I'd learned on my first trip to the Balkans when some of the captured Serb grenades were found to have instantaneous fuses. Either they were factory jobs made for booby trapping, or some fiendish and clever son of a bitch had shortened the fuses. We lost a few guys in Croatia that way before someone caught on.

As it was all old hat to me, I sat unconcernedly in a corner reading a March 1981 issue of Playboy that I'd discovered in the cottage. I found it quite interesting to be reading the first Playboy magazine I could have legally purchased. Miss March 1981 was even better twelve years later than she was when I was eighteen. In over a decade of soldiering around the globe, with long periods akin to enforced monasticism, I've definitely acquired a great appreciation for the female form. My professional interest as opposed to libido was aroused, however, and Miss March's feminine charms forgotten, when various small arms began appearing from storage. Of note was one of the unique 9mm

Croat Defense submachine guns, a Zagi-9, basically an improved Sten submachine gun. The Croats produced at least three different models of hybrid submachine guns designed to make use of available parts, materials, ammo, and magazines. They also produced an Uzi from factory dies, plus their own designs of pistols, and even a sniping rifle.

We discussed the merits of various small arms. Like in Croatia, German G-3 assault rifles and Argentine FN FALs Modelo 3s were available in Bosnia, if only in limited quantities. All the Brits wanted an FN because the British Army SLR (self loading rifle) was basically a Belgian FN FAL, but the Croats who had them didn't want to give them up. The King Tomislav Brigade's armory included a hodgepodge of weaponry: bolt-action Yugo Mausers, Yugo versions of the SKS carbine (a dependable, robust weapon), various Zastava hunting/sniping rifles, World War II Russian PPSH-41 or look-alike Yugoslav Model 49 submachine guns, and even a box of poorly maintained Thompson .45 SMGs. Unfortunately there wasn't any .45-caliber ammunition for the old Chicago equalizers. Just as well, as I don't think I really wanted to tote one of those eleven-pound submachine guns up and down the Herzegovina mountains. But it would have been fun to have one to play with. The PPSH-41 World War II Soviet submachine gun is easily recognized by its distinctive ventilated cooling jacket and 71-round drum magazine. The Yugos copied it as the Model 49. These weapons saw extensive use in the Balkans, but are really only suited for personal defense or close-in work in urban areas or trench lines. Obsolete subguns like this are better than nothing when small arms are scarce, but no substitute for a modern assault rifle.

The King Tomislav Brigade had recently received two hundred G-3 magazines, but no rifles. Colonel Glasnovic and his driver had the brigade's only two G-3s. Zeljko eventually swapped some of the mags off to another unit. The supply system supporting the HVO was hit and miss at best. Ammunition resupply wasn't that difficult because almost everyone in the HVO was equipped with an AK-47 assault rifle, either Yugoslav, Chinese, new Serb manufacture, or Romanian. As always, the Romanian Kalashnikovs were the least favored because of their reputation for having a barrel that burned out after about five thousand rounds. Besides that, the vertical foregrip had to be cut off to ease magazine changes.

A few days previously, I had also had my hands on an AK-74 (5.45mm), physical proof that Russian volunteers were bringing their own toys with them. I would have liked to have kept it and carried it, but there was only one magazine and less than thirty rounds for it. The AK-74 was the current standard Soviet (Russian) infantry rifle firing a 5.45mm cartridge that replaced the 7.62 x 39mm round used in our AK-47s. The cartridge was light, high-velocity, and known to inflict some wicked wounds. I've used an AK-74 in combat since then and even own a semi-automatic version of the weapon: I think it is a fine little bullet launcher. The 5.45mm bullet inflicts wicked wounds.

In the morning while the others were sleeping off their drunks, I hitched a ride back to Tomislavgrad just in time to meet Colonel Glasnovic for our scheduled trip back up to the frontline. He was impressed to see me because he knew it had been a late night out on the nighttime FTX and he knew I'd been at the cottage. As we drove up to the line, I briefed him on the training exercise and the live fire. As always, the time spent with Glasnovic was both informative and entertaining. Driving along the front, he pointed out a spot where a group of Croat soldiers stripped to their t-shirts were playing soccer when an infiltrating group of Serbs fired them up. With both his legs blown off by a grenade, one of the Croats tied off his stumps and continued fighting, driving off the enemy soldiers. He later joked, "When my friends take me swimming they'll have to leave me in the shallow end."

We stopped in Suica for lunch and retrieved Howard's Kalashnikov from the Viking Platoon. Glasnovic was still angry at him over the whole situation. The Viking Platoon was staying busy in Suica. After being hit by Serb artillery fire a week previously, the Viking Platoon had dug in behind their comfy billet in a cottage on the outskirts of town. I looked over an old US Army "crackerbox" ambulance, bought surplus in Germany. The locals came out to greet Glasnovic and we ended up having a beer for lunch. We chatted with many of them, mostly old ladies and a couple of codgers who probably fought in World War II. Glasnovic was a hero to these people. The Canadian-Croat and the young militiamen of the King Tomislav Brigade were the only thing standing between them and the predations of the Chetniks, the weekend warriors from Serbia who would loot, rape, and pillage these quaint mountain villages.

We said our goodbyes and got back into Nick's jeep. We inspected a sector where he'd been shelled twice (third time lucky?) and did a terrain walk, what they call a TEWT (Tactical Exercise Without Troops) at Fort Benning, which I say is the same thing as a PENIS (Practice

Exercise Not Involving Soldiers). Looking over the terrain, Glasnovic and I discussed likely avenues of approach, mounted and dismounted. Because the Chetniks continued to bring up their heavy weapons, everyone expected a full-blown Serb offensive sometime in mid- or late April. The Colonel wanted to emplace some minefields in two areas to deny the enemy's approach. He also decided to put in some more OPs and defensive positions around some key terrain, a hilltop that offered good fields of fire and observation of a large sector of his front.

I think Glasnovic was bouncing a lot of his tactical ideas off me to see what the graduate of Fort Benning's Infantry Officer Advanced Course thought or had to say about them. Nick Glasnovic was an able commander, but his entire military career prior to the outbreak of war in Croatia was as a corporal. He'd never been taught company and battalion tactics.

I was lucky that for such a junior officer in the US Army, I had already commanded two infantry platoons and an infantry company; served as an executive officer in two companies; served as an assistant operations officer (assistant S-3) on a brigade staff and three different battalion staffs; and served as a Special Forces group assistant logistics officer (assistant S-4), all before my twenty-seventh birthday. Hell, at thirty I was a has-been! If I'd been called to active duty on the eve of World War II, with that kind of experience, I would probably have been given a battalion to command--during the American Civil War I would have led a regiment. Here I was working as a light infantry battalion S-3 (training and operations officer) in the rank of major in a foreign army. It's all about your place in history, I guess.

We made some terrain sketches and notes on Nick's map. As we walked by one bunker, he spoke with his troops and they told him some engineers were going to blow some ordnance in place. We walked on another twenty meters, and the engineers blew their charge. Shrapnel whistled by us with a quarter-sized chunk landing between Glasnovic and me. He tossed it at me and said, "Good thing it didn't hit the old noggin, eh?" Neither of us was wearing our Kevlar helmets. What a dumb way that would have been to buy the farm: getting hit by shrapnel caused by friendly EOD.

I tossed the still hot piece of shrapnel from hand to hand until it cooled, slipping it into my pocket as a souvenir. Picking up a near-miss piece of shrapnel during a firefight has never been one of my priorities in life, so except for a few small pieces still lodged in my ass (almost

literally), I don't have too many other souvenirs like this.

The Colonel and I wandered on down the line inspecting some more positions, lingering, longer than I really cared to, by a five-ton truck that had been destroyed by Serb artillery fire. A tough way to learn not to skyline your vehicles. We discussed the upcoming training of two companies of his troops. In his opinion, they were the worst he had and needed some training and discipline. It was up to me and his cadre of foreign volunteers to take care of that. Colonel Glasnovic told me he'd get us some dinars, a partial payment of our month's pay, so there'd be some money for cigarettes and the occasional pivo.

Speaking of pay, HVO pay at that time was eighty Deutschmarks (about one hundred US dollars) a month, which was quite a bit less than the two hundred fifty Deutschmarks per month paid by the *Hrvatski Vojnik* when I had been in Croatia in spring 1992. Inflation had really hit hard. In 1992 a pack of Croatia Filter cigarettes cost about fifty dinars, and a year later about eight hundred dinars. The pay didn't go far. Among mercs, it was typically referred to as beer and cigarette money. No one actually expected to get rich serving as a foreign volunteer in the Balkans save for a few naive dreamers and individuals of a criminal bent.

The Serbs supposedly promised Romanian volunteers land, houses, cash and loot, and they flocked to Belgrade in respectable numbers. Russians were also entering the fight on the Serb side, but up to the time I got there they had only fought in the east. This changed when a group of Russians moved up to the front opposite the King Tomislav Brigade. Some were supposedly former *Spetsnaz* (Soviet Special Operations). The captured Soviet AK-74 I had had my hands on was from one of their dead. I told my troops that if an organized unit of Russians, especially Spetsnaz and/or Afghan War vets, came west, things would really get interesting. They laughed off the idea of fighting highly trained, experienced Russian mercenaries motivated by cash and loot. Before I left Tomislavgrad we received Intelligence reports indicating significant numbers of Russians had arrived in Donji Vakuf about fifty kilometers from Tomislavgrad. The overriding motivation for the Russian volunteers, besides being closely linked with the Serbs culturally and historically, was economic. You've got to figure that things couldn't be any worse in Bosnia for an unemployed Russian soldier than they were in Mother Russia in 1993.

To supplement the meager pay that the HVO volunteers were get-

ting, it wasn't unknown for a soldier or a "volunteer" to engage in some good old-fashioned looting. Liberating the spoils of war, so to speak. Some of the foreign mercenaries in Tomislavgrad were self-admitted looters. As Pat Wells told me when we first met, "I've only made about five hundred pounds sterling (about seven hundred fifty US dollars) here in the last year, though it has its perqs, you know what I mean? You run by a dead body, and he's wearing a Rolex. What the fuck." Because there are way too many guys like this running around war zones, I tend to leave my Rolex and my gold baht bracelet at home. As in Nairobi, my combat-tested Seiko dive watch is temptation enough.

Later Pat told me a bit more about the various methods of looting. "When the shelling is going on is best. Also, if people put down covering fire to keep the snipers off you, you can run up and down the street with a hammer, smashing in the windows and stuffing your shirt, right? Filled our shirts with bottles of perfume, we did. One bloke ran into a store full of Adidas trainers (sneakers) but they was (sic) all little kids' sizes." Pat also told me a story about how he and two other mercs looted the body of a wounded Croat. The soldier was about to be carried away on a stretcher by other Croats, when Pat noticed the trooper was carrying a pistol. During the war any pistol was worth at least two hundred or three hundred Deutschmarks. Pat and the other two mercs rushed over and acted as if they were trying to give the wounded soldier first aid, while stretcher bearers protested. During the delay, Pat looted the pistol from the wounded man's belt. "Fuck it," he told me. "Some other bloke would have just nicked it at the hospital anyway."

These were some of the people I was soldiering with. I could just imagine being wounded and having him and the others pulling off my boots, stealing my gear, and going through my pockets before they gave me any first aid—if they even bothered to unwrap a bandage.

Now I'll be honest—good, clean-cut All-American Catholic boy, not to mention officer and a gentlemen, that I am—as for looting, well, a Renoir might tempt me (just to save and protect it from the vagaries of war, of course), but cheap perfume and a pair of sneakers aren't enough to get this guy to run across the street while under fire. I'm against looting for various moral and tactical reasons. Besides, Glasnovic believed in summary execution for looters. That was reason enough not to loot.

Preventing atrocities and curbing looting was, in fact, one of the very challenging leadership responsibilities during the war. Looting had cost the HVO control of some villages and towns, where troops were so busy looking for loot that they hadn't fully secured their perimeter, and got themselves whacked as a result. Looting occurred on both sides of the conflict. Chetnik counter-attacks were successful because Croat troopers were searching for goodies and partaking of the spoils of war, rather than reorganizing their unit and consolidating their defensive position. Some western military analysts have described the Chetniks as the world's best-equipped and most well-trained looters. They took rape and atrocity to a new plane of heinousness. Atrocities were committed by all the participants in the Balkans war: no one is totally without fault, but the Serbs were definitely the worst with their ethnic cleansing, rape camps, massacres and concentration camps.

Because of the viciousness of the Serbs and the atrocities that the Croats had endured at their hands, I could understand, but not excuse, some of the brutality my fellow soldiers showed the enemy. Admittedly, after you've come upon the remains of a three-year old girl shortly after she has been fed through a wood chipper by a band of slack-jawed Chetniks, the black and white of the law-of-the-land warfare tends to blur. Compared to many of the atrocities perpetrated by your enemy against your civilian population—even your own family—torturing a couple of prisoners for information seems relatively inconsequential. The war in Bosnia provided me ample evidence that man's inhumanity to man knows no bounds. Pat saw two Chetnik prisoners being beaten so badly by Croat troops that he and some other mercenaries intervened. They managed to get one into some kind of civilized custody where he could be treated for wounds. The other had been mutilated and beaten so badly that he was shot out of mercy. Some of the German mercenaries and their Croatian friends took Serb ears as trophies. I expressed my disapproval as tactfully as I could. Those I spoke to ceased such activities, at least while I was around.

The King Tomislav Brigade probably had the best discipline of any unit in the HVO, and that was due largely to their commander. A tall, muscular ex-boxer, Glasnovic wasn't afraid to get physical with a disciplinary problem. Our group had a platoon leader who refused to train. He'd supposedly been a corporal in the old JNA. He told me he knew all there was to soldiering and walked off, leaving his troops in the field and under my control. I took charge of the platoon and put them through our training course without his help. Glasnovic found him in the school's office talking to the secretary and the female medic. I was called out of the field and quizzed as to why the platoon leader wasn't undergoing training. Glasnovic had seen me leading the platoon together with a group of Internationals and wanted to know why. So I told him. When Glasnovic started in on the platoon leader, the recalcitrant troop got mouthy with his brigade commander so Glasnovic just beat the shit out of him, took his weapon, and told him to go home. Right on the front steps of the training school in front of everyone.

The poor attitude and general lack of discipline of some of the troops was disheartening. They failed to understand the importance of training. Until then there had been little emphasis on an organized training program. The negative attitude of the troops toward training was itself a product of the war. Many were more concerned with styling the latest fashions, MTV haircuts, and new earrings than learning to soldier. This was the Pepsi generation, Croat style. Tomislavgrad is located in a prosperous section of the country, and many of the troops barely out of their teens were driving Mercedes and BMWs, courtesy of daddy who was in Germany making some big bucks, usually in the building trades and construction business.

The King Tomislav Brigade troops liked their *pivo* and *rakija*, as proven by the empty cases stacked behind bunkers. Glasnovic later got upset with me, when he saw a rough draft of a story about the King Tomislav Brigade where I mentioned this. But it's a fact: I saw the empties stacked by the case near bunkers. I am neither a propagandist nor an apologist; I tell it like it is. But by way of explanation, I should also mention that the Balkans has fostered several hard-drinking cultures, and those of us who are accustomed to the American military experience are often shocked by the amount of alcohol we see European troops consuming. Another thing I noticed was that the troops, with a lot of downtime on their hands, spent most of their free time hanging out in bars and cafes in typical European fashion. They didn't realize it, but some of them were just waiting to fill a body bag.

There were some veteran fighters, real hard corps, who knew what they were doing and would soak up training like a sponge, but others, kids mostly, had just blown off a few rounds towards the Chetniks and had begun to think they were combat soldiers—and fully-trained combat soldiers at that. Leadership at the small unit level was non-existent. Basic tactical principles like camouflage; noise, light, and litter discipline; providing security during halts on the move; and not skylining yourself or your positions were alien concepts. They had a lot to learn, so I was busy.

That said, the troops were motivated fighters in combat. As Glasnovic was fond of saying, "They know how to give it, eh." Tales of extraordinary heroism abounded. One of the most chilling war stories I ever heard happened right outside of Tomislavgrad. While covering the withdrawal of his unit from a trench line, a very well-known and popular King Tomislav Brigade trooper was wounded in the head by a Skorpion machine pistol bullet, which entered just under the eye. The pain was excruciating. Incapacitated, facing certain capture and torture by the Chetniks who were already overrunning his position, he fired off his last rifle magazine, and drew his pistol. As the Chetniks swarmed his position, he placed it under his chin, and pulled the trigger. Save the last bullet for yourself.

But the lack of strong leadership at the small unit level had caused problems in the previous year. Discipline was a problem, though it was certainly not as bad in the King Tomislav Brigade as in some other HVO units. Although you can't compare the King Tomislav Brigade's discipline to, say, units of the British Army or the US Marine Corps, Glasnovic ran a tight ship. Called "local defense forces," many HVO units were little more than mobs or gangs raised from young men living in a certain municipality.

The idea of suddenly living in a democracy brought with it some mistaken ideas of total libertarianism bordering on anarchy and went to their heads. They failed to understand that military units within a democracy are not democracies themselves. Besides the total absence of anything resembling an NCO cadre, which causes a major breakdown in unit leadership dynamics, part of the problem was that the troops weren't centrally billeted. After serving in the line for four days or so, they would return home and spend as much as twelve days of downtime, much of it lounging about in the Tomislavgrad pubs.

This led to other problems. A story Glasnovic told me is illustrative of what happens when too many troops have too much time on their hands and too easy access to weapons and booze. It was just another day in Tomislavgrad, much like any other, and two troops were standing at the bar in the one of the numerous little kaffee-bar establishments and arguing loudly. One was bouncing an old US Army steel-pot helmet on the bar and shaking his head negatively while the other shook his head positively and crossed his arms. Then, a couple of their buddies got into it. Just when it looked like there was going to be real trouble, the guy with the crossed arms who'd been nodding his head "yes, yes," decided to limber up a little by drawing his Tokarev. Uh-oh. Screw real trouble, this was a *situation*. But wait, amongst all the screaming in Croat, the drunks started to slam wads of dinars down on the bar. Translation: the guy with the helmet said the .30-caliber Tokarev pistol bullet would not penetrate his US Army steel pot.

I've seen discussions like this before: argue, make some bets, throw the helmet, flak jacket, etc. in the alley and fire it up. Inspect the holes. Come back inside. Have some more drinks. No problem. Standard scenario. But in this case, more bets were made. Then the guy with the Tokarev cocked the pistol, grabbed the helmet, and plomped it on his head. Oh Shit! *Ka-Blam!* Instant Jackson Pollock canvas.

If only he would have asked me, I could have told him.

Some of these Croat civilians-turned-defenders-of-the-homeland had a strange attitude towards firearms. To use the word "lackadaisical" would be generous. The fact that some of them were even carrying weapons scared the hell out of me. The Muslim and Serb yahoos were no different. Ignorant *slivovitz*-swilling pig farmer gets automatic weapon. Yippee!

Ever wonder what became of the banjo boy in "Deliverance"? They gave him an AK and sent him to Bosnia.

One of the kids in Tomislavgrad had an uncle or third cousin six generations removed or some damn thing in New York, Chicago, or Toronto (take your pick). Anyway, he wrote a letter begging for a bullet-proof vest. So in the mail comes a Second Chance ballistic vest. Good quality stuff. Probably about six hundred dollars worth of Kevlar. He's so proud of his bullet-proof vest that he wore it around town outside of his shirt, shiny, bright white cover and all. Because otherwise who would know he had a bullet-proof vest, right?

But of course, a few of the boys, jealous no doubt, started to make comments to the effect that it might not be as good as he thought. This soon began to gnaw at the sensibilities, limited as they were, of our combat fashion victim. One day he's at home sitting in the kitchen showing off the vest to grandma. She thinks it so nice that her boy Damir or Vlad or Stefan (take your pick) has this nice vest. So attractive too! He takes it off and says, "Here, Grannie, you try it on." So the sweet little old ninety-some pound Croatian *baka* tries on the vest. (Know where this is going already, huh?) Grandson has a bright idea as Grannie pirouettes, so he draws his Tokarev and . . . *Bang! Bang! Bang!* He hits Grannie three times, point-fucking-blank. She lives. Couple broken ribs, no problem. Grandson then showed the vest around town to all his buddies, proud as punch. Hey, it worked, and what the hell, the bullet dents in the Kevlar weren't a problem.

They were in the back.

CHAPTER 8

LIFE DURING WARTIME

"I think perhaps Special Forces guys and other people like them have depressed metabolisms and they have to be exposed to some sort of danger to feel normal.... [B]efore going to Nam I didn't know that everyone wasn't paralyzed by boredom all the time."

—Jim Morris, *War Story*

On March 25, myself and eleven other foreign mercs, all "volunteered" by me, accompanied a work party made up of occupants of the brigade's stockade to the front. It was the same area where the Germans had ambushed the Chetniks. The work party would dig in some new positions and OPs on the hilltops while we provided local security. We would conduct combat patrols in the area and watch over the labor detail. Two patrols were already out securing the area for the engineers who were busy emplacing minefields.

We loaded up a truck at brigade headquarters and rode up the hill. The weather was warm and sunny, but of course as soon as we got out of the truck it began to rain and sleet. Taking three Internationals with me for security and extra firepower, I led us on a recon patrol through no-man's-land for about four hours. We needed to know what was going on out there. This part of the line was only lightly defended. There were just a few observation posts; the frontline was actually very porous in the mountains. You could move small groups of infantry through here and that was all. Infiltration didn't seem to be much of a problem though.

A wet icy snow, almost sleet, was falling lightly and there was at least a foot of it on the ground. We were in the forest, skirting through groups of evergreen trees and birches. Visibility was poor. I'd only been on the ground fifteen minutes and my pants were already soaked through. I was wearing a US Army ECWS Gore-Tex jacket, courtesy of a friendly supply sergeant in 10th Special Forces Group, and a battered

BDU patrol cap that dripped water from its brim. Cold, icy rainwater trickled down my neck.

We covered as much ground as quickly as we could without giving up our stealth. There was one area where we spotted some Serb bunkers, and another where we found old tracks now filling with snow. The Chetniks had their own patrols out. We were mindful of bumping into them in the thick forest. There was some light automatic weapons fire off in the distance further down the ridge from us, but nothing directed at us. We returned to our own lines and the work party as dusk approached.

I trooped along the forward trace to see how the new fortifications were progressing. As the sun started to die on the horizon and the cold misty rain picked up, I started to shiver slightly inside my soaking wet Gore-Tex. As I walked along the front I was singing to myself a Talking Heads tune called "Life During Wartime." It was very apropos. Hell, it might as well have been our personal anthem. The song talks about having multiple passports and visas, the sound of gunfire up in the distance, being up on a hillside with loaded guns and getting ready to roll and having some peanut butter to last for a couple of days. "This ain't no party! This ain't no disco! This ain't no foolin' around!" Yeah, Baby, tell me about it. Great bass line, too.

I stopped singing under my breath as I approached the guys, lest they think I was some demented headbanger or MTV refugee. As I neared the positions my good buddy Homes was putting in, I noticed the holes were fairly deep. I couldn't figure out why these prisoners were digging so well. Some of them were lazy drunks on their best day. It was especially amazing given the atrocious weather, until Homes told me what was going on. The hard-looking German mercenary was standing behind the group of jailbirds with his machine gun while they dug. The Croat bad-boys thought we were there to make them dig. I laughed. Usually when a German "Nazi" with a machine gun makes you dig a hole in the ground, you have to lay in it when you're done!

With the last bit of daylight we pulled in all our security, loaded up the diggers and their tools in the truck, and drove back to Tomislavgrad. There wasn't much more activity. It was like a *Sitzkrieg*. A few days later Pat and James took two sniping rifles, which they had spent days repairing and cleaning, out on an uneventful patrol with me and Homes. It then snowed for the next week. Tomislavgrad was snowed in, giving a couple of hot shots from brigade HQ an excuse for racing the unit's two snowmobiles up and down the streets. There was no movement at all for the first few days, and after that combat operations were minimal.

We did, however, get most of the guys together again for some training on the Faggot, a Russian anti-tank weapon. The Faggot is a tube-launched, optically-tracked, wire-guided, command-linked, semi-automatic, command-to-line-of-sight (SACLOS) ATGM (anti-tank guided missile). How's that for a mouthful? It's basically a cross between an M47 Dragon medium anti-tank weapon and a TOW, two US Army anti-tank weapons systems. It was a generational improvement on the Russian Sagger. The NATO nomenclature is AT-4 SPIGOT. It has a minimum range of only seventy meters and a maximum of two thousand. Maximum flight time is estimated to be eleven seconds. It has an armor penetration capability of 500 to 600mm. First round hit capability is 90 percent. We watched a Russian training film on the missile. Just watching an old Soviet Army training film was interesting in itself. The Croats could understand it fairly well because of the linguistic similarities between Russian and Serbo-Croat. After watching the pride of Mother Russia rush into mock combat with their Faggot missile launchers, we rode up to the frontline to one of the anti-tank positions to get some hands-on training with it.

The King Tomislav Brigade had some French MILAN anti-tank weapons, used extensively by Croat forces in Bosnia as well. I had already heard rumors that some of the foreign mercs in Bosnia had sold MILAN serial numbers to French Intelligence, who were interested in how some of their weaponry ended up in the Balkans. As soon as we got there, Pat became engaged in frantically scribbling down the serial numbers, hoping to sell them to somebody in the French Embassy in Zagreb. I was prevented from taking photos, as this obsolete missile launcher seemed to be considered top secret by the Croats in charge of it.

Besides the Viking Platoon, the Germans, and the Frenchman Christophe, there were two other Frenchmen. Ex-paratrooper François (a *nom de guerre*), twenty-one, another two-year French Army vet; and Bruno Ruso, twenty-one, a French-Spaniard who had served in the Spanish Paras. Bruno was one of the survivors of Juri Schmidt's disastrous engagement at Duratbegov Dolac, but he never wanted to talk about the ambush. The only comments I could elicit from him were, "Bad, very bad." Bruno had a good-looking, auburn-haired Muslim girlfriend, Amra Jerlagic, who was only about sixteen or seventeen years old. Her English was pretty good—good enough to tell me one day, "I like so much to make the love with my Bruno." Strangely enough, Bruno often had problems with his wounded leg, forcing him to forego field duty and stay in Tomislavgrad to be attended by Amra.

The French and Germans usually got along, but occasionally were antagonistic towards each other, the underlying reason usually being women. The French may think they have a way with women, but compared to the Germans they weren't doing so well in Tomislavgrad. Uwe, with his angel face, was the darling of several older Croat girls. Andy, who bore a striking resemblance to the American movie actor and teen heartthrob Corey Haim, did fairly well with his excellent command of English. Even the tough-looking Homes had a few female admirers.

That week we trained another platoon of troops and watched a live fire demonstration put on by a sister brigade. One of the Sagger anti-tank rockets that was fired went out of control, hit the ground, and exploded behind the observers and the troops maneuvering on the ground. Some people hit the ground as shrapnel, dirt, and rocks flew everywhere. Things were a little tense for a while until it was ascertained that no one was injured. Everyone had a good laugh. The highlight of the day was getting a ride in one of the Russian jeeps the Swedes drove.

The Viking Platoon had increased their number by one with the addition of Carlo, an Italian merc. Carlo was a real ladies' man who spoke no English save for, "Hey, baby, baby." It was his favorite expression next to, "Spaghetti, spaghetti," which is probably more Italian than English, but then again, so was his rendition of "Hey, baby, baby." For some reason the women loved it, and would smile at him when he made kissing noises at them from across the street. If I did that, I'd get my face slapped. The Swedes had to communicate with him through Tony Vucic (aka "Loverboy"), their Croat interpreter, because Carlo did speak a little Croat. The two of them together made quite a pair anytime they even got near anything wearing a skirt.

I wasn't looking for female companionship in Tomislavgrad, but found it anyways. Or rather she found me. One day after coming back from the line, I was having a beer with some of the troops in one of the small hole-in-the-wall bars across the street from the Hotel Tomislav. I left before the party got too wild, and on the way back to my billet I met a Croat girl. I had just crossed the street and lit a Croat filter when a dark-haired beauty came up to me and asked me for a cigarette. While I was lighting it for her, she introduced herself. Martina. She was twenty-two and definitely cute.

Croat girls generally had a low opinion of most foreign "volunteers," but she thought I was different. Later she would tell me that she had seen me a few days before when some of the Internationals were cutting up in the Hotel Tomislav bar. She'd noticed the expression on my face that meant I wasn't happy with their behavior. She decided I was a decent guy when I told one of them to knock it off.

We got to know each other over the next few days, whenever I had some free time after conducting training or running a daylight recon patrol, and before long she was occasionally spending the night with me in my quarters at the Hotel Tomislav. She had to sneak up to my room late at night and past the room next door. Martina didn't care all that much, but I didn't want the others to know I was spending time with her; otherwise, they might cause a problem just out of spite and jealousy. Consequently, our lovemaking was quiet, almost furtive, with me clasping a hand over her mouth more than once. This usually resulted in a fit of laughter by both of us and caused us to bury our faces in the pillows.

Neither one of us thought it was a relationship that was going anywhere. I'd just had two break-ups with girlfriends in the US in the space of about five months, so I wasn't interested in a serious girlfriend or any lasting relationship. And Martina wasn't interested in settling down. She had studied nursing for a while in Zagreb. Her grandmother and a brother lived outside Tomislavgrad and her father was, like so many Croats, a *gastarbeiter* (guest worker) in Germany, where he made good money in the construction business. She let me know right off that she wasn't looking for a free ride to America. We had a few good weeks together and then she went to Split to work. We exchanged addresses and I promised to visit her in Split, but we lost touch. There wasn't time for sightseeing and I had no reason to be in the rear anyways.

Not as many of the guys had indigenous girlfriends in Bosnia as they did in Croatia. Most of the women in Tomislavgrad exhibited the chic sophistication of European girls found in any town of that size. The "in" fashions seemed to be velvet minis with knee-high suede boots. And they wore this stuff within a few klicks of the front. But I never did grow accustomed to seeing the hairy legs of an otherwise très chic Dalmatian beauty encased in panty hose. Someone needs to introduce them to an Epilady. There is something to be said for American girls and their penchant for razors and depilatories. As the joke went—when eyeing the local lovelies it was important to keep in mind the mercs' mustache/teeth rule: "Women here have either a mustache and teeth, or no mustache and no teeth." I once joked among some of the guys that a good pick up-line would be, "Marry me, I'll take you to America, I'll get you a dentist, and we'll live in Santa Barbara.

I say Santa Barbara because the girls all watched re-runs of the TV soap opera Santa Barbara on Croat TV. I had no idea how important it was to the women, though, until one day when I went to Mass. There was a nice-looking Catholic church in town. Quaint and old, in a way we Americans never see unless, well, unless we go to Europe. I'd enjoyed going to mass in Sisak so I went to mass one day in Tomislavgrad. It's true what they say about there being no atheists in foxholes. I like to cover my bets, like the Marine first sergeant played by R. Lee Ermey in *The Siege of Fire Base Gloria*, who told his men, "I talk to Mohammed, Buddha, Jesus H. Christ, and any other religious honchos I can come up with. There is no such thing as an atheist in a combat situation."

The old women were saying the rosary, and after they finished, one of them stood up and addressed the priest. This little old *baka* all dressed in black, with white hair and stout, sensible shoes, started haranguing the padre, begging him for something, and was soon in tears. Geez, what was going on here? This poor woman, I thought. Then a couple of the others joined in. I whispered in German to my buddy Drago, "*Was ist los? Was sagt Oma?*" He said they were asking for a special prayer. The women went on and on. Then Drago smirked a bit, leaned over to me and said, "They want this couple to get back together . . . *sich von einem scheiden, ein Trennung, lassen.*" (They're getting a divorce.) Well gee, I thought, that's nice, these old women are taking an interest in their neighbors, that's the way things should be. The woman finished her plea and they all started praying. I asked Drago if he knew the couple. "Oh, hell no," he said, "I don't watch *Santa Barbara*."

Santa Barbara? These women were saying a prayer, a novena, for two blow-dried character actors on a third-rate soap that no one in America even watched, but which seemed to be the cornerstone of contemporary Croat pop culture. All these women had lost family members in the war—sons, grandsons, nephews. Many had been burnt out of their homes, seen young girls in their family raped—yet here they were caught up in a soap opera, and like good Catholics, they were praying. The whole damn country was being shot up and generally going to hell in a handcart, and they were wasting their prayers on serialized fictional characters whose greatest worry was picking out the right color evening gown and arranging an adulterous tryst before the next commercial. We were pushing the envelope on the outer edge of the surreal. I felt like I'd been painted into a Salvador Dali canvas.

I reached up to touch my face to see if it was melting.

One of the local women, a good friend of most of the guys and almost a big sister to Uwe, was an interpreter for British UNPROFOR. She was missing quite a few teeth and wasn't very attractive, so Uwe nicknamed her "Goofy." She was a real sweetheart and a very well-educated lady fluent in several languages. Besides Johanna, the Swedish journalist, I saw two other foreign women in Tomislavgrad. There was a British UNPROFOR female captain who said she was a PAO-type (public affairs officer), but she could just as well have been Intelligence. She was good looking, on the voluptuous side, and very interesting to talk to. I don't think she really believed I was a former US Army infantry captain. She schizophrenically alternated between wanting to know what I was up to and acting like soldiers of fortune like me were just a rung above pond scum on the evolutionary ladder. If she was Intel, she wasn't very adept at interrogation. After a month or two every female in town, foreign or domestic, was soon a familiar face and after another month or so even the hairy-lipped ones missing teeth began to look good to some of the boys.

Then one day we had a visitor in the restaurant and lounge of the Hotel Tomislav. I pegged her as soon as she walked in. Cold, wet, and tired from a patrolling mission, we had just come in from the field and were sitting down around our usual table drinking espresso while waiting for some hot soup. Pat was already sucking on a Tokat, the vile Turkish cigarettes that were issued with our rations. Usually we smoked the better Croatia Filters, and if somebody bummed a cigarette you passed them a Tokat. No one was moving around much up at the front yet, since we'd just been snowed in for three days, and not all the roads were completely cleared.

The woman was rather attractive, about thirty-five with shoulder length brown hair. I couldn't believe her clothes though. She was wearing a short velvet skirt, silk blouse, nylons and high heels. She flashed a smile and walked over. Female reporter in search of mercenaries acquires target. One or two of the boys looked at her in a way that foretold possible murder, mayhem, and crimes against nature if they managed to get her somewhere alone. Steve and a couple of the Germans boogied. The Germans were wanted men in Germany, and Steve made a habit of calling more attention to himself by acting all nervous about maintaining his anonymity and jumping around than if he had just shut up and stayed out of the way. Pat and Mejor stayed.

Glasnovic had sent her over. Her name was Nancy Nusser and she wrote for Cox Newspapers' Washington bureau. She had heard at the press bureau in Split that there were foreigners serving with the King Tomislav Brigade. The topic of "mercenaries" always makes for cheap and easy sensationalistic copy. After she made a nuisance of herself at the Brigade headquarters, they told her to check the restaurant-bar of the Hotel Tomislav for mercenaries. Hell, where else would they be but in the bar? It should've been her first stop.

She didn't know it, but she'd missed a real scoop. Years later I talked with a SF Chief Warrant Officer, WO5, of Croat ancestry at the Croatian Embassy in Washington, DC, while I was being honored at a formal reception and decorated with the *Spomenicom Domovinskog Rata* medal by the Croatian Prime Minister, Ivica Raca. He was on active duty with the 10th SFG (A) in 1993 and was a frequent visitor to Tomislavgrad. He knew who I was and my background. But he avoided any contact with me or other foreigners. His advisory job with Glasnovic was covert. I had an inkling something was going on—that somebody was in town—just by the way I was sent on missions at times to get me out of the area, or by the lengthy delays in waiting to get into the brigade headquarters to see Nick. Anybody who broke the story at that time of US Army Special Forces actually on the ground in Croatia probably could have grabbed a Pulitzer.

She wanted an interview, of course, and Pat said, sure, no problem, as long as I did most of the talking. I think the only reason he stayed was because he was worried about what I might say. We chatted a little and I mentioned the dangers inherent in being a female journalist wandering around Bosnia. She said something really inane like, "Well, I'll be okay, won't I, I mean, I'm a journalist, I have a press card."

"You mean like this one?" I said, as I flipped out my press card issued in Zagreb. Pat did likewise.

"We'd heard," she said, "that you guys all carried these, but I wasn't sure if it was true. Will they help you?"

"Probably not, even if we're in civvies. The Serbs kill anybody they want," I said, "and if they get you, they'll do more than just execute you."

"Well, I'm not scared of being raped, but I'm worried about being tortured."

Pat and I exchanged glances as if to say, "What a fucking idiot—this chick is totally clueless." The Germans still sitting at the table looked at her with renewed interest, because if she didn't *mind* being raped. . . . I turned back to Nancy and said, "Well, lady, how do you think they're going to torture you?"

Then she said, "Well, I've heard that you guys all save the last bullet for yourself. Is that true?" Pat rolled his eyes yet again. Then he told her about Ted Skinner and Derek Arnold (two volunteers tortured and murdered by their Bosnian Muslim hosts) and a few other atrocity stories just for good measure. Still sitting at the table, everyone agreed that they'd rather do themselves than be captured by Chetniks or Muslims all wound up from the heat of battle.

When a round of drinks came she said, "Oh, let me. I'll pay. How much of this do I need?" as she whipped out a wad of Muslim money. You could've heard a pin drop. I thought the waiter was going to drop his tray. "Not with that you won't," I said, and grabbed the wad of Bosnian money from her before she could wave it around any more. Her big hulking Croat driver-interpreter (who should have been in uniform rather than making big money off the press corps) wasn't clued in enough to make sure she knew enough to pay with Croat dinars. The B-H money was worthless in the HVO-controlled areas of Bosnia. This was basically Croat-occupied Bosnia, annexed as Herceg-Bosna. We explained that the crowded room full of troops had all killed Muslims and lost friends in battles against Muslims. They used Bosnian-Muslim dinars for toilet paper, not to buy drinks with. Just because the line on the map said Bosnia-Hercegovina didn't mean diddly and she better wise up real quick.

Nancy said she wanted to go up to the front and wondered if that was possible. Pat rolled his eyes again and began muttering under his breath. I grinned at him and winked. This was fun. For laughs it was even better than watching Croat militiamen attempt close order drill.

This lady, despite having covered the war in Nicaragua, had obviously not learned a damn thing. I can imagine the accuracy and slant of her reports filed from Managua. Everything about her screamed sixties radical wannabe and left-wing bleeding heart. Regardless of all that, she was an idiot devoid of common sense, but possessing a great set of legs. A combination that some men really like in a woman. Me, I thought that this was the best entertainment we'd had in weeks. It sure beat hell out of the lousy reception on the old black and white TV the guys had "found." It was even better than James' homemade Ouija board, which really freaked out the Brits.

So I told her, "Sure, let's go, I've got a clean uniform you can wear and I've eaten and recharged my batteries and can't get any wetter or muddier than I already am." I told her to go get her boots out of the car. Nancy said she didn't have any boots. No boots? No blue jeans and sweater, etc.? No, she said, just what she was wearing. That was it. Everybody at the table looked at her like she was the dumbest person they'd ever met. It was either that, or she was suicidal. She actually intended to tour the frontline in winter in a miniskirt and high heels. There was snow on the ground and we were in the mountains of western Bosnia. Maybe she thought we'd just drive up to the heated walkways and wheel-chair access ramps to the climate-controlled, wood-paneled bunkers?

I tried to give her some advice. She didn't exactly act like she cared. Then again, who am I, right? What would I know about staying alive in a war zone? When she started to tell me she knew what she was doing, I read her the riot act, as they say back home. She and her driver (I told her to ditch him and find someone who would take care of her before she got herself whacked) had driven from Split to "Tommy-town," just for the day. Just a Sunday drive (it was a Sunday) without food, water, outdoor clothes or survival gear of any kind, but with a wad of the wrong kind of money into the middle of a war zone. A war zone that already had claimed the lives of over forty journalists. If Nancy Nusser was in any way representative of the press corps that covered the war, I understand why so many journalists got themselves whacked in the Balkans. I guess there's something to be said for natural selection and Social Darwinism.

She's just lucky she wasn't wearing a Rolex.

CHAPTER 9

MAD DOGS

"Mad dogs and Englishmen go out in the midday sun."
—Noel Coward, "Mad Dogs and Englishmen"

British mercenaries played a minor, but interesting role in the Balkans conflict. There were many reasons why there were so many Brits fighting in the Balkans. The British do have a reputation for providing mercenaries, with the British regular forces having cranked out some of the most professional fighting men the world has ever seen. Some of it is due to the nature of the British personality and also to the lack of work and the high unemployment in the UK. Just as in any other developed nation, there's obviously not much in the way of exciting employment with a difference to appeal to a former soldier. And of course there was the possibility of money. As Pat Wells loudly announced to everyone within earshot in the Hotel Tomislav bar: "I don't fight for causes or all that. I fight for little slips of paper." Money.

It was also easy for British soldiers of fortune to travel to Croatia. British mercs could cross the channel and then, once on the continent, could ride trains or buses, drive cars, or even hitchhike all the way to the war zone. Some of these guys were in and out for two or three years. It was a damn commuter war.

Unfortunately it was British volunteers who caused the worst mercenary scandal during the war. During the winter of 1991-92, just outside the beleaguered city of Vinkovci, two British mercenaries robbed and murdered a taxi driver. Much like the British mercenaries in Angola under Mad Dog Callan, who killed their own black African troops nearly two decades ago, they did it for simple amusement. One was arrested, but the other managed to avoid apprehension and escape to the UK. This incident became the oft-cited reason or excuse for the eventual termination of the International Brigade and the expulsion of most foreign volunteers.

According to Pat Wells, about three hundred British volunteers served in the Balkans at sometime from 1991 to 1993. This number was arrived at quite simply: Wells and several other British mercs sat down one day and compiled a list of all the Brit volunteers they had met or knew of in the Balkans. They numbered nearly three hundred. Out of this total, a good proportion were cutthroats, wankers, wind-up merchants, time wasters, and bonafide oxygen thieves, but there was also a significant number of professionals.

By spring 1992 when I was in the International Brigade and the war was less than a year old, many British volunteers had already garnered an unsavory reputation, deserved or not. "Colonel" Willi van Noort, who was trained by the British Commandos during World War II, said of the British volunteers then in Croatia, "They're no good, all the time getting pissed up." Interestingly enough, I also heard a very professional Brit merc make the same comment about some of the Dutch volunteers; a few of them were absolutely worthless as well.

Van Noort told me about his run-in with one teenage British "hero." He gave Willi a big sob story about not having enough money to buy a train ticket home to be with his poor, sick mother. "Me mum really needs me at home, she does." Willi, the kind-hearted soul and good man that he is, felt sorry for the teenager and gave the kid money from his own funds, telling him, "Get out of it. This war is no place for you. Go home to England." Weeks later Willi bumped into the beneficiary of his charity in Zagreb, extremely "pissed up." The young "merc" had a bandaged hand and told Willi a long story about having gone back to the front "to help me mates," rather than returning to his mother's sickbed in England. According to our hero he was wounded in the hand while fighting in the trenches outside of Vinkovci. Willi later found out the kid had been on an extended drunk courtesy of the Dutchman's handout, and had lost his finger when he caught it in a tram door while drunk!

During my combat tours in the Balkans I personally served with seven British volunteers, and have since dealt with several other British veterans of the Bosnian War. I met my share of characters. There were some very interesting individuals in Tomislavgrad courtesy of the United Kingdom, including John MacPhee, a huge Scotsman and ex-convict who wore a Black Watch glengarry, boasted that his father was a general in the Black Watch during one of the world wars (a lie), and ran around handing out coins to children. He was harmless enough, I guess, and provided a bit of a diversion when he was talking about feeding some poor unsuspecting bugger haggis. He published a book in Great Britain, *The Silent Cry*, full of fanciful stories and lies about atrocities. I and some others who met him in Bosnia consider him a liar and a nutcase.

Branko Barbic, an Australian-Croat and member of the Croat Parliament, helped a lot of foreign volunteers by sending them on to units, often reaching into his own pocket when they needed funds. In a letter to me in 1994, Barbic said, "Major difficulties seem to have [been] British soldiers probably because they did not succeed to produce the changes they wished. But I have to add that some of them who were highly respected for their professionalism are still members of the Croatian elite units and [a] few of them are married [to] Croatian girls. . . ."

Some British mercenaries found love in other places as well. In that regard I heard a truly sad story. There was an Irishman with "the Crazy Ones" of the Grdani Brigada, who'd been in the Balkans for two years. This Irishman, whose dream was to become a game warden in Tanzania, fell in love with Collette Webster, twenty-seven, an American volunteer nurse. Unfortunately the Irishman lost both of his legs in combat. She nursed him until he was well enough to travel and sent him back to Ireland.

In January 1993, Collette, a store owner from Michigan, decided she wanted to help refugees in Bosnia-Herzegovina. She contacted Suncokret (Sunflower), a Croatian aid organization. She went to work in a camp in the little village of Medjugorje, Bosnia. Medjugorje, the site of repeated apparitions by the Virgin Mary, first seen by six Croat children in 1981, was in 1993 home to both Croat and Muslim women and children forced to flee the heavy fighting in Mostar some fifteen miles away. Collette soon moved to a camp in an abandoned school at Posusje, the temporary home of nearly two thousand Muslim refugees from the Travnik area, and taught English, mathematics and art.

In July, Collette volunteered at Mostar's General Hospital to work in triage, helping to assess and prepare wounded for surgery. But after a month she volunteered as a combat medic with the HVO. On September 27, Collette was in west Mostar, the scene of particularly heavy combat, in an area known as The Rondo. Collette was in a room at the top of an abandoned apartment block with a group of International volunteers when an RPG-7 round came through the window and exploded behind her. She was blown to the far side of the room, conscious but mortally wounded, with serious lacerations to her stomach, liver, pancreas and right arm.

Collette was rushed to the hospital where she had previously worked. Treated by the same doctors and nurses she had recently worked with, Collette died amongst friends. Her body was driven to Split the next day and then flown to Zagreb for cremation. At the morgue in Split, twenty nurses were in attendance, each holding a white rose in one hand and a candle in the other. On October 5, 1993, a memorial service was held in Collette's home town. In attendance, much to her family's surprise, were Croatian expatriates from all over the United States. They had come to pay their last respects to a woman they had never met, but who had done so much to help their people.

While I was in Bosnia in spring 1993, there was a mercenary recruitment fiasco involving some British soldiers of fortune. Intending to form a "crack Commando unit" of twenty to twenty-five men, Bob Stevenson of Shrewsbury, Shropshire, recruited eighteen British "mercenaries," including his own brother. Stevenson, forty-two, had previously served in Bosnia where he'd got himself shot in the leg. He was going back, he hoped, as commander of his own personally raised unit of British mercenaries, the likes of which hadn't been seen anywhere in the world since Angola, 1976. Wages were to be extremely high by Balkan mercenary standards: two thousand pounds sterling a month, about three thousand five hundred US dollars at the time. This was reportedly later changed to two thousand US dollars per month, but it was still excellent pay for a mercenary soldier in the Balkans, most of whom weren't getting paid more than a few hundred a month, if at all. Official rates of pay were paltry at best. A wealthy Bosnian Muslim businessman residing in Great Britain supposedly provided the funds for the relatively high wages. This created quite a stir in the international mercenary community (if such a thing exists) because it all happened when Croat Army pay was only about two hundred US dollars a month and pay in Bosnia for the HVO was between thirty and eighty dollars a month. .

When the mercs showed up for transport to Bosnia they were given a plane ticket and pocket money. Stevenson consented to both print and TV interviews prior to their departure. So much for operational security. Then, in what wasn't exactly a very bright move, he took all eighteen mercenaries into Zagreb en masse. Croatian authorities in Zagreb were, predictably, less than enthusiastic about Stevenson's plan to support Bosnian Muslim units that had by that time been in active combat against the Croat HVO in Bosnia. The Croatians promptly expelled the British mercenaries with their passports stamped, "No entry to Croatia."

Despite the assistance that many British volunteers provided the Bosnian government's *Armija*, Muslim extremists targeted British soldiers of fortune as enemies of their jihad. Ted Skinner and Derek Arnold, two British adventurers, were training Muslim militia forces near Travnik, Bosnia. They were abducted from their quarters by foreign Muslim fundamentalists or mujahideen and local Islamic extremists belonging to the MOS (Muslim Defense Force) of the B-H *Armija*. The two were tortured and then executed in the village of Bijelo Bucje. It's rumored that they were shot in the back of the head execution style. Skinner, who joined the Croatian Army's 77th Brigade during the summer of 1992, claimed to be ex-Australian special forces—he often wore a green beret with a kangaroo badge—and ex-British Army as well. Other Brit mercs who served with Skinner in Bosnia have questioned his background and the extent of his supposed special operations experience.

Skinner was considered very high profile by other mercs. When off-duty he was usually seen in the company of his interpreter, an attractive Bosnian-Muslim woman "soldier." A real cutie. I've seen photos of her sitting on his lap. Not a good idea when there are fanatical Iranian, Syrian, Afghan, Turk and Saudi *mujahideen* running around. He also gave a television interview detailing his cooperation with British Intelligence-gathering elements of UNPROFOR, and was seen in the company of British UNPROFOR personnel several times. Jim Hooper, a professional war correspondent and author, was detained by Bosnian *mujahideen* in the same village, Bijelo Bucje, where the two British mercenaries were executed. Hooper, threatened with execution by some of the local Muslim troopers, was eventually released, just two days before Skinner and Arnold were executed.

Another British mercenary thought that suspicion of Intelligence-gathering (spying) was probably the cause of Skinner's abduction-execution, and that Derek Arnold was killed for guilt by association and for being a westerner. It's possible that the Muslims involved were suspicious of Skinner and distrusted his motives. Simple jealousy can't be ruled out either. Nor can hate. Whether they were executed by fanatical foreign *mujahideen* or the local homegrown variety recently converted to the one true faith is unknown.

After the execution of Skinner and Arnold, other British mercs in Bosnia became very cautious in their dealings, if any, with Bosnian Muslims. When I was in Bosnia, shortly after Skinner's death, they'd all quit working entirely for the Muslims, especially after the fighting broke out between the Croatian HVO and their former allies, the B-H *Armija* Muslims. Several foreign volunteers were killed and a number of others wounded in the internecine fighting. Some of these mercenaries had served with the Muslim forces in the past. They hid their old B-H *Armija* identification cards on their persons, just in case.

British soldiers of fortune fought on all sides of the Bosnian war, including the Serb side. Whether these volunteers were true mercenaries, or Brits of Serbian descent is unknown. Zak Novkovic, a Serb-American who served as a Serb-Bosna Army captain in Sarajevo, says there weren't any British volunteers fighting in units he served with. But Pat Wells claimed that he and another British mercenary were talking in their bunker on the Croat side of the frontline in Vidovice, about fifty kilometers south of Vinkovci, Croatia, one night, when they heard English voices shouting from the Serb side, just to say hello.

In Bosnia there were spooks everywhere. British Army Intelligence agents, aka "green slime" in British Army slang because of their bright green berets, were on the lookout for British soldiers AWOL from their units. A significant percentage of the British mercenaries in the Balkans were deserters who had left the boredom of peacetime army life to fight in a real war in Bosnia. There were also a few volunteers wanted for crimes in the UK. British Military Intelligence was undoubtedly compiling dossiers on their citizens fighting in the Balkans.

At our training center in Crvenice, I had a British Army captain-chaplain ask me some very pointed questions concerning the whereabouts of "the lads." My attitude was that if "the lads" wanted him to know where they were, they'd bloody well tell him themselves. Meanwhile two of the Brits on my team, Mike Cooper and Steve Green, were slipping out a back window of the school building.

"I just want to make sure they're getting their tea, you know. Would you know any of their names?" The "chaplain" was very interested in one particular Brit. "You know, the one with the tattoo of a star on his ear, um, I forget his name." Hmm, a very old technique, that one. The merc he was looking for was AWOL from the British Army, and I knew for a fact he wouldn't associate with this "chaplain" as, according to his fellow British mercs, he was staying as far away from British UNPRO-FOR as possible. Although I'm a lapsed Catholic, the whole episode was upsetting to me, the graduate of a Franciscan university. As a former regular army officer, I'm accustomed to addressing a chaplain with respect and warmth as "padre." I didn't especially care to have some MI puke impersonating a man of the cloth. Besides that, Howard, who'd been in country maybe all of twenty-four hours, was being too cooperative and hanging around instead of beating feet. I tried to get him to leave while the "chaplain" was asking me if I was Canadian or American. He'd heard me yelling at somebody as he drove up. I pretended not to speak English (it makes life easier sometimes if you don't), and at the same time was trying to get Howie to shut up. We didn't need someone from UNPROFOR taking too much of an interest in our operation or us.

Occasionally someone from British UNPROFOR attempted to eavesdrop on a conversation, and I would invariably make a wise-ass statement like, "So, how's the plan to bomb Buckingham Palace going?" Although most of the Brits wore their surplus DPM (disruptive pattern material) battledress uniforms and their beloved SAS smocks, thus making no attempt to hide their nationality, they avoided most of their countrymen in the press and UNPROFOR. This was also a wise course of action in light of the recent torture-murders of Skinner and Arnold. It was quite interesting to see groups of both, in nearly identical kit, sitting at opposite ends of a pub and attempting to ignore each other's presence. Only the English could carry off such a situation with aplomb.

Anytime you get a bunch of itinerant soldiers together cleaning weapons and drinking a cold one you're bound to hear some good stuff. The first time I ever heard of Eduardo Flores it was from Pat Wells while we were drinking a couple of Karlovackos in the Tomislav Hotel pub. Wells had served under Flores in Osijek. A Spanish journalist with no military experience, Flores received a command in the HV because he spoke some Croat and was able to BS the local commander. This incompetent typewriter jockey sent scores of Croat soldiers to their deaths on ridiculous, ill-planned missions. Despite wearing a French parachutist's badge as a "decoration," he constantly denigrated professional soldiers.

Wells and his companions decided to frag Flores during a firefight with Serb forces. As he told it: "We were shooting at him from behind and the bastard kept dodging them. The bloody idiot thought it was incoming. No matter how hard we tried we couldn't hit him. The bastard just wouldn't die."

JoMarie Fecci, one of my generation's most talented combat photojournalists, knew Flores when he was a journalist. She told me she was really surprised when he showed up one day carrying a weapon and bragging to her about commanding a unit of Internationals. JoMarie questioned the wisdom of giving a combat command to a journalist just because he wanted one. Then again, nothing much about the Balkans really surprised anybody anymore. Eduardo Flores would go on to receive the fifteen minutes of fame that Andy Warhol promised everybody. El Commandante Flores got his in a TV documentary. Posthumously.

That TV documentary, *The Dogs of War*, fairly typifies the British mercenary experience in the Balkans. One of the better depictions of mercenary soldiering, it follows the training and operations of Flores' English-speaking mercenary unit in Osijek. According to the documentary, many of their nighttime operations involved setting off explosive charges in Osijek to make it appear as if the Serbs were violating the ceasefire. "Kit," the head trainer of the *Prva Internacionalna Brigada* (First International Company), aka "the Freedom Fighters For Croatia - 3FC, had a well known British mercenary, "Karl Finch" (actually Karl Penta, more recently the author of *A Mercenary's Tale*, a memoir of his experiences in Surinam), for a 2IC (second-in-command) and several other former British soldiers as instructors.

Karl, forty, was formerly a mercenary in Suriname under the *nom de guerre* "Mark Finch," where he and John Richards were the subject of two *Soldier of Fortune* magazine articles. He was one of several English mercenaries recruited for Ronny Brunswijk's Suriname National Liberation Army or "Jungle Commando." Brunswijk, one-time bodyguard for Desi Bouterse, Suriname's Marxist dictator, defected to the opposition as "commander" in 1986.

Kit claimed to be both former 2 Para with service in the Falklands and ex-French Foreign Legion. He was also facing a prison term if and when he returned to the UK. Wells served with Kit and didn't think he was ever 2 Para, but vouched for Kit's French Foreign Legion experience. It is probable that Kit deserted before finishing his five-year

Legion enlistment. As "Colonel" Wim "Willi" Van Noort once complained to me, "Of course these Brits here were all either SAS or Parachute Regiment and they were all in the Falklands!"

Another Brit assigned to the unit was Dave, a crew-cutted redhead with a gold-capped tooth. Dave had "Yorkshire Ripper" painted on his helmet and wore a hand grenade on a cord around his neck. The ex-bar bouncer had obviously watched too many movies. The "Sailor" character, played by ex-boxer Randall "Tex" Cobb in the Vietnam POW rescue movie *Uncommon Valor*, wore a grenade around his neck, just in case he had to pull the pin "and see what comes next." Dave was obviously mimicking this character. Dave said he was just there to kill people. Oh happy day. He was later jailed following the stabbing of a German journalist in a bar room brawl. According to Pat Wells, Dave Stone (supposedly the same guy) was later killed in a gun battle with British police during a bank robbery and he may also have been involved in the murder of the Croat taxi driver that caused so much trouble. Finch, the professional mercenary, said it best when he told the camera, "There's no money in this place so you're gonna get riffraff; there's a lot of 'em."

Some British soldiers of fortune served honorably and with distinction. In doing so, they often went to great pains to avoid the "riffraff" as Finch called them. Military professionals who got down to work and did a job were a godsend to the hastily formed and ill trained HV. While some of these individuals and others of their ilk may have given British soldiers of fortune a bad name, others through their professionalism, bravery, and dedication to their paymasters have only reinforced the worldwide reputation of the British man-of-arms. Unfortunately there weren't enough of those men in Bosnia to go around.

CHAPTER 10

GOING HOME

"And when people are entering upon a war they do things the wrong way around. Action comes first, and it is only when they have already suffered that they begin to think."

—Thucydides, *The Peloponnesian War*

One of my friends in the brigade, Drago, came to me one day while I was eating another greasy cheese omelet breakfast. He was going to the front further north near Suica to visit some friends and wanted to know if he could borrow my helmet. He favored my US Army Kevlar over the steel Yugo Army or East German helmets that most of the troops were issued. He never got my helmet, as he soon invited me to go along.

I quickly ran upstairs and grabbed my LBE, helmet, AK, toothbrush, and spare socks. I piled my gear into the trunk of a battered Audi and squeezed in the back with two others. Drago sat up front with the driver. After a quick stop at the grocery store for a case of *pivo* (which I paid for) and some junk food, we were off for our road trip. Drago slammed a Nirvana tape into his car stereo, and it was like we were a bunch of college boys off to Daytona Beach for spring break. But instead of swimsuits and towels we had a trunk full of assault rifles and hand grenades. The roads were alternately well paved or rutted and mostly covered with snow, but we were there in a few hours.

We drove around a little, bouncing up and down in the decrepit Audi and asking a few people for directions as Drago found our way to his friend's unit. After some handshakes and backslapping I was introduced. We followed a guide to a house near the frontline, where we sat around a typical Herzegovinian living room the grunts had taken over. Some had a *pivo* and others drank Nescafé instant coffee. Cigarette smoke hung heavy in the air. I sat on an old divan with Drago and one of the local grunts, Stefan, who was Drago's cousin. We smoked some of my cheap coronas. Occasionally I could hear the *pop-pop-pop* of rifle fire punctuated by a *brrrp! brrrp!* that I took to be a Sarac machine gun because the cyclic rate was so high.

Drago said that part of the village had taken a real beating. There were many destroyed buildings, and any left standing were pockmarked by shrapnel. Rubble closed off many side streets, and I saw an over-turned car, maybe an old Yugo, I don't remember exactly, burned and stripped, resting on its chassis. No doubt about it, this was a war zone.

As we moved to the front, the banter amongst our group died down and all the noise we made was the clink and the rustle of our gear and a nervous muffled cough or two. Approaching the line of bunkers and open positions along the hillside, we were greeted by several other soldiers, no doubt happy to see some new faces and hear the news from the big city of Tomislavgrad. I wandered around a bit, careful not to skyline myself or walk where there might be landmines. Rejoining Drago, Stefan, and four others, I moved down along the ridgeline to a well-built bunker. Some of the larger bunkers were solely sleeping positions, but this one was set up with observation/firing ports. I really wished I had some binoculars to survey the frontline. Only a few minutes after I had settled inside the fighting position, someone opened up with a Sarac. This was joined by some rifle fire and soon everyone in our bunker was elbowing his way to a firing port opening.

I fired off most of a magazine in rapid-fire semi-auto mode. Braced against a timber, I was sending rounds down range as quickly and as accurately as I could hope. The range to the Serb positions was at the maximum, and I really doubted whether some of the guys with our Romanian AKs had the range. With everyone burning off mags of 7.62mm ammo on full auto, the smell of cordite and hot gun grease soon mixed with the odors of sweat, urine, unwashed clothes and fear in the close confines. The noise of the weapons reverberating within the bunker was deafening. My ears were soon ringing and acrid gun smoke stung my eyes. Stefan started laughing. I don't know why.

One of the guys started yelling and another popped inside and then ducked back out. We all followed him. I didn't know what was going on, but decided it was a smart move to be in the middle of the group that was hastily beating feet out the door. Just as I got outside I saw someone fire an RPG. Whoosh! Oh, Yeah! Now we were starting to put the damn-damn on them! This exchange went on for about half an hour until someone passed the word to ceasefire. Later I walked around with Stefan as he pointed out where the in-coming enemy small arms fire had hit several of the positions. Fortunately we hadn't received any artillery fire as expected.

That night, after helping put a dent in the *pivo* supply, I slept on some old couch cushions laid on the floor. Breakfast was feta cheese and a loaf of bread followed by a half-dozen Croat Filter cigarettes. We said our good-byes and loaded up the Audi for the ride back to Tomislavgrad. So much for a day off. Now it was back to the less glamorous and unexciting job of training HVO soldiers.

The first day back at the schoolhouse brought a surprise. Another Englishman showed up. Jeff (a *nom de guerre*) was a former Brit squaddie and a friend of Pat's. He came down to Bosnia from Zagreb for a few days' visit just after Mike, our demo expert, returned to England. It wasn't a good trade. Another American who joined me later described Jeff as "the most disgusting, infantile person I have ever met." This might be because Jeff's right forefinger was permanently entrenched in his right nostril. He also thought flatulence was the most hilarious thing in the world. Jeff was only in Bosnia for two days before he had a Croat, the training school OIC, reaching for his pistol. Jeff pointed his Kalashnikov and words were exchanged. Not good. It all started because Jeff was teaching some really obscene and rude Croatian phrases to James in the office, in front of Aisha, the medic, and Ankha, the secretary, who had such a nice butt that she drew a crowd every time she walked towards a filing cabinet.

I told Jeff to knock it off. He kept going on and on, and I could see two of the Croats getting a little upset. I'd get upset too, if a bunch of trashy foreigners showed up in my hometown and started swaggering around with automatic weapons and harassing my women while I was in the middle of a war. Then Jeff began breaking wind on purpose in the close confines of the training school office. No wonder many of the Croats hated foreign volunteers, when many of them were low-life, ignorant gutter-scum like Jeff. So that's how it started.

Then, instead of being a man and knocking Jeff on his ass, one of the Croats ran outside to complain to Daddy Glasnovic. On his way he bumped into me, almost bowling me over. I stood in the doorway blocking his way and demanded an apology. This didn't help matters any. I was hoping to stall him and cool him out. Jeff followed him outside and called him a Communist, which is something you simply do not do. That's when the Croat went for his pistol and Jeff leveled his Kalashnikov at him. Never try to play Quick Draw McGraw with a pistol in a flapped service holster against a man cradling an automatic rifle. Dumb, very dumb, but fortunately no one got killed.

To put it succinctly, Jeff was a real piece of trash. Later that same day, during some range firing, he noticed a Croat trooper carrying a nickel-plated Tokarev. Jeff said out loud, "I could get two hundred Deutschmarks for that. He's dead if I get the chance." Great, the guy would shoot you in the back for about a hundred and fifty US dollars. He actually put his foot up against mine to measure my Goretex boots for size, and later admired my beat-up Seiko. After all this James later said to me, right in front of Jeff, "Hey, if we stay past the time our return tickets expire, you'll buy us tickets with your American Express, and I can pay you back, right?" Jeff said, "You've got an American Express?" Oh, did I mention that Jeff was also an ex-convict wanted for various low-life crimes in England including credit card fraud?

At about the same time, a friend of Chris's showed up from Australia. Max (supposedly Chris's cousin) was also of Croat ancestry, and like Chris (how coincidental!) claimed to have been 2 Commando Australian SAS. That was something no one believed, probably because he didn't know one end of a rifle from the other. In fact, he seemed to have no military experience at all. Chris later confided to me that Max wasn't a 2 Commando vet, but yes, he, Chris, was a genuine SAS trooper. Right.

Max fit the image of the stereotypical Balkans merc psychopathic nutcase that he was, and everyone, including his "cousin," called him "Mad Max." According to Chris, Max had done time for bank robbery in Australia. Max was quite proud of his history as a professional stick-up man, despite the fact that he was a failure at it and had gotten caught. That's the interesting thing about ex-cons: they'll brag about the crimes they've been convicted for and the time they've served in prison, obvious proof of a reverse value system and sociopath behavior. I guess in their own weird, twisted way, they think it makes them tough, or a "real man." It's proof only that they're not just scumbags, but stupid, inept scumbags. James was always telling stories in his very irritating black LA gang patois about ripping people off or beating them up. He sounded like the soundtrack for a bad low-budget, rap-gangster movie.

The number of ex-cons, thieves, and mercs of dubious character was starting to multiply in town at an alarming rate. One day Chris, the military policeman, passed me a small parcel to give to Pat. It was marijuana. Oh great, I thought, if I hold onto this and Chris is setting me up, then I'm busted. The idea of an extended stay in a Croat-Bosnian military jail was decidedly unappealing. The problem was, if I ditched it or took it back to Chris, I wouldn't be one of the boys and they'd worry about me turning them in. I would then be viewed as a threat and a liability. Not good, but a good way to get back shot. I solved the problem by stashing it in a potted plant in the hotel hallway until Pat showed up, and then told him to keep the stuff away from me. As for hard drugs, I had to keep my supply of injectable pain medications from my aid bag stashed, because Pat had mentioned mercs dipping cigarettes in morphine stolen from aid kits and smoking them. I knew somebody would try to black-market the stuff if I left it, so while I donated all the rest of my medical supplies to the brigade, I took my Nubain (a morphine substitute) and most of my syringes with me when I left.

That night, after they got the marijuana, Pat, James, Jeff, Green, Pingo, and whoever else got drunk and high. This was the first of several times I had to run next door into a room full of armed, drunken, screaming mercs, wrestle James to the ground, and pull a grenade from his hands. He would hold a grenade in his hand and then threaten to pull the pin. On occasion he tried to pull the pin as my hand was gripped around the frag. He said he just wanted to see what everybody would do. He was a nut for attention.

It's bad enough worrying about Serb artillery, mines, snipers, etc., but after I (the former law enforcement professional) heard first-person stories of rape, murder, burglary, looting and attempted fragging from the men I was supposedly commanding, well, I began to worry about my wallet—and my back.

There were about twenty of us in Tomislavgrad. I was the nominal leader, though for some it was only when they wanted something. Steve Green, the British troublemaker, frequently got his buddy Anders, Jeff the flatulence king, and James going on some criminal scheme, or would incite them with rumors. Pat and Mejor would follow along. Several of the Germans and the French were good, but I didn't have much use for the British. Those in Tomislavgrad at that time were thieves, deserters, and troublemakers. Unfortunately the bad apples damned the rest of us by reputation. Because of this, some Croat troopers and some staff officers in particular were outright hostile to me and other volunteers.

But others were very friendly, especially the more experienced professional types. One of Glasnovic's staff officers, whom I admired greatly, was always telling me jokes. He often referred to me as his

"American *Ustasha*" or "my favorite terrorist." He was not alone in his opinion. One day we were having a fish dinner in a lakeside restaurant with Glasnovic when a Croatian woman asked if I was married. Before I could answer, Glasnovic laughed and said, "Krott? Married? Who would marry a terrorist like him!?"

You couldn't blame some of the HVO officers for harboring resentment towards us, especially when some of the mercs would interrupt Glasnovic with the most mundane problems. The man was trying to run a brigade. Some foreign volunteers, like Roger Risberg and his platoon (who were actually assigned to a different brigade, the Jajacka Brigade) were self-sufficient professionals, but most of the others treated Glasnovic like their own personal squad leader and supply sergeant. If they wanted another magazine for their Kalashnikov, they went running to Glasnovic.

Although Anders conveniently left Tomislavgrad the day after our fight to join another brigade—a smart move on his part—I didn't like the idea of working in an atmosphere where foreign mercs were beginning to turn on each other. I had a talk with Glasnovic before he heard about it from somebody else. When I explained the incident with Anders, he wanted to lock Anders up but I dissuaded him. Anders had already wised up and asked permission to leave town. He left on the bus that morning nursing a badly bruised face.

But the fight was still going to cause some problems. Loud partying two nights before had woken up one of Glasnovic's staff officers, a major, who had complained. The fight and the noise the previous night were sure to generate another complaint. It did. This was the final straw, and the other mercs living in the hotel were sent to a house in the countryside. Glasnovic and I played it off as avoiding trouble because of the complaints, but he really wanted them out of town. I think at that point he would have been happy to see them leave Tomislavgrad altogether.

Nothing much was happening in the war anymore. The Bosnian Serbs were supposed to sign the ceasefire and Glasnovic planned to stop any offensive action at that time. As he told me, "I've got a town full of refugees to worry about. I can't break a ceasefire. If I do, we'll get shelled by the Serbs."

Most of the foreign mercs, save for the Scandinavians, were going to train for another week and then patrol for a week before the ceasefire. My plane ticket home expired in a week, and although I had a thousand dollars for emergencies plus my American Express card, I didn't really want to buy another ticket. And I wasn't going to make enough cash to buy another with my HVO pay being only a hundred dollars a month, and rapidly dwindling due to inflation. Uwe had already invited me to go to Germany with him for Hitler's birthday celebration. Masquerading as an American "Nazi" comrade from the war in Bosnia, I would be able to infiltrate the German right-wing Neo-Nazi underground and write a feature article for *Soldier of Fortune* magazine (which I did). I figured I could do that and then stay with friends stationed at the American army base at Hohenfels, near Ravensberg in Bavaria.

The Germans and French had managed to distance themselves from the others so that they could stay in town. They had a real dump of an apartment, usually littered with trash. It was stocked full of weapons, ordnance and equipment, some of which was undoubtedly bound for Germany or the black market. They could remain there for a while, but would have to move into the house that Glasnovic was setting up for the troublemakers. James was to be the leader. This was laughable as he had, at best, a room-temperature IQ, was functionally illiterate, neurotic to the point of insanity and couldn't read a map. Homes kept quiet about this, but exchanged glances with me when it was discussed. I was sure he was going to keep the Germans from getting whacked under James' "leadership." Pat, the most experienced soldier of the bunch, had elected himself "officer in charge of administration and logistics" for a four-man group, which would grow to seven if Bruno, Christophe, and Fran played along. The Germans wanted nothing to do with it, and the Viking Platoon wasn't officially in a part of the KTB. Sounded like a good way to keep his ass out of the line of fire. He had more military experience and much more time in the Balkans, yet he was going to let James plan the missions. A good way to avoid a psycho. Colonel Glasnovic was just happy they were twenty kilometers outside of town.

Another American, Mike McDonald (a *nom de guerre*), twenty-five, a pre-med student from Springfield, Missouri, and a former US Army Ranger corporal and reserve Special Forces sergeant, showed up at this time. He was lucky to be alive. Mike had traveled to Zagreb and then gone to Croatian Army headquarters. They sent him to some type of Bosnian Defense Force office where he was given a bus ticket to Tuzla. At the last minute, he bought a ticket to Tomislavgrad because he'd read Colonel Brown's article about the King Tomislav Brigade in *Soldier of Fortune*—a decision that saved his life. Tuzla was a Moslem stronghold, and the cadre of Iranian fundamentalists there would have had a lot of fun with an American Ranger.

Many intentional soldiers of fortune traveled to Zagreb and left for home after spending a few weeks and, in some cases, only a few days in country. A significant number of ex-military types decided that the whole fucked-up show just wasn't for them, thank-you very much. Several of these mercs were young Americans, ex-GIs in their early twenties who had expected to find professional units of elite foreigners. They showed up in Croatia or Bosnia, took a look around at the whole unorganized mess, and unceremoniously beat feet for the nearest train station. Young men with a thirst for adventure, but a smattering of experience in dealing with an organized military bureaucracy, were shocked by what they found. Not only was the whole situation chaotic and unlike anything in their national armies, but after a few days or weeks of listless activity punctuated by all-night drunks and no promise of active combat, they got bored and left

I bunked Mike with the Germans and gave him most of my combat equipment, including my web gear and a US Army flak vest I brought back from Somalia. Mike, who had once worked as a bodyguard on a protection detail for Barbara Bush, was only around for about three days when he was in on one of James' "mission briefs," which consisted of James strutting around waving his Kalashnikov in the air and yelling something like, "We gonna get down, muthafucka, we gonna get funky." His plan was to go straight across no-man's-land—disregarding the minefields—and continue to raid the same section of the Serb lines. Night after night. A real tactical genius.

Mike, the former Ranger, was completely dumbfounded when he witnessed this. Definitely not how a patrol order is given in the Ranger regiment. Then, despite the fact that they had all the food they could possibly eat, James, with his uncontrolled criminal tendencies, started talking about stealing pigs and chickens from the neighboring farmers to eat. It wouldn't take long for the farmers to put two and two together: "Hmmm, before foreigners move next door, I have all my pigs and chickens, but after they move next door, I start to lose animals and they start having barbecues."

The crackpot criminal schemes expanded. McDonald decided he'd heard enough of people's plans to rob banks, smuggle weapons into Germany, deal drugs, and sell stolen weapons on the black market. He became worried about his own personal security and decided to leave.

It was a smart move on his part. In that kind of environment, if you don't enthusiastically join someone's criminal plans they consider you a security risk. He knew he wouldn't be safe staying in the brigade, so Mike decided his best bet was to join Uwe and me for the ride out of Bosnia. James' homeboy patois was also starting to annoy him, so after one final nerve-grating day, he packed a few things in a rucksack and snuck out of the billets at about 0300. He was worried the whole time that someone would catch him, and the drunken mercs would hold a kangaroo court and shoot him for "desertion." According to Mike I was tried, convicted in absentia, and targeted for execution because "I knew too much." Knew too much about what, I don't know. Maybe they meant their frequent use of marijuana and their plans to black-market weapons. Mike left all his gear behind, including the LCE and flak jacket I'd given him and his Kalashnikov, so no one could accuse him of stealing a weapon. He legged it cross-country at night, covering about twenty klicks of unknown terrain until he got to Tomislavgrad. A real feat with no map or compass in the pitch-black night of the Herzegovinian mountains. The hard-as-nails ex-Ranger slept in the snow and the bushes outside the hotel awaiting my return.

Meanwhile I was out with Howard, Tony Vucic (the Viking Platoon's loverboy Croat), Uwe, and a couple of the Viking Platoon troopers at the Crvenice "disco" for my send-off party. Roger had left for Sweden to sort out some finances and two others had gotten fed up with the Balkans and left, but most of my Viking Platoon buddies were there. My little departure celebration was abruptly cut short on our way out the door when a drunken Croat (sometimes a redundant phrase) stuck a pistol in my face and told me to draw or he would shoot. Slight problem there, as I didn't have a pistol. I was not having a good week.

Hell, everyone wanted to shoot me.

We got the hell out of Dodge before the Croat gunslinger could ventilate us. Maybe he thought we were UNPROFOR, or maybe his girlfriend told him she liked me or something—who knows? As it was, I almost had to knife him to get out of the damn club. That was something I really didn't want to do, because if I survived the resulting brawl or firefight, I would go straight to a Croatian jail. We treated the whole incident as just another night out. At home in the US it would've been a major event and resulted in the cops showing up, arrests, a trial, etc. Here in the war zone it was just business as usual, and we were just happy to have survived another day of insanity in the Balkans.

We stopped by a house out in the boonies accompanied by much boisterous revelry to retrieve Tony, the platoon Lothario, from the warm embrace of one of the local maidens. I hit the hotel, checked that my bags were all packed, curled up with my Kalashnikov, as was my habit, and crashed out for a few hours. There was a knock at the door and I came straight out of the rack with my AK locked and cocked. I heard the knock again and someone calling my name, a very odd circumstance at 0600 in the morning, because most of the other foreigners could no longer be counted on getting out of bed before 1000, or even noon. I answered the knock with my AK flipped to full automatic. It was Mike. He told me what had transpired and begged me to get him out. I pulled some money from the thousand-dollar stash taped to my leg, and we went straight to the little bus kiosk near headquarters and got him a ticket.

We went downtown to the Germans' apartment to get Uwe. He was very grateful because his alarm hadn't gone off and he almost missed the bus. While we were waiting for the bus Jeff showed up. He had a weapon. Uwe and I had turned our AKs into the arms room, while Mike had left his at the farmhouse. I had my Bowie knife inside the waistband of my jeans and under my jacket where I could get at it.

Mike's disappearance had been discovered, and Jeff had immediately hitched a ride into town. What his motivation was can only be guessed at. It sure wasn't to see his good buddies, Rob, Uwe, and Mike off. We all hated his guts, thought he was a scumbag, and had let him know it on several occasions. It was strange to see Jeff up and around so early in the morning, or anytime before noon for that matter. He was looking very shifty. In fact, his whole demeanor was extremely strange, and he kept loitering next to us like he was up to something. Maybe he was planning on ripping us off—money, watches, credit cards, anything. Fortunately it was daylight and there were people in the street, including soldiers we knew from the brigade. We boarded the bus without any trouble.

The ride out of Bosnia was fairly uneventful. Because he was still wanted for bombing a Communist bookstore in Germany, Uwe was traveling on Andy Kolb's passport. They didn't look the least bit alike, but by some strange coincidence, Uwe looked exactly like Andy's passport photo. We were worried about Uwe and his passport, but we all cleared the police and border checkpoints without any trouble, though

Mike's and my American passports raised some eyebrows. We were so happy to be on our way that we really enjoyed our lunch stop in peaceful Slovenia, where we were so busy slamming Slovenian beers that we nearly missed the bus. We jumped up and ran across the roadside tavern's parking lot shouting obscenities as the bus driver started to pull out without us. We sweated out a couple more police checks at the Slovenia-Austria border, wondering if we'd get questioned or if Uwe would get nabbed with Andy's passport.

The next little bit of excitement was at the end of the line in Salzburg. We had our bags searched after we unloaded at a bus station in Austria. The cops were just walking by. Before we could get into the station they stopped us. The Austrians began asking Uwe questions. They asked him where he'd been. He shrugged and said, "*Urlaub*" (vacation). They asked why he was in Bosnia, and again he replied, "*Urlaub*." After the third question and response of *Urlaub*, I was ready to scream. Mike was faking shivers and trying to look miserable. I eyed the Glock 9mm pistols hanging from their belts. The policemen then checked our bags. One looked quizzically at the movie film can-shaped Russian DP machine gun magazine I was taking home. "Souvenir," I said. If we'd been smuggling war souvenir weapons, we'd have been busted right there.

I loaned Mike some more money for a train ticket to Milan so he could catch his flight, and saw him off. Then Uwe and I caught a ride across the German border with his Nazi friends who came down to Salzburg to pick us up so we could avoid a border check.

I was out of Bosnia and I didn't plan on going back anytime soon. Besides, I had heard there was work in Africa . . .

EPILOGUE

After I left Bosnia in 1993 I returned to my home in Olean, New York for a short while before visiting special operations units in Estonia and Latvia. In January 1994 I traveled to the Sudan, spending nearly five months in the field with the Sudanese People's Liberation Army. I got a lot of combat experience versus Islamic *mujahideen*, including firing a 12.7mm machine gun into a 250-man human wave attack. I got wounded and was rocketed, bombed by Antonovs, and sniped at. Before returning home I visited friends amongst the Samburu tribe of Kenya and looked up an old acquaintance, Wilfred Thesiger, noted author, explorer, eccentric adventurer, and ex-SAS major, in Maralal.

Upon my return home I worked briefly in corporate security before being hospitalized with an unknown viral infection that attacked my liver and brought on a case of Bell's Palsy (facial paralysis). A few weeks after leaving the hospital, I visited the French Foreign Legion base at Kourou, French Guiana, as a guest of the 3rd *Regiment d' Infanterie Etrangère*, and in November I visited the Jugoslav 63rd Airborne Brigade in Nis, Serbia, with a group from the Hellenic (Greek) Commando Association. There I re-fought the defense of Mostar on cocktail napkins with Serb paratroopers who had fought on the other side of the Neretva.

At the time of the first draft of this book (1995), I hoped to return to the Balkans and make a meaningful contribution toward a lasting peace. I soon changed my mind.

In February 1995 I observed winter warfare training exercises conducted by the Canadian Army before I returned to work in the corporate security field. In January of 1996 I made a parachute jump in Honduras with their Paratroop and Special Forces (Teson) units after jumping with my friends in the El Salvadoran Special Forces for the first time since 1989. In the spring I journeyed to South East Asia. I worked on a medical mission in Cambodia and was ambushed by Khmer Rouge at a roadblock on my way to sightsee in the Killing Fields. In Thailand I jumped with the Royal Thai Marine Corps Recon battalion and I also jumped in Myanmar (Burma) with the Burmese Army. I then infiltrated back into Burma where I spent time with the Karen guerrillas and helped train a sniper platoon. After four days at home I went on to jumps in Holland and jumps and scuba diving in Estonia with my good friends in the Estonian Special Operations Group. During the summer of 1997, I finally found myself in Malongo, Angola, training a 125-man paramilitary guard force for Chevron and the Cabinda Gulf Oil Company

In 1998 I traveled around the world on a twelve-country adventure, seeing action in Afghanistan with Taliban troops and later in Sudan with my old friends in the SPLA. These adventures showed up on the Discovery Channel and I even got a camera credit. During that trip I survived a terrorist bombing of my hotel in Kampala, Uganda, and treated the wounded there and at a subsequent bombing at the Nile Grill nearby a few hours later. A month after returning home I returned to Africa and made a parachute jump with the South African National Defence Force's 44th Parachute Brigade and spent some time with various South African police agencies and got in a little action with them.

Over the next two years I made trips to war zones in Colombia, Sudan, Uganda and Burma. In Burma I made a grueling foot infiltration across the Thai border and through the mountains to a jungle clinic and then survived the "escape and evasion" back as Tatmadaw forces hunted for us. In 2001 I made parachute jumps in Czech Republic, Slovakia and the Ukraine, and I caught the tail end of the war versus Albanian guerrillas in Macedonia where I nearly got my ass blown away by both sides. The next year I jumped in India with their Special Forces over the Taj Mahal. In 2003 I went to work for a Canadian oil company in Yemen and then as a civilian security "contractor" in Iraq in the winter of 2003, where at this writing (2008) I am still employed.

To the best of my knowledge via correspondence and through word of mouth, this is what's happened to some of the characters in this book in the last fifteen years or so.

Anders "Pingo" remained in western Bosnia for a while, but according to Wells, Anders left the Tomislavgrad area around Christmas of 1994. He is a member of a foreign volunteers for Croatia association.

Christophe and his sidekick François returned to France after the abortive amphibious recon-raid. Chris found work in his chosen civilian vocation: filmmaker. The last I heard, he was a direction assistant, but had put all his money (and hopes) into his own film, for which he was producer and director. He expected to release it in 2001.

Howard proved himself to be a competent mortarman. As of spring 1994, he was rumored to be back in the United States and delivering pizzas for Dominos somewhere in the Midwest.

Mike Cooper is back in England. For several years he lived the life of a country squire and wrote technical manuals. He currently lives in London and works in concert productions. We correspond occasionally.

The Croat Commando unit saw heavy combat outside of Dubrovnik in the fall of 1992. They executed a night infiltration attack on a Chetnik bunker complex, receiving light casualties, but overrunning the position and wiping out the Chetnik defenders. They suffered two killed. Blondie received a discharge and was last known to be working in Sisak. Italiano likewise received his discharge, and was known to be hanging around Sisak, still chasing the ladies and his fortune. Pedrag, the commander, was wounded by mortar fire in the Dubrovnik action. He was sent to Holland for facial reconstructive surgery. Pedrag was later killed in the Krajina campaign, as were several of the others, most of whom had returned to active duty for the Krajina Offensive aka "Operation Storm" in August 1995. According to a Croat general I spoke with, Pedrag's brother Drago was the commander of the Croatian Army's training command in June 2002.

Bruno Ruso left Bosnia in July 1993 with Amra Jerlagic, his Bosnian-Muslim girlfriend, who was pregnant. Lucas, their son, was born in Madrid in January 1994. Bruno worked for some time in private security before rejoining the Spanish Army Special Forces. Amra abandoned Bruno and their child and works in Spain as a high-speed train stewardess. Bruno has served in Spain's "green berets" since 1995, including a two-year assignment to the Eurocorps in Strasbourg, and was promoted to staff sergeant in 2003. He deployed to South Lebanon in 2006 with his A-Team and is now serving a tour in Afghanistan. He still yearns for a life of even greater adventure, however, and is considering leaving the army to be a private security contractor.

Karl Penta, aka Karl Finch, was arrested in Osijiek while serving with an English-speaking merc unit, imprisoned, then repatriated. In 2002 Penta published *A Mercenary's Tale*, a memoir of his experiences as a mercenary in Surinam.

Eduardo Flores was court-martialed by the HV and executed for the black-marketeering of stolen weapons.

François, aka "Fran," was one of the two Frenchman (the other being his friend Christophe) who served with the King Tomislav Brigade in spring 1993. He later fought along with the Karen in Burma in 1994, was a participant in the Comoros Islands coup with the infamous mercenary Bob Denard in 1995, and was jailed in France for more than a year because of his merc activities in Burma. I was told he committed suicide in Paris with a .45 pistol January 9, 2000 (ironically, the birthday of Lucas Ruso, the son of his KTB comrade, Bruno).

Davor "Joe" Glasnovic was ransomed for twenty thousand Canadian dollars after spending fifteen months in Serb captivity where he nearly starved to death. While a POW he received brutal beatings that broke ribs, and he was periodically tortured by the Serbs. He underwent reconstructive surgery for his mutilated face. As of 2003 I heard he was living, as I was at the time, in Edmonton, Alberta.

Zjelko "Nick" Glasnovic became a colonel general in the new Bosnian Army. He was sworn in on May 26, 2000 as Entity Armed Forces Inspector General by LTG Ron Adams (SOFOR commander) for the term of one year. He continued to serve with distinction, until resigning to enter politics.

Steve Green attended the 1993 SOF convention in Las Vegas with Mike Cooper. I was dissuaded from beating him senseless by the simple fact that I couldn't figure out how to do it without being arrested. He kept his distance. According to Cooper, Green married, had three kids, and divorced.

Thore Hansen is back in Norway, working for a security company and very bored. He actively pursues contracts with corporations, governments and private individuals.

Heiko was wounded by friendly fire in the summer of 1993. His whereabouts are unknown.

Uwe "Honecker" Herker was still wanted by the *Bundespolizei* when he returned to Germany. He did his prison time (taking computer courses) and was released in early January 1996. He spent New Year's

1996 with Homes Homeister and Tom Kelly, a King Tomislav Brigade veteran and close friend whom I knew from Fort Benning. It is rumored that German Intelligence wanted him to return to Bosnia as a confidential informant. Another KTB veteran told me that Uwe died in mid-October 1996 in Germany of a heroin overdose.

Michael "Homes" Homeister: though I expected he'd marry the daughter of the HOS commander who owns the *Za Dom* (The Homeland) bar in Tomislavgrad, Homes returned to Germany and was picked up by police. Homes traveled on a Finnish passport belonging to "Marco," who looked somewhat like Homes. Marco Casagrande, a Finn with the Viking Platoon, later wrote a bestseller, *Hitchhikers on the Road to Mostar*, under the pseudonym Luca Moconesi. Marco's book upset the sensibilities of a female left-winger in the Finnish government, and he was threatened with indictment in international court for war crimes. The German police found Home's own passport on his person and sent him off to do his prison time, where they let him out on weekends. He was released in the fall of 1996. We corresponded regularly for several years. Homes became gainfully employed, joined the *Bundeswehr* Paratroops reserve, and became a husband and father.

Werner Ilich, according to Kev Von Rees (an American who served with the MUP), was seen on a TV program wearing his HV Brigadier's uniform. A friend on the Croat General Staff told me that Ilich is indeed an officer, but in a position of little consequence.

The International Brigade, established by Branimir Glavas in October 1991 and previously headquartered at Operativna Zona Zagreb, Ulica 292, Kagarna 1, in Zagreb, became officially defunct in spring 1992. The powers that be in Croatia decided they had no need of foreign volunteers. Most foreigners or "outsiders" in Croatia proper received their discharges sometime in 1992 and went home. Some, mostly those of Croatian parentage, are still in Croatia. Others remained because of their political connections and/or involvement in training programs. In late 1995 some foreign volunteers were still finding it possible to sign on with a unit, and saw combat in the last battles before the Dayton Peace Talks. In March 1996 I learned that all Internationals in the HVO (Bosnia) were thrown out of the country, save for three who received Croat citizenship. A few others stayed on as civilians.

"James" is probably still wanted in Los Angeles County for some crime. According to Wells, in 1993 he was allegedly popped at the

Slavonia border and his military contraband confiscated. He then went back to the States and later returned to Bosnia. He had his photo taken with Bob MacKenzie in the winter of 1994-1995, and was last seen by Pat Wells (whom he stayed with in Bristol) in Bosnia in February 1995. In September 1995, Tom Kelly informed me that JR had lost some toes to a landmine during the past summer.

"Jeff" was, according to Wells, caught stealing weapons to sell on the black market. He was requisitioning explosives, grenades, mines, and anything else he could get his hands on, and signing Pat Wells' name. Wells went into one of his psychotic tempers and nearly beat him to death with a tire iron. Would've been no great loss.

Andreas "Andy" Kolb, aka "Bismarck," was killed in action in or near Gornji Vakuf on November 15, 1993. He was struck in the head by shrapnel and was dead on arrival at the hospital. I first learned of his death from his mother. Homes later provided the details of his death.

Eugene Lee: after returning to the States in 1992, the self-described Dead Head shipped supplies to his old unit in Croatia, getting them scopes and scope mounts for M-44 Mausers so they could use the old bolt-actions for sniping. Lee was awarded the *Spomenicom*, the HV Service Medal for the War of the Homeland, by a grateful Croatian government. He finally returned to Croatia in fall 1995 with Carl Graf. Eugene visited his old friends from the Brinja Black Wolves and was recommended for a lieutenancy in the HV. The last time we spoke "Geno" was designing crystal jewelry in Nevada.

John Major, aka "Mejor" or "Meyor": Wells last saw the Franco-Hungarian Legionnaire in February 1995. He was doing well and attempting to get a Croat passport. Tom Kelly reported to me in March 1996 that he received his papers.

Mike McDonald: I visited McDonald several months after we left Bosnia. He was back in college in Springfield, Missouri, co-habitating with a very pretty nurse, and looking for a good war. In early 1995 he was shot, under mysterious circumstances, in the leg with a .357 magnum, shattering his femur. He recuperated and moved to Arizona to pursue a private pilot's license with his GI Bill, hoping to fly cargo in the Third World. In 1997 I arranged a position for him on my training team in Angola. In 1998 he was in Santa Cruz, California, a serious student of Eastern philosophies, and planning a move to Hawaii.

We caught up with each other recently while I was working in Yemen and Mike was working in Kuwait. He became one of the new breed of corporate mercenaries working as a contractor in Iraq. We both went to work in Iraq in 2003. During a break from Iraq, we were on the same Blackwater security team for the hurricanes in Louisiana. He returned to Iraq as a "shooter" on a Protective Security Detail, and we worked together for the same company briefly. He was wounded by an IED in 2007 and a year later is still recovering from wounds. He owns an eco-travel lodge in the Amazon.

Robert Callan MacKenzie: a memorial service was held for Bob in Coronado, California. His remains were never recovered.

Alex McColl retired from *Soldier of Fortune* magazine. He died in a car accident in Nebraska in October 2002.

Andy Meyers is still MIA in Sierra Leone and presumed dead. A captured RUF guerrilla claimed he saw a captive Meyers suffering from a stomach wound a few days after the firefight.

Johnny Rajkovic turned down a promotion in the HV and took his discharge to pursue a civilian career in Sisak. He twice visited my home in Olean, New York.

Somali Interpreters: I bumped into two of my interpreters as well as the lovely Suad Yusuf in Nairobi, winter 1993–1994. I was told that two interpreters had died during the Battle of the Black Sea ("Black Hawk Down") while riding on a rescue convoy with 10th Mountain Division troops.

Joe "Crazy Joe" Stelling continued to serve in the Balkans and eventually returned to the Netherlands. A somewhat inaccurate UN Human Rights Report concerning mercenaries by Enrique Bernales Ballesteros referenced Joe and some others. Joe sent me a Christmas card a few years after our time with the Sisak Battalion, so I guess all was forgiven.

Bob Stephenson reportedly went to prison in the UK for a spate of armed robberies committed with some of his would-be mercenaries.

Douwe Van de Bos went back to Holland and became actively involved in the Netherlands-Croatian Work Community.

Viking Platoon (or *Viking Vod*): one of the Scandinavians went on to serve with Karen guerrillas in Burma. We keep in contact. Another, a Dutchman who joined after I left Bosnia, contacted me in 2003 while I was in Holland and threatened my life. Why, I don't know. We'd never even met. I told him what hotel I was staying in and waited up all night in the lobby for him. The hero never showed.

Wim "Willi" Van Noort, the Dutch colonel, worked on training a Croat airborne unit in 1993 taking a ten-man cadre to Texel Island,

Holland, for parachute instruction. He was later promoted to brigadier and was involved in the planning of a bloodless coup in Croatia. It was pre-empted and Willi's patrons fell out of political favor. Willi took a round below the left knee while on the frontline near Stankovci south of Zadar. He went back to Holland for surgery and married one of his nurses. He visited me at my home in Olean, New York in February 1996. He currently lives in Holland and in Florida, USA. I still hear from him occasionally.

"Pat Wells" returned to Bristol. According to several British volunteers and Tom Kelly, Pat shot and killed the French Foreign Legionnaire veteran Ronnie Pereversov, an Anglo-Canadian volunteer in Bosnia, who was also a good friend of Kelly's. The head of a Croat volunteers' association in the UK maintains that Pereversov "was shot whilst asleep, reportedly by a British volunteer whom Ronnie had recently uncovered masquerading as an ex-Legionnaire in the village of Zupanja near Mostar in 1995."

Pat attended the SOF convention in Las Vegas in 1995 with another Bosnia vet, "Ian." They were guests in my home in Olean for several days until Pat got drunk, went off on one of his violent rages, beat up Ian in the back seat of my car as I was driving, and threatened to kill both of us. The police (in neighboring Bradford, PA) got involved, but fortunately we all stayed out of jail. I drove them both to Niagara Falls to see the sights, a cocked .380 in my pocket, and then took them to Buffalo and put them on a bus for New York City. Other than that we're still "friends." Ronnie Pereversov is still mourned by many and a payback for his murder is a distinct possibility.

GLOSSARY

AATV—Australian Army Training Team Vietnam. Raised in 1962 to train units of the army of South Vietnam, it consisted of approximately thirty officers and warrant officers. The unit increased to approximately one hundred. The AATTV had the longest tour of duty of any Australian unit in Vietnam, serving from 1962–1972, A total of a thousand men (990 Australians and ten New Zealanders) served with the unit). Of these, thirty-three men were killed and 122 wounded. Amongst other decorations awarded, the unit received four Victoria Crosses.

AO—Area of Operations.

APC—Armored Personnel Carrier.

Armija, B-H—The army of the recognized state of Bosnia-Hercegovina. Initially composed of units from all three major ethnic groups, it is now almost entirely Muslim.

ARVN—The Army of the Republic of Vietnam. (Pronounced "Arvin.")

A-Team—The twelve-man "Operational Detachment–A," or ODA of the US Army Special Forces.

BDUs—Battle dress uniform, the standard woodland camouflage combat-utility uniform of the US Army.

Blue-on-blue—Slang for friendly fire exchange. Blue is always used to denote friendly unit dispositions on situational maps and overlays, while red denotes the enemy.

Bojna—Battle.

Boonies—The woods, jungle or other wilderness terrain, also to describe a jungle hat, aka a "boonie hat."

BOQ—Bachelor Officer's Quarters.

Camp MacKall—The location of the US Army's Special Forces Qualification Course near Fort Bragg, North Carolina, where "Green Berets" receive much of the training. Recently re-named after my former commanding officer, Colonel James "Nick" Rowe, assassinated in the Philippines.

Chalk talk—To explain something on a chalkboard, etc.

Chetniks—A generic term for Serbs and Serb nationalists used by Croats and Muslims. "Ceta" was a Serb word for "armed unit." The Chetniks are a Serb nationalist movement that originated in the nineteenth century after the founding of the Serbian kingdom in 1830 when the *Hajduka Cetniks* (armed brigands) became an irregular, but recognized militia within the royal Serbian Army. During World War II, they initially wanted to ally themselves with the Nazis, and under Mihailovic fought a patricidal war against their fellow Serbs in the "partisans," massacred Croats and Muslims, and even fought alongside the Italian Fascists and the Croat *Ustasha* (something they are now loathe to admit). Symbolism includes the skull and crossbones, the Monarchist crown, and the "Four C's": *Samo Sloga Srbina Spasava* ("Only Unity Will Save the Serbs"). It is said that the "Serbs kill without compunction and die without complaint."

Claymore—The US Army M18A1 anti-personnel mine or "Claymore" is named after the Scottish broadsword. Weighing only 3.5 pounds, it is a directional, fixed fragmentation mine emplaced with its adjustable scissors-type legs. Primarily designed for use against massed infantry troops, it is command-detonated by means of an electrical firing device colloquially known as a "clacker" and firing cord with blasting cap. When detonated, a 1.5-pound charge of C-4 plastique explosive sends a matrix of steel spheres (all packed into an OD green plastic rectangle with curving bow facing the direction of fire) out in a sixty degree fan two meters high and fifty meters wide at a range of fifty meters. The

Soviets and the JNA had their own copies of this weapon. Local fabrications also existed in the Balkans.

Combat Arms—The fighting branches of an army: infantry, artillery, armor, combat engineers, and of course, Special Forces.

CZ-75—Czechoslovakian (now Czech) service pistol made by Ceska Zbrojovka. A 9mm semi-automatic, it was the "best" sidearm available.

Crater and Fragment Analysis—Proper field analysis of artillery and rocket craters and the surrounding debris to provide information for accurate counter-battery fire.

Delta Force—The 1st Special Forces Operational Detachment-Delta (SFOD), more commonly known as Delta Force, was activated at Fort Bragg, North Carolina on November 19, 1977. The unit was the brainchild of Colonel Charlie Beckwith, an SAS trained US Army Special Forces Officer. Beckwith commanded Project Delta in Vietnam, a forerunner of SFOD-D, and was selected by the Pentagon to form and train an elite counter-terrorist unit. Delta was the unit involved in the aborted rescue of the Iran hostages in 1980, and has carried out several successful counter-terrorist missions around the world. The US Army does not officially acknowledge its existence to the media.

Desants—From the Slavic (Russian) for a landing by helicopter (descent), and can also mean a unit. In Russian a *desantnik* is a paratrooper.

Dittybopping—Walking in a combat zone in something less than a fully alert manner.

EOD—Explosive Ordnance Disposal.

Faggot—Soviet ATGM (anti-tank guided missile).

Frag—A shrapnel fragment from a grenade, rocket, or shell. Also, to frag someone: to kill a commanding officer with a fragmentation grenade (or any other means).

Freak or freq—Military slang for radio frequency also known as a "push."

Front leaning rest position—jocular description of the pushup starting position. Since pushups are sometimes used as punishment (especially for recruits), putting someone in "the leaning rest" is meaningful. Extended time in this upright pushup position quickly causes fatigue and pain.

Fougasse—Homemade jellied gasoline, usually stored in 55-gallon drums with a "kicker" charge in the bottom and detonated by command as a perimeter defense weapon. A French innovation in Indo-China, it was a popular improvisation of US forces in Vietnam.

GPMG—General purpose machine gun.

Hajduk—Mountain bandit.

Hooah—US Army motivational exclamation.

HOS—*Hrvatske Odbrambene Snage*, or Croatian Defense Force, the military wing of the HSP. Pronounced "hoss."

HSP—*Hrvatska Stranka Prava*, or the Croatian Party of Rights. Founded in 1880 and revived in 1991, this conservative right-wing nationalist organization has historical links to Ante Pavelic's World War II *Ustasha* party, the NDH. The HSP and the HOS are often referred to as "Nazis." Dobrislav Paraga, the HSP leader, has said the World War II *Ustasha* (who were entrusted by the SS to run the Jasenovac concentration camp themselves) were "too liberal."

HV—*Hrvatska Vojska*, or the Croatian Army. Pronounced "haw-vay."

HVO—*Hrvatsko Vijece Odbrane*, or the Croatian Defense Council, the Army of the semi-independent Croat state of Herceg-Bosna in Bosnia. Pronounced "haw-vay-oh." A running joke in Bosnia was that HVO stood for "*Hvala* (thank-you) Vance-Owen."

Indigs—US Army slang for "indigenous personnel," meaning natives or locals.

JNA—*Jugoslovenska Narodna Armija*. The Yugoslav People's Army. Sometimes mistakenly translated as Jugoslav National Army.

Kabar—A fighting knife, originally the USMC fighting knife of World War II; so-called because its best-known maker was KABAR of Olean, New York.

Kaserne—German for "barracks" and also US Army slang for the same.

Killzone—area in front of an ambush where the enemy is trapped and annihilated by concentrated fires.

Klick—Military slang for kilometer.

Kosovo—*Kosovo Polje*, "the Field of Blackbirds," Serbia's historical Golgotha, has been "turned into an infinite expanse of Serbia's imagined glory." As early as 1992, many Internationals were predicting an inevitable civil war in Kosovo.

Krajina—Borderlands of Croatia, from *Vojna Krajina*—military frontier.

LCE—light combat equipment, also LBE – load-bearing equipment, aka web gear, TA-50, and ALICE (from its US Army acronym); also for Brits, "kit." A soldier's LBE (usually web suspenders and belt) with canteens, magazine pouches, and ancillary equipment is the bare minimum necessary for survival in combat and the field.

LRRP—Long-Range Reconnaissance Patrol. Pronounced "Lurp."

Mad minute—When soldiers put their weapons on rock n' roll (automatic) and expend large quantities of ammunition. Support weapons may be fired as well. In a real-world tactical situation, this is called firing the FPF (final protective fires) to halt an attacking unit that may overrun your position, or to delay same, preparatory to "bugging out."

MILAN—*Missile d' Infanterie Léger Antichar*, a French anti-tank rocket. MILANs were used extensively by Croat forces in Bosnia.

Milicija—police. A *milicionar* is a policeman.

NCOs—Non Commissioned Officers (sergeants). An NCOIC is the NCO in charge.

NDH—*Nezavisna Drzava Hrvatska*, the Independent State of Croatia (World War II) led by Ante Pavelic.

NODs—Night Observation Devices, also referred to as STANO—Surveillance, Target Acquisition, Night Observation.

O'dark-thirty—An ungodly unreasonable early hour of the morning when normal people (civilians) are still sleeping.

OPSEC – Operational Security.

Panama Triangle—Supposedly so-named by instructors at the old US Army Jungle Warfare School in Panama. Technique of putting a unit into 360-degree security. A triangle is formed to circle the wagons; e.g., a company sets in with 1st platoon on the left side of the triangle, 2d platoon on the right, and 3rd platoon forming the base. Machine guns are usually sited on the points so that they can fire down along the front of the unit. This technique is more tactically sound and easier to implement than putting the unit in a circle. It also provides the best interlocking fields of fire and works well for large patrol bases as well.

Phoenix Program—The organized targeting of the VCI (Viet Cong Infrastructure) for assassination by US special operations during the Vietnam War.

Pivo—Beer: the popular Croat brand was *Karlovacko*.

Praga—Slang for multi-barreled anti-aircraft gun.

PT—Physical training.

Puska (or *puska mitrajet*)—Rifle, machine gun.

Rakija—Plum brandy or *slivovitz*. The popular Croat brand was *Loza*.

Recon—To reconnoiter or, pertaining to a military reconnaissance, what the Brits call a "recce."

Ring-knocker—Slang for a USMA at West Point graduate because of the school ring, usually worn.

RPG/RPG-7—Rocket anti-tank grenade launcher. Of Soviet design (but widely copied), the *Reaktivniy Protivotankovyi Granatomet* was introduced in 1962. Weighing only 19.6 pounds, it was designed principally for use versus armored vehicles. It can also be employed against bunkers, fortified buildings, and troops. It's an "all-purpose bazooka" and remains in wide use throughout the world.

Rucksack flop (also "to go tits up")—To sit down and lean against your rucksack. A very untactical position.

SA-7 SAM—Soviet hand-held surface to air missile. A.k.a *Strela* or Grail.

S-3—The staff section designation for training and operations in an American battalion or brigade HQs. Division staff is G-1, G-2, G-3, etc.

Sabor—Croat parliament.

Sahovnica—The crest of Croatia, a red and white checkerboard shield surrounded by a wreath and surmounted by a five-pointed crown which contains five different historical and heraldic symbols.

SAMs—Surface to Air Missiles.

Sand tables—Terrain model used for briefings.

SAS—An elite British special operations unit. The British SAS (Special Air Service) was founded by David Stirling during World War II. SAS troopers are experienced, mature troopers who have volunteered from other units and passed a rigorous selection course. Australia and New Zealand each have a SAS Regiment and the now-defunct nation of Rhodesia had an SAS Regiment.

SDO—Staff Duty Officer.

Slivovitz, sljivovic—Balkan plum brandy.

Spetsnaz—Elite Soviet (now Russian) Army special operations unit of Parachutist-Commandos. *Spetsnaz* is an acronym for *voiska spetsial'nogo naznacheniya*, "forces of special assignment" or "special-purpose force."

Spoon—The safety lever on a grenade that is held down before and after the pin is pulled. "Letting the spoon fly" means releasing it and arming the grenade.

T-62—Soviet Main Battle Tank (MBT), a further development of the venerable T-54/55 series. It has a crew of four and mounts a 115mm main gun and two machine guns (one 7.62mm and one 12.7mm). Widely exported.

Toe-popper—A small anti-personnel mine detonated by foot pressure. It's designed to wound, usually just blowing off part of the foot or toes.

Tokarev—A 7.62mm (.30-caliber) Soviet-designed automatic service pistol, similar in design to a Colt or a Browning. The Tokarev is a good, robust weapon without any annoying safety devices, etc. The Jugo version incorporates a magazine that holds an extra round, making Soviet and ChiCom magazines incompatible with the Jugo weapon.

Tommy Town—Foreign volunteer slang for Tomislavgrad, Bosnia.

TOW—The current US heavy anti-tank rocket launcher, TOW stands for Tube-launched, Optically-sighted, Wire-guided command-linked anti-tank missile. It's a tank killer pure and simple. It is in use by several foreign countries.

Trombone – Slang for attachment for launching rifle grenades. Much-coveted accessory. It increased barrel length by about eight inches, which many Brits (accustomed to long-barreled FNs) found comforting.

UNHCR—United Nations High Commission for Refugees.

UNPROFOR—United Nations Protection Force (Croatia and B-H). The UN troops were as useful as eunuchs at an orgy. A common observation was, "He's not a player, he's a UN observer." The first proposed name was UN Intervention Force Former Yugoslavia; however, the acronym would've been UNIFFY, which would've been too accurate. Relief organizer Fred Cuny (later killed in Chechnya) once quipped in his Texan drawl, "If the UN had been around in 1939, we'd all be speaking German."

Ustasha—Nazi; from the NDH-era and Ante Pavelic's fascist Ustasha Movement.

Ville—US Army slang for village, town, any urban area.

VJ (*Vojska Jugoslavije*)—The army of Jugoslavia; successor to the JNA.

VOPP—Vance-Owen Peace Plan.

Willy Peter—Military slang for WP, white phosphorous. The M34 White Phosphorous Smoke Hand Grenade currently in use by the US Army contains fifteen ounces of white phosphorous inside a rolled steel body, serrated to facilitate fragmentation. The WP filler burns for approximately sixty seconds at a temperature of 5,000 degrees F. It is a very nasty bit of ordnance. White phosphorus' effect on human tissue is quite simple: it will burn straight through to the bone and out the other side unless deprived of oxygen. Packing the wound with mud is a common first aid field expedient.

XO, Executive Officer (aka "exec" or "2IC")—The second in command of a military unit. He usually supervises the support and headquarters elements and acts as the commander's right-hand man.

Zagi 91—Croat 9mm submachine gun. The Croats produced at least three different models of hybrid submachine guns designed to make use of available parts, materials, ammo, and magazines.

Zengees- The ZNG (*Zbor Narodne Garde*—National Guard Corps) sometimes mistakenly called the Zagreb National Guard, the precursor of the Croat Army.

Zero—Battlesight zero, to sight-in a battle rifle.

ACKNOWLEDGMENTS

Having read many books with just the barest of acknowledgements, I'm a little self-conscious about writing this. Well, screw it. In completing (and re-writing) this manuscript, I owe several people who helped along the way a great deal of thanks: Gary Linderer of *Behind the Lines*, Bob Brown of *Soldier of Fortune*, and former *Behind the Lines* Senior Editors Kregg Jorgenson and Kenn Miller (both accomplished authors and much better writers than I) for their support and encouragement. Jim Morris, author of *War Story*, for his exemplary example and encouragement. To Greg Walker, my friend, brother and mentor, SF operator, fellow Iraqi roadrunner, and accomplished author, thanks for the constant encouragement. Mark Gatlin of Naval Institute Press provided early encouragement.

Ray Lane Aldrich (CW3 USA retired) and Linda Aldrich (RIP) and their daughter Rae Ann Voelkner and her husband Bill (LTC, USAR) have my deepest gratitude for giving a bum like me three hots and a cot whenever I was in town, whether it be Warrenton, Virginia or Ravensburg, Germany. Mike "Major Mike" Williams, one of the Special Forces "Originals," for his mentoring.

Not enough published authors thank the unsung heroes of literature, our public school teachers, so to my high school English teachers, Richard Brown, Avis Harwick, Mary Harvey, and Karl Shuey, my sincere thanks for pounding in the basics. Any butchery of the English language that I perpetuate in this, my first real effort at writing anything beyond five thousand words, is solely my own fault. For this final version I owe much appreciation to my agent/editor, Gayle Wurst of

Princeton International Agency for the Arts, and my publisher, David Farnsworth, for their hard work and guidance.

I thank Sergeant Major David Lewis (USA retired) of the Saint Bonaventure University ROTC program and First Sergeant John Neuschwanger (company first sergeant, Co A, 1/17th Infantry, Camp Casey, Korea, 1985–1986) for keeping a young infantry second lieutenant out of trouble and showing him what it meant to soldier. Sergeants train officers and very rarely the other way around.

I also want to express my thanks to four very good soldiers: John Rajkovic, Richard Vialpando, Michael Homeister, and Ranger Mike "McDonald" for watching my backside in the Balkans and giving it a good swift kick when it really needed it. Finer friends no man ever had. I would be remiss not to mention good friends like Mike "Connors," "Tom Kelly," and Zak Novkovic, who shared their experiences, and in Connors' case, his ammo, with me. This is their book, too.

And of course, Mom and Dad, thanks for never worrying, or showing it if you did.

Rob Krott
Mahmudiyah, Iraq, 2008

BIBLIOGRAPHY

BOOKS

Curtis, Glenn E., Ed. *Yugoslavia: A Country Study.* DA PAM 550-99, US Government Printing Office, 1992.

Dempster, Chris and Dave Tompkins. *Firepower.* New York: St. Martin's Press, 1980.

Dizdarevic, Zlatko. *Sarajevo: A War Journal.* New York: Henry Holt and Co., 1994.

Dragnich, Alex N. *Serbs and Croats: The Struggle in Yugoslavia.* New York: Harcourt Jovanovich, 1992.

Drakulic, Slavenka. *The Balkan Express.* W.W. Norton and Company, New York, 1993.

Ezell, Edward Clinton. *Small Arms of the World.* Harrisburg, PA: Stackpole Books, 1988.

Gilbert, Adrian. *Sniper: the World of Combat Sniping.* New York: St. Martin's Press, 1995.

Glenny, Misha. *The Fall of Yugoslavia: The Third Balkan War.* New York: Penguin Books, 1993.

Grundy, Kenneth W. *Soldiers Without Politics: Blacks in the South African Armed Forces.* Berkeley and Los Angeles: University of California Press, 1983.

Hoare, Mike. *The Road to Kalamata.* Lexington, MA: Lexington Books, 1989.

Hogg, Ian V. and John Weeks. *Military Small Arms of the 20th Century.* 6th edition. Northbrook, IL: DBI Books, 1994.

Malcolm, Noel. *Bosnia: A Short History*. New York: New York University Press, 1994

Mallin, Jay and Robert K. Brown. *Merc: American Soldiers of Fortune*. New York: MacMillan Publishing Co., 1979.

Moore, Robin. *The Crippled Eagles*. Miami: Jennifer Publishing Co., 1980.

Morris, Jim. *War Story: The Classic True Story of the First Generation of Green Berets in Vietnam*. New York: St. Martin's Paperbacks, 2000.

Vulliamy, Ed. *Seasons in Hell*. New York: St. Martin's Press, 1994.

West, Rebecca. *Black Lamb and Grey Falcon*. New York: Viking Press, 1943.

Windrow, Martin. *The Waffen SS*. revised edition. London: Osprey Publishing Ltd., 1987.

Williams, L.H. "Mike" with Robin Moore. *Major Mike*. Ace Charter, Popham Press Book, 1981.

MAGAZINES

Brown, Robert K. "SOF Team Trains the King's Cadre," *Soldier of Fortune*, April 1993.

Hooper, Jim. "War in Bosnia, Part II," *Combat and Militaria*, October 1994.

Krott, Rob. "Looking For War In All the Wrong Places." *Soldier of Fortune*, September 1992.

_____. "*Zelene Beretke*: Tigers of the Croatian Forests," *International Military Review*, May/June 1993.

_____. "Knife Fighting in Croatia," *Fighting Knives*, July 1993.

_____. "*Achtung* Baby!" *Soldier of Fortune*, August 1993.

_____. "Special Forces in the Balkans," *Behind the Lines*, November / December 1993.

_____. "Serbia's *Amerikanac* Commando," *Soldier of Fortune*, April 1994.

_____. "Outlaw Merc," *Soldier of Fortune*, April 1994.

_____. "Battle Blades in Bosnia," *Fighting Knives*, November 1994.

_____. "Little Nancy and the Big Bad Mercenaries," *Soldier of Fortune*,

MacKenzie, Robert C. (as "Bob Jordan") "Combat Zone Croatia," *Soldier of Fortune*, February 1992.

_____. "Shoot and Scoot," *Soldier of Fortune*, October 1993.

_____. "Looking For a Few 'Pretty Good' Shots," *Soldier of Fortune*, May 1993.

_____. "SOF Editor's Final Firefights," *Soldier of Fortune*, September 1995 (posthumously from notes).

Wallace, Jim. "Yanks In Yugoslavia," *Soldier of Fortune*, January 1992.

ABOUT THE AUTHOR

Rob Krott was raised in McKean County, Pennsylvania, and educated at St. Bonaventure University and Harvard University. A former US Army officer, he has traveled to over sixty countries and received military awards and decorations from ten foreign governments including Croatia's *Zahvalnica*, awarded by the defense minister for combat missions along the Kupa River, and the *Spomenicom Domovinskog Rata* medal awarded by the Croatian president and personally presented to him by Ivica Racan, the Prime Minister of Croatia. Krott has also served in the field with guerrilla armies including the Karen National Liberation Army in Burma and the Sudanese People's Liberation Army. He is the military affairs correspondent for *Small Arms Review* and was previously mastheaded as chief foreign correspondent for *Soldier of Fortune* and as a columnist and foreign correspondent for *Behind the Lines: The Journal of US Military Special Operations*. At this writing he was working in Iraq as a private security contractor.